THE
RUNNER'S
BUCKET LIST

200 RACES TO RUN BEFORE YOU DIE

— DENISE MALAN —

D0958499

TRIUMPH
BOOKS

Library of Congress Cataloging-in-Publication Data

Malan, Denise.
    The runner's bucket list / Denise Malan.
        pages cm
        ISBN 978-1-60078-838-3 (pbk.)
    1. Marathon running—Guidebooks. 2. Running races—Guidebooks.
I. Title.
        GV1065.M34 2014
        796.42'52—dc23

                                                          2013040304

This book is available in quantity at special discounts for your group or organization. For further information, contact:

Triumph Books LLC
814 North Franklin Street
Chicago, Illinois 60610
(312) 337-0747
www.triumphbooks.com

Printed in U.S.A.
ISBN: 978-1-60078-838-3
Design by Andy Hansen
Page production by Alex Lubertozzi

For my grandparents and Mike

THE RUNNER'S BUCKET LIST

001

BAG THE BEST SWAG

The roar of the crowd, the thrill of the chase, the triumph of the finish…

Oh, who are we kidding? Sometimes we're in it just for the swag.

Runners love T-shirts, jackets, hats, medals, and pretty much anything else with a race logo they can show off. And race organizers love swag too; it not only attracts runners to their races but gives the events some good, cheap advertising. It seems every year races up the ante on the best giveaways to make their events stand out.

From the coolest medals to the most unique swag (harmonicas, anyone?), these races get creative so you can feel pampered and earn some souvenirs to be proud of.

BUILD THE BUCKET LIST

There are many more races than could fit in this book that are well-run, unique, and deserving of being on your bucket list. I realize this.

That's why *The Runner's Bucket List* is a work in progress. I'd love to hear about all the great races out there that rise above the average event. What makes them one of a kind? Why do you keep coming back year after year? In short, why should they be on the bucket list?

Contact me at www.runnersbucketlist.com, www.facebook.com/runnersbucketlist, or @runbucketlist on Twitter, and you just might see your suggestions in the next edition.

Happy running!

HOW TO USE THIS BOOK

Those patterns evolved into the 25 chapters in this book, each representing a unique type of race, each an event that should be on your bucket list. They are large and small, indoors and out, easy and hard, fully clothed and, um, less so. Some you have no doubt heard of, including the New York City Marathon. Others are a bit more under the radar but just as deserving of being on any runner's must-run list. Each is unique in its own way.

With the goal of making the list as accessible as possible, every chapter contains races of varying distances held in different areas of the country. Many are marathons but each section contains at least a 10K and usually a 5K, so beginning runners and walkers can experience the same type of race. There are a few ultra marathons, listed because of their iconic status, but those races (anything longer than 26.2 miles) are only for the toughest of runners.

Most of these races are in the United States, but there is one full chapter on international destination races, something every runner should experience.

The idea is that each runner can make his or her individualized bucket list and work to start checking off the races.

Of course, I wanted to run all 200 races and write about my experiences firsthand. Unfortunately I didn't have a luxurious five-year deadline to do that, so much of the information on races in this book was compiled from interviews with runners and race directors, online results and reviews, and race websites. But I still wanted to provide that personal touch, so each chapter also contains at least one first-person race report written by myself or a contributor who experienced the event.

Each race capsule contains information about the race's location, distance, month, and website where you can find more details. While these details are as up to date as possible, please keep in mind that races change often. The dates, distances, and even the courses can vary from year to year. Every effort was made to ensure the races in this book were stable and would be there for readers to enjoy, but circumstances unforeseen can lead to races shutting down. Be sure to check a race's website for the latest details.

INTRODUCTION

The inspiration behind *The Runner's Bucket List* is simple: running is an adventure.

You can race a train in Connecticut or commemorate a prohibitionist's bombing of three bars in the middle of the night in a tiny Kansas town. You can feel free as you run through the towering redwoods in California or confine yourself to a gym and make 204 trips around a tiny indoor track in Indiana.

The Runner's Bucket List started with my own personal list of races I was dying to run. When my grandfather told me about a race in Kansas City that was run completely underground (and cleverly scheduled around Groundhog Day), I became obsessed with finding more unique races around the country.

Pretty soon, I had compiled a list 50 races long. The Talladega 21000, a half marathon around the famous superspeedway in Alabama. The Guinness Challenge in Tulsa that involves drinking three stouts in only four miles. The Hatfields and McCoys Reunion Marathon that pits the feuding families against each other.

I wanted to run them all!

But faster than I could tick them off, the list continued to grow. As it did, I started noticing patterns in the events. Many fit themes, such as costume races, adventure and obstacle course races, night races, indoor races, and hot and cold races. *The Runner's Bucket List* was taking shape.

CONTENTS

A blues CD, harmonica, and guitar medal are among the Mississippi Blues Marathon swag.
Photo courtesy of Denise Malan

MISSISSIPPI BLUES MARATHON
You won't be singing the blues over this swag

Some places are country. Some places are more rock 'n' roll.

But Mississippi *is* the blues.

That's exactly what race director John Noblin thought when he helped start the Mississippi Blues Marathon. Other cities like Nashville were capitalizing on their musical histories with destination marathons, so why not Jackson?

LOCATION: Jackson, Mississippi
DATE: early January
DISTANCE: marathon, half marathon, marathon relay (five runners)
FIELD SIZE: 3,000
WEBSITE: www.msbluesmarathon.com
RACE HIGHLIGHTS: unique swag like harmonicas and blues CDs; scenic and historic course through Jackson

The blues was born in the Mississippi Delta's fields and, later, its juke joints, thanks to artists such as Robert Johnson and Muddy Waters. The Mississippi Blues Trail celebrates this heritage with more than 150 historical markers throughout the state, including a dozen in Jackson.

A couple of the markers, and some blues venues, are on the marathon route, along with the state's original Capitol, three universities, and several historic neighborhoods.

"We thought, *If a person comes to Jackson for only one day, what would you want them to see?*" Noblin said. "The route takes in just about every historic point in Jackson."

The Mississippi Blues Marathon was first run in 2008 and from the start has had only one sponsor, BlueCross BlueShield of Mississippi. By 2013, 3,000 racers competed in the full, half, or relay marathon distances, and the race was recognized as one of the best deals for your money.

This race is blues through and through, from the bands playing at the expo to the beneficiary of the money raised—the Mississippi Blues Commission's Musician Benevolent Fund, which helps established blues musicians during times of need.

And, of course, there's the bluesy swag.

Each participant receives a CD of blues songs from Broke and Hungry Records and a commemorative harmonica made by Hohner. The finisher's medal is different each year—in 2013 it was a rocking, glittery guitar with a pick attached.

"I think there's a feeling that a lot of races are getting more and more expensive," Noblin said. "Our race packet value, what folks take away from our race, is a large percentage of what they give to put in it."

GASPARILLA DISTANCE CLASSIC
Two days. Four races. More than 30 miles. No problem.

You're going to need an entire medal rack just to show off the bounty you earn at the Michelob Ultra Challenge at the Gasparilla Distance Classic.

Taking on the challenge means competing in all four of this racing festival's distances—the 15K and 5K on Saturday, with a half marathon followed by an 8K on Sunday.

Challenge racers get the T-shirts and other goodies for each distance, plus the four finisher's medals. The ultimate reward, though, is the giant challenge finisher's medal and embroidered finisher's jacket at the end of the fourth race.

Put that all together, and you can see why the pirate-themed festival's motto is, "It's all about the booty."

LOCATION: Tampa, Florida
DATE: late February
DISTANCE: half marathon, 15K, 8K, 5K
FIELD SIZE: 28,000 (1,100 in the challenge)
WEBSITE: www.tampabayrun.com
RACE HIGHLIGHTS: run multiple races to earn a treasure trove of medals; earn an embroidered finisher's jacket and challenge medal for the full four-race challenge

"We try to make sure our runners walk away with something special," said Susan Harmeling, executive director of the Gasparilla Distance Classic Association. "They earned the medal they wear around their neck."

The challenge started somewhat by accident. The association used to host two race weekends in Tampa: a marathon and half marathon in December, and the 15K/5K in February. The weather was proving too hot for the marathon weekend, so organizers combined the racing events into one weekend in cooler February.

There was an immediate uproar from runners who were used to doing both events, Harmeling said.

"We thought, *Okay, we'll create an opportunity for you to do all of them*," she said. "And they did."

For those not quite ready to do the full Michelob Ultra Challenge, the Gasparilla offers shorter race combinations: the Beck's Light Challenge, which includes the half, 15K, and 5K; and the Select 55 Mini Challenge, which includes the 15K on Saturday and 8K on Sunday. You'll still get extra swag—and extra bragging rights—over the rest of the pack.

The popularity has only grown since the challenges' first running in 2004. About 1,100 of the 28,000 racers in the festival now compete in the Michelob Ultra or one of the shorter challenges.

"There are some crazy runners out there," Harmeling said. "The hardest challenge you can throw at them is the one they want to do."

FLYING PIG MARATHON
Make it to the finish swine

Many races have themes, but the Flying Pig Marathon takes it to the extreme.

The Flying Pig—whose name is a nod to Cincinnati's meatpacking history—has "grunts" for volunteers. The most spirited aid stations compete in a "Ham It Up" contest. Along the course, runners can refuel with "Pig Newtons," and at the end they cross the "Finish Swine."

LOCATION: Cincinnati, Ohio
DATE: early May
DISTANCE: marathon, half marathon, marathon relay (four runners), 10K, 5K
FIELD SIZE: 30,000
WEBSITE: www.flyingpigmarathon.com
RACE HIGHLIGHTS: fun pig theme and medal; beginner-friendly marathon

I could go on; the pig puns are never ending. They are also marketing gold, apparently.

"The brandability of the pig has helped," race executive director Iris Simpson-Bush said. "Just that name has allowed us to grow in leaps and bounds."

The marathon started in 1999 with a few thousand entrants. By 2011, more than 30,000 people competed in all weekend events, including a half marathon, 10K, and 5K.

The race has more than just a catchy name and fun theme on which to build its reputation, however. The Flying Pig is known for its hospitality—and its swag. Runners get tons of freebies at the race expo sponsored by local mega-company Procter & Gamble, and each entrant receives a premium bag, technical shirt, and a poster.

The finisher's medal is among the most coveted in marathoning. As you guessed, I'm sure, it features a pig, a 3D version smiling and flying toward you from the front and flying away on the back, complete with a curly tail.

Simpson-Bush said the Flying Pig has always tried to offer runners something extra since its inception.

"We understood that Cincinnati is not typically a destination city," she said. "We felt to attract out-of-towners we might have to do a little bit more."

That has made the race popular, especially among first-time marathoners who at one time thought they could run 26.2 miles only when pigs fly.

ROUTE 66 MARATHON
Find yourself at the Center of the Universe

A little-known fact about Tulsa, Oklahoma: it contains a tiny spot that is the Center of the Universe. And those who don't mind adding an extra .3 miles to a marathon can run right through it and earn an extra medallion to pair with the Route 66 Marathon's award-winning medal.

"We call it the world's shortest ultra," race executive director Chris Lieberman said.

The Center of the Universe is a spot on a pedestrian overpass over some railroad tracks in downtown Tulsa where you can hear your voice echo. (No, of course it's not really the center of the universe. It earned its nickname because it's a very particular spot. Even someone standing next to you won't be able to hear your echo.)

LOCATION: Tulsa, Oklahoma
DATE: late November
DISTANCE: marathon, half marathon, marathon relay, 5K
FIELD SIZE: 7,500
WEBSITE: www.route66marathon.com
RACE HIGHLIGHTS: extra .3-mile detour that earns a medallion; party zone in the "Center of the Universe"

The bridge was near the marathon route, so organizers decided to make it an optional detour.

"There are so many races these days to chose from, you have to differentiate yourself," Lieberman said.

Runners have about 16 miles to think about it and can make a game-time decision.

If they take the extra route, they're rewarded with beer, music, and a party atmosphere packed with spectators, plus a medallion to carry with them the rest of the race signifying they finished 26.5 miles. About one-third of racers choose the detour, Lieberman said.

The Center of the Universe medallion isn't the only Route 66 swag you'll be proud of. The regular finisher's medal is an award winner.

In the first few years of the race, the medals were in the shape of the Route 66 road sign. But Lieberman said the organizers wanted something more imaginative, something that really honors the heritage of the historic highway.

"We figured out what's cool about Route 66," he said. "It's the cars and the chrome and the paint."

Now, each year, Lieberman and assistant race director Kim Hann spend hours researching the antique autos that used to travel the route. And each year, they design a new medal honoring one of them. The 2012 medal overlayed chrome and translucent paint in homage to the 1936 Dodge pickup, symbolizing strength and endurance. The year before, the medal was in the shape of the flying lady, the hood ornament of a 1941 Cadillac.

First-time marathoners or those belonging to clubs such as the 50 States Marathon Club or Marathon Maniacs also get special medals with their designations.

"Kim and I spend a lot of time thinking of the medals," Lieberman said. "We just don't stop until we think it's a first-class medal."

That work has paid off: in three years the medal climbed from third to second and finally first place in *Marathon & Beyond* magazine's annual list of best medals.

RUN NIKE WOMEN SERIES
A finisher's medal you'll actually want to wear

Sorry, guys; these races are all about the ladies.

And they're all about the bling—genuine Tiffany & Co. necklaces are the finisher's medals for these girly-girl races in San Francisco and Washington, D.C. (Men are still welcome as participants; the races are just really geared toward women.)

Kacey Faberman, of Charlotte, North Carolina, ran the Nike Women's Marathon in 2012. She didn't sign up necessarily for the necklace, but it ended up being a major bonus (and it didn't hurt that each one was handed out by a cute guy in a tuxedo at the finish line).

"I love having a race medal that I actually wear," Faberman said. "When I've received finisher's medals in the past, I've felt way too silly to wear them—I'm 27, not seven."

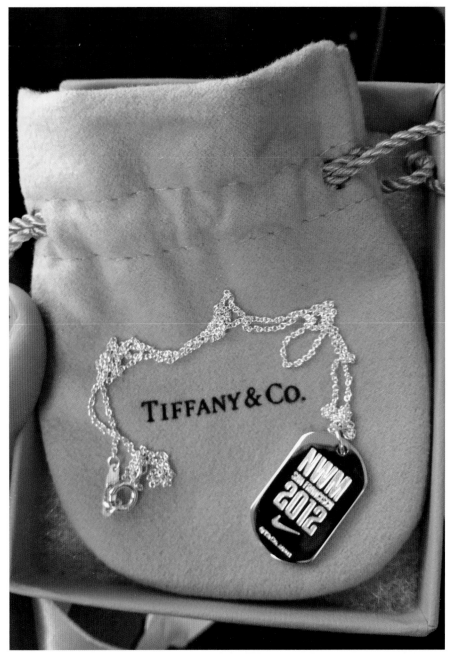

The finisher's "medal" for the Nike Women's Marathon is a Tiffany & Co. necklace with a unique pendant each year. Photo courtesy of Kacey Faberman

The pendant that year was a commemorative dog tag with the Nike swoosh that came in the signature light-blue Tiffany's bag. Faberman put the necklace on after the race, then wore it back to the hotel, to a celebratory dinner, and to the airport the next day. She still wears it sometimes.

LOCATION: San Francisco, California; Washington, D.C.
DATE: mid-October (San Francisco); late April (Washington)
DISTANCE: marathon, half marathon (San Francisco); half marathon (Washington)
FIELD SIZE: 30,000 (San Francisco), 15,000 (Washington)
WEBSITE: www.facebook.com/ RunNikeWomenSeries
RACE HIGHLIGHTS: Tiffany & Co. finisher's necklaces for both the half and full marathon; cute guys to hand them out

"The fun thing about wearing the necklace, and seeing others wear it as well, is that you can't help but ask one another about their experience of running this women power event," Faberman said. "And like most runners, I can talk ad nauseam about the races I've run, so I never hesitate to share my San Francisco experience when asked about the necklace."

The Nike Women's Marathon began in San Francisco in 2004 to commemorate the 20th anniversary of the first women's Olympic marathon, which American Joan Benoit Samuelson won in Los Angeles. Since that year the Nike Women's Marathon has raised more than $134 million for the Leukemia & Lymphoma Society.

The pendant on the finisher's necklace has been different for each race. Some are a simple circle or rectangle, and others are more elaborate. The 2005 pendant was a silhouette of a woman in full stride.

The San Francisco marathon and half marathon are so popular that in 2013 Nike started a half marathon in Washington, D.C., also with a specially designed necklace from Tiffany's.

There could be some drawbacks to these races—the marathon gets low marks on some race review sites for being disorganized, pricey, and overly commercialized (you must be a Nike+ member to register). But the San Francisco course is gorgeous, and if you're in it for the swag, you can hardly beat a "medal" you'll actually want to wear.

WINEGLASS MARATHON
One of the classiest races around

Some runners come for the fast course which winds through several small upstate New York towns. Some come for the beautiful fall foliage or the small-race feel.

But many come for the champagne and the stemware.

In the home of the famous Corning Inc. glassmaker, the Wineglass Marathon keeps it classy with some of the best swag around (and don't forget to visit the Corning Museum of Glass while you're in town).

LOCATION: Bath to Corning, New York
DATE: late September or early October
DISTANCE: marathon, half marathon, 5K
FIELD SIZE: 5,500
WEBSITE: www.wineglassmarathon.com
RACE HIGHLIGHTS: wine glass, champagne, and glass finisher's medal for racers; gorgeous fall foliage and flat course are bonuses

The Wineglass swag bags that include champagne and a wineglass, plus unique handmade glass medal for finishers, have earned the Wineglass praise in top running publications. Even with the great swag, the registration price has remained reasonable.

Add that it's one of the highest-ranked races in the country for percentage of its field qualifying for the Boston Marathon, and it's easy to see why the Wineglass has grown rapidly in the last decade.

It took 25 years for race registration to double (from 250 runners at the first Wineglass in 1982 to 500 runners in 2007). By 2010 the race sold out for the first time at 1,800 participants. The next year, the field capped at 3,000 sold out three months before the race. A half marathon also was added in 2011, followed by a 5K the next year.

So register early if you want to get your hands on some of the best race packets in the country, and get ready for a scenic, fast course followed with a little bubbly at the end.

FORT LAUDERDALE A1A MARATHON
The best beach-themed medal

For nearly the entire Fort Lauderdale A1A Marathon or Half Marathon course, the Atlantic Ocean is either on your right or your left as you cruise the famous A1A Coastal Byway, and the race finishes on the beach.

It's only natural that the finisher's medal continues the theme.

LOCATION: Fort Lauderdale, Florida
DATE: President's Day weekend in February
DISTANCE: marathon, half marathon, 5K
FIELD SIZE: 5,500
WEBSITE: www.a1amarathon.com
RACE HIGHLIGHTS: cruise the famous A1A highway; earn one of the most creative medals in racing

Race organizers come up with a new medal for each running, a task that becomes harder and harder each year, said Matt Lorraine, who owns race parent company Exclusive Sports Marketing. Organizers start working on the next year's medal practically as soon as the race is over.

Previous medals have included sea turtles, sandals, and clamshells, which won the *Marathon & Beyond* medal contest in 2010 with a truly unique feature—the clamshell was hinged and opened to reveal the engraved medal.

In 2012, the race put two medal finalists to a vote of the runners—sandals vs. seahorses. The sandals won, and though they didn't have a locket, they were larger than most medals at about six and a half inches for the marathon and four inches for the half. The seahorses were a close enough second in the voting that they became the 2013 medal, which featured two seahorses, back to back, with a hinged locket in the middle.

The medal is one way for Fort Lauderdale to stand out, Lorraine said. The popular Miami Marathon nearby attracts 25,000 runners, while Fort Lauderdale has grown to about 5,000 in the half and full marathon since it started in 2006.

"It was wildly expensive, the amount of money we spent on the medals," he said. "It was very pricey, but we look at it as an investment in the race."

Little Rock Marathon
A medal that will weigh you down

Denise Malan

You'll never run the same Little Rock Marathon twice.

The course doesn't change, but a different theme each year makes it a completely new, and completely fun, experience. Of course, the centerpiece of each theme is Little Rock's famous finisher's medal—a giant, one-of-a-kind hunk of metal that you will definitely want to show off.

LOCATION: Little Rock, Arkansas
DATE: early March
DISTANCE: marathon, half marathon, 10K, 5K
FIELD SIZE: 9,000
WEBSITE: www.littlerockmarathon.com
RACE HIGHLIGHTS: one of the largest medals in racing; fun new theme every year

The 2011 Little Rock Marathon was my first full marathon, and I chose to run it specifically for the medal. The race theme that year was "A Race of Mythic Proportions," a nod to Greek mythology. Greek pillars and volunteers dressed in togas greeted us at the expo. The marathon medal—"a medal of mythic proportions"—weighed a full pound and featured a flat, spinning Earth on top of a man's shoulders. A little over the top, sure, but doesn't finishing a marathon deserve such a big reward?

Actually, it seems that Little Rock's medals get a little more over the top each year. The 2012 race, with the theme "Celebrate," featured disco-costumed volunteers and a glittery medal the size of a dinner plate with a spinning disco ball in the center. It was something to celebrate indeed.

Even with that large medal, the marathon is still affordable at $85, so I splurged and spent an extra $20 for the VIP perks tent—probably the best money I've ever spent on a race. The tent had a pre-race smorgasbord of candy, nuts, fruit, and bagels, plus heaters to keep us warm (the temperature was hovering around 30 degrees that day) and

One of the best bits of swag at the Little Rock Marathon is a jumbo-sized finisher's medal; the theme behind the awards changes from year to year. Photo courtesy of Little Rock Marathon

VIP portable toilets with shorter lines. Post-race, massage therapists awaited to soothe one's aching muscles.

But another one of the best perks of the race is free for runners: the post-race party features delicious barbecue; tubs of munchies including Oreos, chips, and nuts; an open bar; and live music and dancing. And in a brilliant move, organizers schedule it for 4:00 PM, late enough for everyone to go home, shower, and catch a nap before the party starts. You can bring friends and family for $20 per person.

The marathon starts downtown in the River Market, travels over a bridge to North Little Rock and back, then meanders through some of Little Rock's most historic neighborhoods. We passed the Arkansas Capitol, which is a replica of the U.S. Capitol and often is used by Hollywood as a stand-in. At the governor's mansion, Governor Mike Beebe himself stood outside and waved as we passed by.

Almost immediately after we passed the halfway point, I learned why shirts sold at the expo featured the slogan, "What hills?" We churned up a three-mile incline, and I realized I had to forget about my goal time and concentrate on just finishing. After reaching the top in the historic Hillcrest neighborhood, we then stampeded down the other side of the hill, a steep, two-mile drop.

When I finally saw the marker at Mile 26, my eyes started to tear up. I had no idea finishing a marathon would be so emotional. With my goal time long past, I stopped to take a picture of the sign. I wanted to remember this moment.

Around that final mile marker is one of the race's quirkier elements: a "lipstick stop" where runners can grab some lipstick and look in the mirror to freshen up for the inevitable pictures they'll take at the finish line. I was too tired to really care what I looked like, but I swiped one of the lipsticks and put it in my race belt for later. More swag!

Soon after I crossed the finish line, a volunteer hung one of those giant medals around my neck. With zero energy left even to walk, I could barely hold my head up from the weight of the dang thing. But I couldn't wait to show it off.

002

PUSH YOUR LIMITS

Think you can beat a train through the hills of Connecticut? Race to the summit of a Colorado mountain—then straight back down? How about finish a half marathon and a marathon in the same weekend?

Then sign up for one of these races and prove it.

Runners are gluttons for punishment. We want to see where our limits are, then push them just a little bit further. And then, of course, brag about it.

The races in this chapter will help you test your speed, endurance, strength on hills, and even, in a couple cases, your mastery of stairs. So pick which limit you're going to push, then start training if you want to earn those bragging rights.

The scenery can help keep your mind off the hills in the Harpeth Hills Flying Monkey Marathon in Tennessee.
Photo courtesy of Elly Foster

HARPETH HILLS FLYING MONKEY MARATHON

"A tough little run in the park"

Race founder and director Trent Rosenbloom doesn't mince words about the Flying Monkey Marathon.

"It is a marathon that is about running," the race website says—or rather, warns. "Running hard. Running over big and memorable and painful rolling hills through dense woods. Running with other like-minded athletes."

This race is meant to be the antidote to flat, fast, big-city races. There are no bands playing inspirational music, no cheering fans, not even a certified course.

LOCATION: Nashville, Tennessee
DATE: late November
DISTANCE: marathon
FIELD SIZE: 300-350
WEBSITE: www.harpethhillsmarathon.com
RACE HIGHLIGHTS: personalized T-shirt with the number of your "Monkey kills" on the sleeve; 7,200 feet of rolling elevation change in an urban forest park

"If you get to the end and you (or your gadget) believe the route to be long, we won't charge you extra," the website continues. "If you believe it to be short, just keep running."

The Flying Monkey is run in the Harpeth Hills of Tennessee, a tough course with 7,200 feet of total elevation change through Percy Warner Park, a completely preserved forest in an urban area only nine miles from downtown Nashville. (Though the only "flying monkeys" you're likely to see are stuffed toys thrown by some volunteers.)

Rosenbloom started the race in 2006 after an anonymous posting on a local online running message board broached the idea of a marathon through the park. Though the race has become more popular, he's kept it small. Runners must enter a lottery for one of the 300 coveted spots in the race.

And there's nothing stuffy or overcommercialized about this marathon. Every runner and volunteer gets a cotton T-shirt with a unique monkey-themed design each year. Technical shirts for participants are devoid of sponsor logos and have the runner's name on the front. Those who have run the Monkey before have the number of their previous "Monkey kills," or finishes, on their sleeve, something to give veterans bragging rights.

When you're going to run that many hills, there's not much you can do but laugh about it. The race director sends emails to runners leading up to the race berating them for even signing up. And runners aren't afraid to dish it right back.

"A friend of mine put it best: 'Don't hate the hills, hate the race director,'" Rosenbloom said. "We really have a fairly strong culture of the mantra, 'Trent sucks,' and they build up a lot of jovial anger at the race director."

Adding to the camaraderie, runners also are asked to bring some food for a potluck after the race. Most racers and volunteers will stick around for a couple hours after the race to swap stories.

Tim Runyon of Illinois, who has run the Monkey three times, said the small-race atmosphere and the bonding among runners keeps him coming back.

"It's basically a family reunion with people you don't know until that day," Runyon said. "I have friends that ask me, 'Why do you want to go do that again if it's so difficult?' I said, 'If you run it you'll understand.'"

GOOFY'S RACE AND A HALF CHALLENGE OR DOPEY CHALLENGE

You have to be a little bit goofy to try this one

So a full marathon just isn't challenge enough for you anymore? It's time to step up to the Goofy Challenge—a combination of the Walt Disney World Half Marathon on a Saturday, and the Walt Disney World Marathon on Sunday. The Goofy Challenge became so popular that it spawned an even tougher physical test: the Dopey Challenge, which includes the half and full marathons that weekend, with an appetizer of a 5K on Thursday and a 10K on Friday.

LOCATION: Orlando, Florida
DATE: mid-January
DISTANCE: marathon and half marathon over two days, or marathon, half marathon, 10K, and 5K over four days
FIELD SIZE: tens of thousands
WEBSITE: www.rundisney.com
RACE HIGHLIGHTS: extra medals for the extra miles; stop and take photos with the Disney characters

That's 39.3 miles of Disney craziness in two days, or 48.6 miles in four days. Is it a coincidence that these challenges are named after Disney's notoriously (and lovably) least-intellectual character?

Runners who complete the Goofy Challenge will win a coveted Goofy medal on top of the Donald Duck medal (for the half marathon) and Mickey Mouse medal (for the marathon) already prized by Disney runners. The Dopey Challenge finishers will receive six medals: the three from the Goofy Challenge, plus 5K and 10K medals, and a Dopey medal. They also will likely earn some very sore legs.

The courses wind through the Disney theme parks, including the Magic Kingdom and Epcot for the half, with both of those plus Animal Kingdom, Hollywood Studios, and the ESPN Wide World of Sports for the full marathon. There are plenty of spectators—Disney characters among them—to cheer you on. Runners and their guests are invited to a cool-down party Sunday night after the marathon in Downtown Disney.

Bill Askew, a self-proclaimed huge Disney fan from Pittsburg, Kansas, had run the inaugural Disney marathon in 1994 and decided to do the Goofy

Challenge in 2013 in honor of the race's 20th anniversary.

He took it easy on the half to save some energy for the marathon and finished both courses, granted with a slower marathon time than he wanted because of temperatures in the 80s that weekend.

With 27,000 runners in the half marathon and 24,000 in the full, Askew said the runners started fairly slow and it was not easy to find a good pace. But he wouldn't trade that for anything—he loved chatting up fellow runners. One was carrying an Olympic torch and let him carry it for a block. Another told him of stopping to try out a ride during the marathon.

"That was the best part of the race—meeting some very nice people and chatting for a bit, learning their story," Askew said. "Both races had plenty of water stations, medical tents, handing out Biofreeze, [petroleum] jelly, food—bananas, gels, chocolate. I don't think you could ask for more of that."

LEADVILLE RACE SERIES
Where running legends are born

The Leadville Trail 100 is the stuff running legends are made of: 100 miles through the Colorado Rockies, on forest trails and mountain roads, from elevations of 9,200 to 12,600 feet, all under a 30-hour time limit that some runners don't make.

LOCATION: Leadville, Colorado
DATE: June through August, depending on race
DISTANCE: 100 miles, 50 miles, marathon (26.05 miles), heavy half (15.46 miles), 10K
FIELD SIZE: various
WEBSITE: www.leadvilleraceseries.com
RACE HIGHLIGHTS: known as one of the toughest ultra races; experience a taste of the legendary Leadville 100 with shorter races

In other words, pure running punishment.

Leadville is a former mining town and the highest incorporated city in North America, hence its nickname, "Two-Mile High City." The city had been the site of numerous mining booms and produced tons of gold, silver, lead, copper, and zinc. After years of decline, the city had the highest unemployment in the country in 1983 when Ken Chlouber started the 100-miler and started to bring in visitors.

Today, the Leadville 100, known as "The Race Across the Sky," is still run each August and has helped build Leadville into a running Mecca. The ultra was immortalized in the 2009 best seller *Born to Run*, and those who attempt it are a special brand of runner and a special brand of crazy (in the most complimentary form of the word, of course).

Fortunately, now those who are just a fraction of the crazy can get a taste of Leadville. The Leadville Race Series has added the Silver Rush 50-miler, the Trail Marathon (actually only 26.05 miles—not that you'll complain), a "Heavy Half" (15.46 miles), and a 10K.

The courses are different, but the terrain is no less mountainous. The marathon climbs from an elevation of about 10,200 to 13,200 feet at Mosquito Pass, then back down to the start with plenty of ups and downs in between. The Heavy Half, about 2.3 miles longer than a regular half marathon, follows a smoother route to Mosquito Pass and back down. The 10K covers the first and last 3.1 miles of the legendary Leadville 100 course.

THE GREAT TRAIN RACE
A fun way to test your speed

So you think you're fast?

Faster than a steaming locomotive?

The Great Train Race in Connecticut puts that to the test. The Iron Horse train typically takes 59 minutes to traverse the precisely 6.816 miles from New Canaan to Wilton. Racers take on the train and try to keep up with its approximate 8:41 minute-per-mile pace.

The train, however, doesn't always hit that pace; it can be faster or slower. Previous results show the train took anywhere from 54 minutes to

LOCATION: New Canaan to Wilton, Connecticut
DATE: mid-October
DISTANCE: 6.816 miles
FIELD SIZE: usually around 100
WEBSITE: www.clubct.org
RACE HIGHLIGHTS: test your speed against a train, not just other runners

1:04, and one year it took a leisurely 1:19 (and every single one of the 76 runners beat the train).

The race pits runners against an imaginary commuter on a real train—actually three trains. To get from New Canaan to Wilton, the commuter would have to take the New Canaan branch line train to Stamford, switch to a train to Norwalk, and then hop on the Danbury line train to Wilton.

"It takes a bit over an hour. In the early years of the race, it was 55 minutes, but the train seems to have gotten slower with age," reads a news account in the *New Canaan Daily Voice* by Jim Gerweck of Club CT running club. "The majority of the runners finish before the train arrives, and they start to cheer wildly when the crossing bell chimes, signaling the train's imminent arrival."

Even if you don't beat the train, just try not to be last. The final runner receives a "Lantern Rouge" award, referring to the red lamp on a caboose.

PIKE'S PEAK MARATHON
A race with altitude

At least at the Pike's Peak Marathon, what you see is what you get: simply straight up, and straight down.

This marathon, the third-oldest in the country, is so legendary an entire book was written about it. The race started in 1956 as a competition between smokers and non-smokers (I can venture a guess which team won) and now calls itself "America's Ultimate Challenge."

LOCATION: Manitou Springs, Colorado
DATE: mid-August
DISTANCE: marathon, 13.32 miles
FIELD SIZE: 2,500
WEBSITE: www.pikespeakmarathon.org
RACE HIGHLIGHTS: thin air, 11 percent grade, and unpredictable weather

The course takes runners along trails from the base of the mountain in Manitou Springs, Colorado, at 6,300 feet elevation, to near the peak at 14,050 feet. If you choose the Pike's Peak Ascent, you stop there for a final distance of 13.32 miles, slightly longer than a half marathon.

If you're doing the full Pike's Peak Marathon, you have to turn around and head straight back down the mountain—which is not as much fun as it sounds—to get the full 26.2 miles. Running downhill for extended distances can be just as hard on the legs as going uphill.

Though there might be some slight downhills on the way up, and vice versa, the overall average grade is about 11 percent. And don't forget that the higher you go, the thinner the air. The weather at such high altitudes is also unpredictable. In 2005, hundreds of runners were stuck at the summit during a huge storm. The temperature can vary wildly too, meaning runners must prepare with layers of clothing.

Clearly, this race calls for some training outside the norm.

The organizers recommend lots of trail running, and if you're stuck on a treadmill, set it to a 12 to 15 percent grade. Those who don't live at high altitude should arrive a few days early to adjust.

Above all else, remember this: don't overdo it. Plan on the ascent taking about as long as your average flat marathon time. The average runner takes about 63 percent of the ascent time to go downhill. The marathon has a total time limit of 10 hours, a good three to four hours longer than many marathons.

RACE TO ROBIE CREEK
"The Toughest Race in the Northwest"

There are no ordinary, boring starting guns here. Each year the Race to Robie Creek committee plans a new quirky starting production to kick this race off with flair.

And it's a good thing—you're going to need some entertainment to keep your mind off of the grueling race that lies ahead of you.

The Race to Robie Creek starts at Fort Boise, Idaho, and climbs 2,000 feet in the first 8.5 miles to the Aldape Summit. While that seems tough enough, that's not the worst of it. In only about half that distance, you'll drop nearly the same elevation as you race toward the party at the end of this half marathon that bills itself as "The Toughest Race in the Northwest."

"It'll beat you up as bad as a full marathon, even though it's just a half," said

LOCATION: Boise, Idaho
DATE: third Saturday in April
DISTANCE: half marathon
FIELD SIZE: 2,400
WEBSITE: www.robiecreek.com
RACE HIGHLIGHTS: 2,000-foot climb through 8.5 miles; quirky theme each year that has helped the race develop a cult-like following

Brian Rencher, a member of the race's organizing committee. "It's the downhill that really beats you."

For some reason, though, runners keep coming back. With a cap of 2,400 participants, the race now sells out just a few minutes after registration opens in mid-February (though this is the rare race that allows its numbers to be resold). That's a far cry from its first running in 1975 that included only 25 participants. As the race has grown, it's become known as a rite of spring in Idaho.

But back to that quirky start.

Each year members of the race committee—known as the Rocky Canyon Sailtoads (long story)—pick a new race theme, which is kept secret until registration opens. Pirates, samurai, Scotland, and "It smells your fear" have all been themes. Then select members of the committee work on a starting production that isn't revealed, even to other members of the committee, until race day.

They've cracked whips, sawed the heads off statues, popped a weather balloon full of fake fur, had a biker gang rev their engines, and made scent hounds howl. The bizarre start has only added to the race's cult-like appeal.

The race theme is carried all through the rest of the event too, from the T-shirts to the finisher's "trinket." You'll be disappointed if you were expecting a medal, but the finish line party and race story you'll be able to tell should more than make up for that.

BISBEE 1000
Be sure to train on the StairMaster

For years since it was first run in 1990, the Bisbee 1000 was referred to as "the 5K that feels like a 10K." The nine staircases totaling 1,000 steps along the course prevented an accurate distance measurement until GPS systems came along and race organizers found out it's really more than four miles.

Distance isn't the point anyway. This is the Bisbee 1000, after all, named after the stairs along the course (the number of which also varies depending on who is counting, but 1,000 is close enough).

Bisbee actually has far more stairs than that—351 staircases spread around the city that would total 33,000 steps in three miles if stacked end to end. The steps started as walking and mule trails during the town's mining heydays in the early 20th century. The trails became wooden steps then finally concrete staircases built by the Works Progress Administration after the Great Depression.

The Bisbee 1000 takes advantage of that heritage and is a good race for anyone who wants to step out of their 5K comfort zone but isn't ready to challenge themselves with a much longer race.

"People who run hills, run trails, or practice on stadium stairs, like lots of people do to train for this, are going to do well," race founder Cynthia Conroy said. "People who are just used to walking around the neighborhood are going to be surprised."

The event is walker-friendly, though, and the organizers place starters in corrals according to their projected 5K time to avoid congestion on the staircases. The race is limited to 2,000 participants and has sold out in recent years. Musicians play on each of the nine staircases to entertain runners.

An event within an event—the Ironman Ice Competition—lets you test your speed up a smaller set of stairs, only 155 this time, for a possible cash prize. Of course, there's a catch: you have to carry a 10-pound block of ice in a set of antique metal tongs, similar to those used to deliver ice to homes before the advent of refrigeration. The record so far is 19 seconds, though the average ranges from 25 to 45 seconds.

LOCATION: Bisbee, Arizona
DATE: third Saturday in October
DISTANCE: about 4.2 miles
FIELD SIZE: 2,000
WEBSITE: www.bisbee1000.org
RACE HIGHLIGHTS: nine staircases totaling 1,000 steps in about four miles; enter an Ironman Ice Competition and test your speed up stairs while carrying a 10-pound block of ice

Runners tackle one of the nine staircases during the Bisbee 1000 in Arizona.

Photo courtesy of Bisbee 1000

The Ironman Ice Competition starts two hours after the first starters take off in the Bisbee 1000, so there's plenty of time to register for both events. The ice competition started as a way to entertain spectators waiting for the awards ceremony.

After the race, stick around for a merchant's marketplace and a craft beer festival to help celebrate your accomplishment.

Dipsea, Double Dipsea, or Quad Dipsea

"Aside from the blood and stinging…"

Scott Dunlap • www.atrailrunnersblog.com

One Saturday in 2005, I joined 330 other trail runners for the 30th running of the Double Dipsea, a rugged 13.7-mile, out-and-back course along the famous Dipsea Trail north of San Francisco.

LOCATION: Stinson Beach, California
DATE: late June
DISTANCE: 7.4 miles (Dipsea), 13.7 miles (double), 28.2 miles (quad)
FIELD SIZE: 1,500 (Dipsea), 630 (double), 250 (quad)
WEBSITE: www.dipsea.org, www.doubledipsea.com, www.run100s.com/qd.htm
RACE HIGHLIGHTS: handicap system that allows older runners and women to win; "allowed shortcuts" if you know what you're doing

This race was new for me in two ways. First, I had never tried the rugged, 676-step, 2,200-vertical feet Dipsea Trail that is legend in the Bay Area (so why not do it twice?). Second, I had never tried a handicapped race, where runners start in waves to give older runners an equal chance to win. Knowing there are few things more humbling than having a 70-year-old kick your butt on some serious vert, I knew this race would be epic.

The Double Dipsea is one of three annual trail races along the dramatic Dipsea Trail. The original race (7.1 miles one way from Mill Valley to Stinson Beach) was a marketing event created to lure city folk out to the Dipsea Inn 100 years ago, and they haven't missed a year yet. Walt Stack, a local running hero, figured one way wasn't enough, and worked with his club, the Dolphin South End Runners, to create the Double Dipsea in 1970. The Double Dipsea is an out-and-back from Stinson Beach, run with same handicap style of the original Dipsea that encourages older runners to compete. If two isn't enough, you can do the Quad Dipsea—28.2 miles and 9,200 vertical feet of quad-burning pain.

From the moment you arrive at Double Dipsea registration, the senses of tradition and camaraderie are evident. Most runners have shared this experience many times already and know every step, root, and crag by heart. The average age is even older than most ultra races—I would guess midfifties, with a solid showing of men and women over 60. When I arrived for my first race, everyone milled around at the beach, sharing stories of Walt Stack (who passed away in 1995), and speculating if a 53-minute head start would be enough for 68-year-old single Dipsea champion Russ Kiernan to hold off local speed demon Cliff Lentz, known to decimate this course at a sub-seven-minute pace. Walt had beaten the young turks many times in his heyday, so this was a fitting memorial to keep Walt's spirit alive. I asked the medics if they expected injury. "Guaranteed. We brought extra stretchers," one said.

As I watched the first few waves of runners head out, I got some tips from the experienced among us. They warned me to be careful of the dizzying, uneven steps at the turnaround in Mill Valley, to take my time on the extremely steep Cardiac and Suicide Hills, and to have some Tecnu ready for the miles of poison oak. Hmmm…maybe I should have studied that map a little closer. My age/sex put me with the "scratch" group (no handicap advantage), so we got to go last.

The Dipsea Trail leaves no time for warm up, and within a quarter mile all of us were chugging up the hills that wound endlessly into the thick, cruel fog that hid any sense of how much more was to come. Three runners in the scratch group took off like jackrabbits, and the rest of us spread out quickly. I soon appreciated the 55-degree weather as my heart rate went through the roof, and given the sound of heart rate monitor alarms going off behind me, I wasn't the only one. The tipsters were right about the poison oak—a few sections were like a poison oak jungle, barely cut back from the narrow trail. But given the amount of vertical that remained ahead of us, poison oak was the least of our worries.

I found a good pace along with Ron Gutierrez, who had challenged himself to "just try and run the whole race" this year. A bold goal for the Dub-Dip, and one I definitely wasn't going to be able to match up the steep stairs. As we traded off the lead (Ron on uphills, me on downhills), we began catching up to the runners from previous waves. Everyone was gracious about letting us pass (and shouting words of encouragement), as long as the narrow trails permitted. I learned quickly that you take your life in your hands if you try to pass outside the trails, as evidenced by some fresh blackberry bush scrapes on my left leg.

As we crested Suicide Hill about five miles in, Russ Kiernan, the 68-year-old phenom, came flying down the trail. Just a few minutes behind was Melody-Anne Schultz, taking the downhills like a champ. Ron and I joked that Russ didn't need a 53-minute head start to beat us, and given his speed, that was probably true.

We climbed another mile up a road (seeing a few more runners coming the other way) and then headed down the steps that weaved through the Mill Valley suburb. Everyone was out cheering on their moms/brothers/grandpas, helping get our minds off the hypnotizing steps that quickly switched from wood to stone, short to long, steep to flat, in no apparent order (this must be what the extra stretchers are for). As a reward for getting down, we got to turn around and go back up!

I checked my watch at the turnaround (1 hour, 2 minutes), and guessed I was in about 50th place, but with the handicap it's hard to figure out who is really in front of you. All you can really do is go as hard as you can. I walked a good portion of the stairs on the way up, saving plenty of energy for the downhill. As I hit Suicide Hill (now understanding its name comes from the downhill section) a bee stung my left arm, so I had to take a few seconds to scrape the stinger out. One woman laughed as she ran by, saying, "A bee sting too? You're having an epic Dipsea!" Epic, indeed.

Aside from the blood and stinging, I felt strong on the second half. I kept seeing runners on nearby trails, so I asked a woman near me if we were lost. She explained that "some small shortcuts are allowed if you know where they are"—another advantage for the locals. My quads trembled as I headed down the last two miles of fun, but my shoes were giving me plenty of traction down the muddy trail. I finished in 2:09 (48th), and chatted with the other muddy/bloody/exhausted runners. Russ, the 68-year-old, had done it, just narrowly beating Judy Rabinowitz. Roy Rivers, 48, came in third, clocking the fastest non-handicap time with a blazing 1:45.

I jotted down some tips for next year (bring Tecnu, hit the StairMaster as part of training, and learn the "allowed" short cuts), and looked forward to the day that my age will give me a boost in starting position. I can only hope to improve enough to match the likes of Walt, Russ, and Judy!

CRATER LAKE RIM RUNS
The view will be worth it

A fellow runner in the 1970s returned from a training run near Crater Lake and suggested to local running club president Bob Freirich that they should start a race there.

"Are you out of your mind? Nobody's going to run that," Freirich remembers replying.

LOCATION: Crater Lake National Park, Oregon
DATE: mid-August
DISTANCE: marathon, 13 miles, 6.7 miles
FIELD SIZE: 500
WEBSITE: www.craterlakerimruns.com
RACE HIGHLIGHTS: long, steady hills, one of them five miles long; unbeatable scenery that can take your mind off those hills

But when he went with another group of runners he realized the views of the lake are worth all the tortuous hills. The first run had less than 40 entrants, but by the next year there were 250. In 2012 the Crater Lake Rim Runs were celebrating their 37th year and had been capped at 500 entrants for years.

Crater Lake was formed 7,700 years ago when a massive eruption caused a volcano to collapse. Rain and snow filled the remaining caldera, forming the deepest lake in the United States at nearly 2,000 feet. The result is a lake about five miles across with spectacularly blue water, cliffs rising nearly 2,000 feet above the lake, and snowcapped mountains in the distance.

And, of course, the setting for spectacularly difficult races.

All three Rim Run distances (marathon, 13 miles, and 6.7 miles) have long, steady, up-and-down grades nearing 1,000 feet at time. Some hills are nearly five miles long. All the races are run on paved roads, except the last four miles of the marathon, which are on a cinder road.

Freirich recommends runners get a good base of hill runs to prepare. But the best training, Freirich says, is a good attitude.

"Just remember [the hills] are coming and they will take something out of you," he said. "If you take your time and remember to look left or right, you're going to see some beautiful, spectacular scenery. It'll take your mind off of it—at least for two or three steps."

RACE REPORT

Blue Ridge Marathon
Big challenge, but even bigger reward

Kacey Faberman

The website touts Blue Ridge as "America's Toughest Road Marathon" due to 7,200-plus feet of elevation change. But completing it is more than just "tough"—I would call it punishing, rewarding, epic, and a true achievement.

LOCATION: Roanoke, Virginia
DATE: late April
DISTANCE: marathon, half marathon, marathon relay (five runners)
FIELD SIZE: 1,200
WEBSITE: www.blueridgemarathon.com
RACE HIGHLIGHTS: take on a race named after a mountain range, so you know it's tough; billed as "America's Toughest Road Marathon"

At times it was hard to decide which was worse, the steep inclines or the dizzying descents. While the uphill climbs exercised my lungs and often reduced me to walking too many times to count, the downhills caused my quads to absolutely scream— and days later, they were even louder. On top of the ups and downs of the road, in 2011 the weather in Roanoke, Virginia, was also pushing my limits. That April, the Weather Channel called for "severe storms," which on Saturday morning meant everything from drizzle and light wind to monsoon-like conditions. A tough race, made even tougher? Bring. It. On.

With the extreme elevation change, it was close to impossible to pace this race. Reviewing my splits, I noticed:

- I started taking walk breaks at Mile 3.

- I ran five miles at a seven-minute-mile or faster pace, including two that were in the six-minute-mile range.

- I ran four miles at an 11-minute or slower pace, including a 12-minute mile.

- My slowest mile was Mile 19, leading me to the conclusion that hills were not my friend. My fastest mile immediately followed, at the dreaded Mile 20—usually when marathoners hit the wall. I blamed this blistering pace, which is faster than my 5K pace, on a shortened stride and that pull we call gravity.

I crossed the finish line, which was right by a railroad track, as the seventh female, good enough to win my age group. The awards were so creative: reclaimed railroad spikes welded to look like runners.

I truly enjoyed this race, even with its challenging elevation changes. I love small-town races, and Blue Ridge shined in the areas that make me enjoy events of this size. In smaller races, I'm less anxious at the start line—there's not a lot of jostling to get a "good" position and you don't have to worry about which corral you're placed in. Once you're running, elbows aren't thrown and I can run all the tangents I want, because there is plenty of room for everyone. And while it may seem contradictory, I always find that I talk to more people when there are just a few hundred participants than when I'm surrounded by thousands. The sense of camaraderie is amazing and so helpful when I'm grinding away on those grueling miles (you know, the ones in the late teens and early twenties). Finally, it's the volunteers and the residents in small-town races that always blow me away. I probably passed more people cheering on the sidelines, offering up gummy bears they purchased and

The Blue Ridge Marathon in Roanaoke, Virginia, awards age group winners with a repurposed railroad tie trophy. Photo courtesy of Kacey Faberman

oranges they sliced and plated, than the number of people running the marathon.

I would certainly say with this race that the bigger the challenge, the bigger the reward. Obviously, this run was hard—any race with "mountain" included in the name, or named after a mountain or range, will be. I wasn't really sure what goal to set for myself when I signed up for Blue Ridge, but upon crossing the finish line, I realized that being on two legs was an accomplishment!

MOUNT WASHINGTON ROAD RACE
Don't worry—there's only one hill

In 1904, a medical student named George Foster was the first man to record a timed run up Mount Washington, the highest peak in the northeastern United States. He made the grueling 7.6-mile climb to impress his friends.

If you want to do the same, enter the Mount Washington Road Race and follow in Foster's footsteps.

The race was established in 1936 by some of Foster's friends, according to the event website, though it went defunct during World War II and wasn't brought back until 1961, becoming an annual event in 1966.

Besides the steep climb to the summit at 6,288 feet, Mount Washington is notorious for its unpredictable and rapidly changing weather. The average wind speed is 35 mph, fog is recorded on most days of the year, and the average temperature is in the 20s. This also happens to be the location where the world-record highest wind speed was recorded in 1934: 231 mph.

LOCATION: Mount Washington, New Hampshire
DATE: mid-June
DISTANCE: 7.6 miles
FIELD SIZE: 1,000
WEBSITE:
www.mountwashingtonroadrace.com
RACE HIGHLIGHTS: climb the highest peak in the northeastern United States; take a chance on weather at the summit

Surprisingly, harsh weather has caused the race to be shortened only once, in 2002, when winds and freezing rain at the summit brought the race to a halt at the halfway point.

Did I mention the race is in *June*?

Now let's talk about that hill. The average grade on the Mount Washington Auto Road is 12 percent, with a cruel 22 percent in the final 100 yards.

To get an idea of how much the climb will affect your time, look at the course record. Set in 2004 by New Zealand runner Jonathan Wyatt, the fastest mark is 56:41, a 7:30-mile pace. Wyatt has run a 2:13 marathon, just over a five-minute-mile pace.

Despite the potentially adverse weather and the relentless climb, the Mount Washington Road Race is growing ever more popular, with only 1,000 entrants earning a spot through the lottery system each year.

If you want an extra challenge, see if you can beat Foster's original Mount Washington time of 1:42.

THE RUNNER'S BUCKET LIST

003

BE PART OF A BIG-CITY RACE

Tens of thousands of runners. Streets lined with cheering spectators standing several deep just to get a glimpse of the action. Elite athletes, television cameras, and all the fanfare that comes with a world-class athletic event.

Every runner really must experience a big-city race.

Most of the largest and most famous events are marathons, such as the New York City Marathon, the world's largest one-day sporting event, and the Boston Marathon, the world's most elite marathon and probably the most-cited bucket list race for serious runners.

But the largest two races in the United States actually are 10Ks, giving non-marathon runners a chance to experience the same exhilaration of competing in a big-city race.

The Chicago Marathon, one of the six World Marathon Majors, attracts 45,000 runners each year. Photo courtesy of Bank of America Chicago Marathon

CHICAGO MARATHON
Fall in love with the Windy City

The Chicago Marathon course has seen four world records and more than a dozen national records. No wonder this race, one of the six World Marathon Majors, has a reputation for being flat and fast. And it's scenic to boot.

The course starts and ends in Grant Park, on the shore of Lake Michigan in downtown Chicago. In between are many highlights of the city: the Chicago Board of Trade, Lincoln Park Zoo, Willis Tower, United Center, the Chinatown Gate, and 29 official Chicago neighborhoods.

LOCATION: Chicago, Illinois
DATE: mid-October
DISTANCE: marathon
FIELD SIZE: 45,000
WEBSITE: www.chicagomarathon.com
RACE HIGHLIGHTS: scenic and historic tour of Chicago; flat, fast course that has seen four world records set

Along the way, the 45,000 runners will be cheered on by 1.7 million spectators.

"My favorite part of the course was undoubtedly the fans!" said Mindy Keller, who ran her hometown race as her first marathon. "There was not a single spot along the course where you did not feel the support of the amazing spectators."

Keller trained for the race with the Chicago Area Runners Association, which offers a world-renowned training program friendly to beginners and advanced runners alike.

"I looked forward to meeting my new friends for long runs along the beautiful Chicago lakefront path each Saturday morning," she said. "The training mileage flew by as we caught up on events of the past week and supported one another in achieving our goals."

When Keller made it to the big day, she found that she fell in love with her city all over again. Some of her favorite sites: beautiful architecture and high-rises in the Loop; historic homes in Lincoln Park; energetic music and dancing in Lakeview; iconic baseball parks in Wrigleyville and Bridgeport; beautiful murals and Latin music in Pilsen; and dragon-costumed dancers in Chinatown.

"Even if you've lived in Chicago for many years, the marathon will provide you with a brand-new perspective on the city," Keller said, "and you will come out of the race with an even greater love for your hometown city."

RACE REPORT

New York City Marathon
Five boroughs of cheering fans

Denise Malan

At the base of the mile-long Verrazano-Narrows Bridge, thousands of runners are crowded together, belting the lyrics to "New York, New York" and barely able to wait another minute to start one of the world's most famous sporting events.

It's just starting to sink in that I'm standing here too, singing with them.

I know I'm lucky to be here. My name was drawn in the 2011 New York City Marathon lottery, which I entered on a whim. Only about one of three people who want to race make it each year, and 2011 had a record field of 47,000 runners, including qualifying, lottery, and charity entrants.

That November day started with catching a bus in midtown Manhattan by 5:30 AM. I was in the third and final wave of runners to take off at nearly 11:00 AM, so I had to wait almost five hours after we were dropped off at the starting village on Staten Island. I just wasn't quite prepared for the cool temperatures and the stiffness caused by sitting on a concrete curb for several hours. Volunteers were handing out free hats, bagels, and hot drinks, so I managed to survive. I kept my eye out for celebrities I had heard were going to run that year: actor Mario Lopez; Olympians Jennie Finch and Apolo Ohno; or supermodel Christy Turlington. I never did see them, but I did spot some contestants from NBC's *The Biggest Loser*. I watched and cheered as the first wave, led by elite runners I'd only read about, took off across the Verrazano Bridge.

> **LOCATION:** New York, New York
> **DATE:** first Sunday in November
> **DISTANCE:** marathon
> **FIELD SIZE:** 47,000
> **WEBSITE:** www.nyrr.org
> **RACE HIGHLIGHTS:** see all five boroughs of New York City by foot; draw energy from the 2.5 million spectators who line up every year to see the race

In a couple hours, it was my turn to stand at the base of the bridge, bursting with energy and excitement. After my wave started, I no longer felt cold. Runners around me were stopping to take pictures of themselves on the bridge, with the Statue of Liberty in the background. Many of us clearly were here to enjoy the race, not to set any personal records.

I purposefully left my iPod at home, ready to soak in the sights of all five New York boroughs—Staten Island, Brooklyn, Queens, the Bronx, and Manhattan—and the sounds of 2.5 million spectators. People lined the streets, with children making their way to the front of the crowd, hoping to score high-fives as runners passed. I would move over and slap their hands when I needed a little power boost, and they would get so excited, as though I was a celebrity. Maybe, to them, anyone running the race is.

Many runners had written or taped their names to the front of their shirts, so the spectators could encourage them personally. I wish I'd thought to write my name, but I felt extra special when I heard someone yell, "Yeah, Green Shirt Girl, go!" and knew they were talking about me.

The steady stream of racers never thinned out, so we all had to be careful not to elbow or trip each other as we ran through the various neighborhoods of Brooklyn, then wound through the boroughs, over several bridges. It seemed help was always there when I needed it—some energy gels and wet sponges around Mile 18, and the most energetic singers, music, and spectators in the Bronx at Mile 20. (There were more than 120 musical acts along the course, so the music never really stopped.)

Around Mile 21, we dropped back into Manhattan and closed in on Central Park for the final leg. The finish line was so close I could almost feel its pull, encouraging me to pick up the speed. My cell phone in my race belt started to buzz with texts from friends and family who had been following me with the marathon tracking app. When I finally crossed the finish line, I was actually glad they were following me that way, because I was pretty sure we'd never find each other in the mess of people in the finish area.

I didn't have a specific goal time in mind, but I wanted to finish fast enough to have my name in the next day's special edition of *The New York Times*. I had just missed the estimated time needed to make deadline, so I was a little disappointed, but that didn't dampen my exhilaration at finishing the race.

Immediately after getting the medal, finisher's food bag, and mylar blanket, we began what previous marathoners have dubbed the "death march" through Central Park. We trudged in a tight pack to the gear check trucks to pick up our bags, though I got mine relatively early and was able to cut out of the park.

My plan had been to catch a taxi back to a friend's apartment where I was staying, but that was next to impossible. My cell phone's battery dead from the tracking app, I trudged a few blocks until I found a bus line that looked promising. By the time I finally made it back to the apartment, more than two hours after finishing, I enjoyed another of New York's unique offerings: Thai food delivered within a half hour.

The next morning, I returned to Central Park to buy a finisher's shirt and have my medal engraved with my name and finishing time. I bought a commemorative newspaper and flipped to the end to check the last published time. It was later than mine! I frantically flipped backward to look for my time and there it was—my name in *The New York Times*.

PEACHTREE ROAD RACE
Run with 59,999 of your best friends

It might be hard to believe, but the largest road race in the United States (ranked by number of finishers) actually isn't a marathon. It's the AJC Peachtree Road Race 10K, which is run every Independence Day in Atlanta and also bills itself as the largest 10K in the world. (The

LOCATION: Atlanta, Georgia
DATE: July 4
DISTANCE: 10K
FIELD SIZE: 60,000
WEBSITE: www.peachtreeroadrace.org
RACE HIGHLIGHTS: largest race of any distance in the United States; attracts a varied field from Olympians to walkers

AJC stands for *Atlanta Journal-Constitution*, the newspaper that has been the race's main sponsor since 1976.)

The Peachtree started with only 110 racers in 1970. Within only 10 years it had a cap of 25,000 runners, and by 2011 the race was selling out within hours and organizers instituted a lottery system to register.

The cap in 2012 was 60,000 participants—60,000! Think about that number for a minute. That's enough people to sell out an Oklahoma State Cowboys football game. Enough people to fill the entire state capital city of Helena, Montana—twice.

If the sheer number of runners seems hard to imagine, check out these numbers:

- Volunteers needed: 3,400.
- Spectators lining the course: 150,000, an especially impressive number for a 6.2-mile race.
- Starting waves: 20.
- Number of portable toilets needed to accommodate the runners: 750.
- Approximate number of calories burned by all participants: 36 million.

Like any big-city race, the Peachtree attracts elite athletes. The past winners list includes such famous names as Frank Shorter, Jeff Galloway, Gebre Gebremariam, and Grete Waitz. The blazing course record of 27:04 was set by Kenyan Joseph Kimani in 1996.

But don't let that intimidate you: the Peachtree Road Race also is walker-friendly and has a much slower field overall than many big races, making it a non-threatening option for many runners. In 2011, only about one in five runners finished the Peachtree in less than an hour, or just under a 10-minute-mile pace. The course is open for three hours after the last wave starts the race.

RACE REPORT

Boston Marathon
The ultimate bucket list item
· ·
Kacey Faberman

Editor's note: Kacey wrote this race report in late 2012, before the tragic bombing at the 2013 Boston Marathon. After the bombing, I chose to leave the report as it was written, an untarnished tribute to the best race in the world. As runners, the greatest way we can honor the victims is to keep running Boston Strong.

I started running because I wanted to run the Boston Marathon.

Yes, you read that correctly. I didn't start running because I wanted to run a marathon, and I wasn't a marathon runner who set my sights on Boston. I started running because I wanted to participate in the best race in the world—the Boston Marathon.

It took me six marathons to qualify, but when I did, I was elated and couldn't wait to register for and run the world's oldest annual marathon and one of the six World Marathon Majors.

Training for and completing the 26.2 mile distance is tough, inspiring, challenging, enjoyable, time consuming, fulfilling, tear inducing, smile inducing, and so much more. But it was the support, encouragement, and sometimes looks of crazy that I've received from my family and closest friends over the years that was crucial in making my running-of-Boston dream come true.

LOCATION: Boston, Massachusetts
DATE: third Monday in April
DISTANCE: marathon
FIELD SIZE: 25,000
WEBSITE: www.baa.org
RACE HIGHLIGHTS: it's Boston, the most elite marathon in the world

To even enter Boston, runners must already have run a pretty fast marathon to meet the strict qualifying times, something only 10 percent of marathon finishers do. Having always obsessed about time in previous marathons, my Boston goal was to finish with a smile on my face. And I'm happy to say I achieved that goal. That smile came from the incredible organization, exciting but still somewhat nerve-calming Athlete's Village, the diverse towns from Hopkinton to Boston, and the spectators who lined the entire course.

The Boston Marathon has been run continuously for well more than 100 years—and it shows. The organization of this race is unlike any other race I've run. The expo is huge but easy to navigate—you can find shoes, apparel (including the must-have jacket), last-minute race necessities you may have forgotten at home, and nonessentials that celebrate the event (like a hand-embroidered pillow with all the towns you run through stitched in every color on the front). They even have a big-screen viewing of a video of the entire course, with Boston Marathon–associated personalities narrating the miles. This preview helped to set me at ease and prepared me for what to expect.

To get to the start, runners board school buses to the Athlete Village in

Hopkinton. Shuttling 25,000 or so runners might sound like a challenge, but if it was for the organizers, I definitely didn't get that impression. Riding the bus from the Common in downtown Boston to the start was a great opportunity to connect with other runners. It's amazing to hear the stories of how people made their way to this famed running event.

After disembarking from the buses at the Athlete's Village, runners have an hour or two to chill before the waves start. The time leading up to a race start can often be tense, but the Athlete's Village had the opposite effect on me, and I found myself not stressing about the race I'd be starting around 10:00 that morning. The Village offered bagels, coffee, a replica of the "Welcome to Hopkinton" sign complete with photographers, a free pre-race massage tent, and port-a-potties galore—it was a runner's paradise!

When my wave was called to head toward the start line, I walked with the thousands of other runners who shared my preassigned wave start. After stepping into the corral that corresponded with the numbers printed on my bib, it wasn't long before I took my first steps along the world-renowned course. Because the course is point-to-point, runners have the opportunity to see many different locales. Before getting to the big city of Boston, I ran through many unique, small towns: Ashland, Framingham, Natick, Wellesley, Newton. Each town definitely had distinct personalities, but the commonality was that they proudly supported the race and loved to let the runners know it. Whether I was running past a biker bar (fully packed, at 11:00 AM) or a university where girls offered kisses, spectators were out in full force. More than 500,000 spectators take to the streets on this state holiday of Patriot's Day, making it New England's most widely viewed sporting event. I'd say that half a million spectators is a conservative estimate.

I ran Boston in 2012, a year of record heat. The spectators really were fantastic in helping to beat the temperatures in the high 80s. They came out from their homes with extra cups of water, ice cubes, and hoses with spray nozzles. The spectators along the course were phenomenal, and certainly a big reason why this big-city race is a success—whole towns get behind it. They encourage, they cheer, and they clang together anything and everything they can find to create enough noise to drown out any negative thoughts that crossed my mind—whether because of the weather or the hills.

I had high expectations for Boston—it is THE marathon. My expectations were all completely exceeded. The organizers, the expo, the Athlete's Village, the towns, the spectators—all top notch. No detail is spared in this marathon, and this commitment to excellence made me feel like an elite runner.

It's easy to say that everyone should run this race, though it's not always so easy to get there. But do whatever you can to toe that start line in Hopkinton, because it is completely worth it.

LOS ANGELES MARATHON

Feel like a Hollywood star

The Los Angeles Marathon's new "Stadium to Sea" route has proven to be a big draw.

More than 23,000 runners take part each year in one of the country's largest marathons with one of the most famous courses.

"I do actually prefer the big races over the small ones—they're just more exciting," said Joel White, a San Diego, California, resident who has run seven marathons, including LA. "LA, I would just say it's a great destination."

LOCATION: Los Angeles, California
DATE: March
DISTANCE: marathon, 5K
FIELD SIZE: 23,000
WEBSITE: www.lamarathon.com
RACE HIGHLIGHTS: get in your LA sightseeing along the course, passing such landmarks as the Hollywood Walk of Fame, the Sunset Strip, and Rodeo Drive

The race actually used to be a looped course, but in 2007 organizers switched to a point-to-point course, finally settling in 2010 on the current route that starts at Dodgers Stadium and ends in Santa Monica.

In between, the runners pass through four cities: Los Angeles, West Hollywood, Beverly Hills, and Santa Monica, with a host of famous neighborhoods included—downtown LA, Little Tokyo, Chinatown, and Echo

Park, the city's first center of movie production.

In LA, you can do your sightseeing and marathon all at once. You'll pass by all these must-see attractions along the course: Grauman's Chinese Theater; the Hollywood Walk of Fame; the Sunset Strip; Hollywood Boulevard; Rodeo Drive; Century City; four sites of Academy Awards ceremonies; and numerous famous diners, schools, theaters, and museums.

And what would a Hollywood race be without the stars? In 2012, a long list of celebrities—chef Gordon Ramsay, legendary runner Dean Karnazes, actor Ed Norton, basketball star Pau Gasol, and even cartoon characters Phineas & Ferb—recorded well wishes for runners that played on the big screen in Dodger Stadium before the race.

While there's plenty to keep runners entertained on the course, White cautions that there are some challenging stretches and you'll want to get some hill training in before the race.

"The course itself is not really easy or hard; it's just somewhere in the middle," he said. "From start to finish it is more downhill than uphill, but the uphill is more toward the end."

You'll probably forget all about that, though, when you see the finish line at Ocean Avenue, running parallel to Palisades Park and Santa Monica State Beach.

PHILADELPHIA MARATHON
A race full of historic inspiration

LOCATION: Philadelphia, Pennsylvania
DATE: mid-November
DISTANCE: marathon, half marathon, 8K
FIELD SIZE: 30,000
WEBSITE:
    www.philadelphiamarathon.com
RACE HIGHLIGHTS: start and finish near the famous *Rocky* steps; course lined with sites from early American history

You'd be hard-pressed to find a more inspirational backdrop for a start and finish line than the Philadelphia Marathon's— the steps of the art museum where Rocky Balboa infamously pumped his fists during the training montages in *Rocky*.

And where else can you run past the Liberty Bell and

Independence Hall, birthplace of the Declaration of Independence and the U.S. Constitution?

Philadelphia's historic and scenic course draws 30,000 runners and twice as many spectators every year. Runners give this race high marks for organization and crowd support. Even the mayor has been known to come out and give runners high-fives.

Those crowds and the race-day atmosphere really help you feel like a champion. Bands along the course frequently play the theme from *Rocky*, and don't forget to take a picture wearing your marathon medal on those art museum steps.

LILAC BLOOMSDAY RUN
Honoring the heroics of everyday life

For runners who want a big-city race without the big city, the Lilac Bloomsday Run 12K in Spokane, Washington, is the answer.

The Bloomsday is the second-largest race in the country, despite being in a city that doesn't even crack the top 100 in terms of population. Olympic marathoner and Spokane native Don Kardong founded this race in the 1970s, during a running boom that was sweeping the

LOCATION: Spokane, Washington
DATE: early May
DISTANCE: 12K
FIELD SIZE: 50,000
WEBSITE: www.bloomsdayrun.org
RACE HIGHLIGHTS: big-city race with a small-city feel; truly earn your T-shirt

country, and it immediately became a hit. The Bloomsday started with 1,000 runners in 1977, and two years later it already had 10,000 runners. By 1988, it had blossomed to include more than 57,000 runners and walkers. Today it consistently has more than 50,000 entrants and has remained remarkably affordable with a $17 entry fee.

The Bloomsday's size isn't its only unique trait.

First, what the heck does that name mean? The interesting moniker actually derives from the James Joyce novel *Ulysses*, about a day in the life of a man named Leopold Bloom in Dublin. That day, June 16, has been dubbed by scholars as "Bloomsday" and has come to represent the heroic odyssey of everyday life. Kardong paired that with Spokane's nickname of the Lilac City, and there you have it: the Lilac Bloomsday Run.

The run also is an uncommon distance: 12K, or 7.46 miles. The first Bloomsday was about eight miles, but the course evolved over the first few runnings as the field grew, and it was officially certified as a 12K in 1984.

And unlike most road races today, this one makes you work for your T-shirt. Most races offer shirts for every entrant, and many larger races and marathons also offer finisher's shirts. But at Bloomsday, you don't get a shirt at all until you cross the finish line.

MIAMI MARATHON
The race that belongs in a movie

The Miami Marathon course might look a little familiar, even if you've never been to the spicy South Florida city.

First, the race starts at American Airlines Arena, home of the NBA champion Miami Heat. And you might recognize some scenes from your favorite movies, like *2 Fast 2 Furious*, *Miami Vice*, *There's Something About Mary*, *Ace Ventura: Pet Detective*, and *True Lies*. In fact, hundreds of movies and TV shows have been filmed along the course, so many that the race organized a seminar at the expo so runners know which famous spots to look out for.

LOCATION: Miami, Florida
DATE: late January or early February
DISTANCE: marathon, half marathon, 5K
FIELD SIZE: 25,000
WEBSITE: www.ingmiamimarathon.com
RACE HIGHLIGHTS: recognize settings from hundreds of movies and TV shows; take a dip in the Atlantic afterward to recover

The race, which draws 25,000 runners, captures true Miami style, from a Cuban coffee stop between Miles 13 and 14, to the course entertainment. Art deco buildings, bridges, and beach views are all part of the scenery.

Matt Reibel has run the Miami Marathon or half marathon since the event started in 2003, partly because it is his hometown marathon, but also because he loves the course.

The Miami Marathon draws 25,000 runners every year to a course along which hundreds of movies and television shows have been filmed. Photo courtesy of ING Miami Marathon/Mara Patterson

"I have run marathons in other cities and towns, but what makes Miami so special is its course," he said. "Where else but the Miami Marathon do you start out in front of the home of a NBA championship team, go past some of the world's most beautiful cruise ships, past partygoers just leaving the clubs in South Beach, past the smell of fresh Cuban coffee and pastries of the cafes and restaurants lined up along the course in Coconut Grove and other areas, past spectators cheering you on in dozens of different languages, and then be able to recover in the pristine waters of the Miami beaches after the race?"

So if you take on Miami, take Reibel's advice: run your best, but don't forget to enjoy the setting.

THE RUNNER'S BUCKET LIST

004

ENJOY THE SCENERY

A gorgeous view can take your breath away—and take your mind off your burning legs or the miles left until the finish line.

It's no wonder that the most scenic races are also some of the most popular among runners, many in such high demand that they often sell out quickly or have to implement lottery registration.

At these races you can enjoy the unparalleled vistas of Big Sur, chart your own course around Maui, and tour the Garden of the Gods.

The Sedona Marathon in Arizona has been growing, but organizers are keeping it small enough that it doesn't lose its boutique-race feel.
Photo courtesy of Sedona Chamber of Commerce

SEDONA MARATHON AND HALF MARATHON

A boutique marathon in Red Rock Country

The scenery around Sedona, Arizona, has a worldwide reputation for its restorative, spiritual, and romantic nature. The small town of about 10,000 is a popular destination for tourists who love the hiking and the outdoors, plus it's only a couple hours' drive from the Grand Canyon.

LOCATION: Sedona, Arizona
DATE: early February
DISTANCE: marathon, half marathon, 10K, 5K
FIELD SIZE: 2,300
WEBSITE: www.sedonamarathon.com
RACE HIGHLIGHTS: explore Sedona's red rock country, some of the most unique scenery in the United States

The Sedona Marathon that explores some of the most unique scenery in the country started in 2006...it almost ended in 2011. The private company that ran the marathon was going to discontinue the race to pursue other interests, but the Sedona Chamber of Commerce stepped in and purchased the event.

"Our board of directors believed in the event and the importance of the economic impact to the region, especially at a time when our primary industry—tourism—is slow," chamber president Jennifer Wesselhoff said of the February marathon.

The full marathon starts and finishes at Sedona Medical Center, following Dry Creek Road out of town, and turning on Boynton Pass Road, which eventually turns into a dirt road through the turnaround. The elevation chart shows a course full of hills, with a steady drop from about Mile 9 through the turnaround at 13.1, then a climb back up again through Mile 17.

"We've been told that the Sedona Marathon is one of the most beautiful, and most difficult, courses in the country," Wesselhoff said. "The combination of breathtaking scenery, a high elevation of 4,500 feet, and an extremely hilly course makes runners/walkers of all abilities feel a sense of triumph."

The marathon has teamed with other local tourist attractions, such as the Sedona Film Festival, Tlaquepaque Arts and Crafts Village, and Oak Creek Brewery, to offer a full schedule of events leading up to race day, making this scenic marathon even more unique.

The race has been growing every year and now hosts about 2,300 runners in all four distances, but the chamber hopes to keep it small enough to maintain its boutique feel.

MAUI PARADISE MARATHON AND HALF MARATHON
Run at your leisure

No aid stations or cheering spectators. No traffic control, starting line, or finish line. No early start time or six-hour time limit.

There's not even a race date or set course (though there are several good suggestions).

But you can still earn a T-shirt and a medal.

The Maui Paradise Marathon earns its name by being quite possibly the most laid-back race in the country and by letting runners explore the natural beauty of the Hawaiian island on their own.

Race founder Jerry Levey, a part-time Hawaii resident, said the non-race started with the idea that costs were getting out of control for so many running events. Much of that money goes to traffic control, police, and other race infrastructure.

LOCATION: Maui, Hawaii
DATE: any, with race party dates in May, September, and December
DISTANCE: marathon, half marathon
FIELD SIZE: 50 a year
WEBSITE:
www.mauiparadisemarathon.com
RACE HIGHLIGHTS: you are in complete control of the course, time, date, and experience

"There are runners out on the streets every day and they seem to be able to navigate without any police protection or anything," Levey said.

He tried once to formalize the marathon, with about 30 runners, but authorities nixed the idea of a sanctioned event without traffic control. So Levey decided to leave it up to the runners.

Tourists can run the Maui Paradise Marathon or Half Marathon any day of the year, whenever they plan their trips to the island destination. The race's website provides a couple scenic course suggestions (one of them even submitted by a race finisher), but you can choose your own path if there are other parts of the island you'd like to explore.

It's also up to you to provide your own water and food. Some runners have their spouse or friend bike alongside them to provide race support. One man's brother followed him on a skateboard.

Runners can blaze their own trails, just as long as they finish the distance. Levey said many runners start right from their hotels. Some have even run on other Hawaiian islands such as Oahu or the big island of Hawaii. Levey still counts those as finishes.

"It's designed to bring back the time when you just stepped out the front door, put on your shoes, and ran," he said.

A few times a year, the Maui Paradise Marathon hosts non-official race days for runners who prefer the camaraderie. There's still no race support on the course, but the runners enjoy chatting and sharing a meal afterward.

About 50 runners a year complete the Maui Paradise Marathon, a figure Levey said depends completely on the honor system. When a runner finishes the course, they contact Levey and pay a small fee for him to send the T-shirt and finisher's medal.

Though it's not required, Levey has had many runners share their GPS records, photos, or other mementos as proof of their accomplishments.

"Generally speaking, runners are very honest people," he said. "They won't have a shirt and they won't have a medal showing on their wall if they didn't earn it."

RACE REPORT

Big Sur International Marathon
Enjoy the crashing waves along Highway 1

Scott Dunlap • www.atrailrunnersblog.com

In April 2010, I had the great pleasure of joining 7,000 eager runners for the 25th Big Sur International Marathon near Carmel, California.

LOCATION: near Carmel, California
DATE: late April
DISTANCE: marathon, 21 miles, 10.6 miles, 9 miles, marathon relay (up to five runners), 5K (half marathon in November)
FIELD SIZE: 10,000
WEBSITE: www.bsim.org
RACE HIGHLIGHTS: run Highway 1, the nation's first designated scenic byway; take pictures at Hurricane Point, on the Bixby Bridge, and with a classical piano player along the course

This was the second leg of the Boston 2 Big Sur Challenge: two marathons in six days, and a great way to ring in my 41st birthday. Thanks to great weather and the incredible organization of the volunteers and race team, it was a weekend to remember.

I pretended not to notice that I was already limping, still healing from a bike accident a few weeks before, and now amplified by running a beer-soaked Boston Marathon just days earlier. But I so, so wanted to experience that feeling of having Highway 1 all to ourselves, drifting up the rugged Big Sur coast. It called me like a siren song.

At 3:00 AM on race day, I chased a handful of ibuprofen with a cup of coffee and hoped for the best. Taking meds before a race is like watching a traffic accident about to happen—you know it's not going to end well. I may not be much wiser at age 41, but I'm as stubborn as ever! The bus ride to the start was an eager mix of first-timers and grizzled vets, all citing that the projected 60-degree weather couldn't be better. Among the runners were 372 crazy enough to tackle the Boston 2 Big Sur Challenge. The things we do for swag...

I got off the bus and sat with two women from Denver as we let the sun slowly warm us up in the starting area. We chatted with a nice couple from Kansas City who looked for any excuse to spend time in Carmel. We learned that all 50 states were represented here, as well as 21 foreign countries. This race attracts the coolest people!

We made our way to the start, just in time to hear the national anthem and see the doves released (much to the liking of the circling turkey vultures). We descended out of the redwoods to the live soundtrack of local bands who braved the early morning to be set up for us. Within a few miles we were spread out along Highway 1, hearing only the popcorn sounds of our footsteps against the crashing waves. Ah, so peaceful...

The aid station volunteers were amazing, per usual, and the mile-marker signs were hilarious. Everyone was chatting away and having a great time. I continued to be surprised by how many Boston 2 Big Sur runners there were—and they were doing great!

At Mile 10, we got to my favorite part—Hurricane Point. This two-mile climb never seems to end but rewards you with the best views of the course. Fresh legs from the relay teams and the 21-milers helped pace us up the hill.

I joked with the Boston 2 Big Sur runners at the top: Which is tougher, Heartbreak Hill in Boston or Hurricane Point? No contest, they said. Hurricane is five times the heartbreak of Heartbreak.

The descent after Hurricane was quick, and we soon found ourselves crossing the halfway point at Bixby Bridge. The photo shooting session next to the piano player was so popular, I couldn't get in! It's definitely a great spot. My watch read 1:53—I was on track to run my slowest marathon of all time, but it didn't seem to matter. I was just glad to share the experience.

The weather held up nicely and started to get downright hot. As the ibuprofen wore off, I found myself yo-yo'ing between seven- and 10-minute miles as I slowly climbed into the Carmel Highlands. I ran with Matthew, whom I've now met at four different races, and he pulled me up to Mile 22 before stopping for the fresh strawberry aid station.

I pulled into the finish in 3:53 and thanked my body for holding up for one last race. Within minutes I had retreated to the Boston 2 Big Sur tent for a couple of beers and another dose of ibuprofen. Normally I would be stressing about it, but my heart was still overflowing from all the beauty, friendly faces, and inviting community that put on an amazing day. It's hard to imagine a better setting for a marathon, and I looked forward to taking a snooze on the beach before hitting the Forge in the Forest for some grub.

GARDEN OF THE GODS 10 MILE RUN
"Pure running nirvana"

LOCATION: Manitou Springs, Colorado
DATE: early June
DISTANCE: 10 miles, 5K
FIELD SIZE: 1,600
WEBSITE: www.gardentenmile.com
RACE HIGHLIGHTS: run by Balanced Rock, a 700-ton rock seemingly balanced on its tip; challenge yourself with hills and altitude while enjoying the views

The Garden of the Gods and its trademark red sandstone formations are a trip back to 70 million to 320 million years ago, as the Rocky Mountains and its predecessor mountain ranges formed.

The rocks first were pushed up as a mountain range formed, then eroded over millions of years to become the towering, fascinating shapes they are today. Layers in the rocks represent different geologic eras in the Earth's history.

Another piece of trivia: the Garden of the Gods is a National Natural Landmark that got its name in the 1850s when two surveyors remarked it would be a great place for a beer garden, fit for the gods to assemble.

But all that will really matter to you while you're running the Garden of the Gods 10 Mile Run is that the course is gorgeous...and hilly...and at high altitude.

The course takes you through the heart of the park and past its most famous formation, the Balanced Rock, a 290-million-year-old, 700-ton rock in a delicate perch atop flat sandstone. The altitude ascends from 6,210 to 6,530 feet just before the midway point, with rolling hills throughout.

This run will challenge your lungs and your legs, but it's so gorgeous, the training group director has labeled it "pure running nirvana."

The event ends with a finish festival in Manitou Springs Memorial Park, where runners love to soak their tired feet in the bubbling Fountain Creek.

MOUNT DESERT ISLAND MARATHON

The way running should be

The Mount Desert Island Marathon is hilly and challenging, but you won't hear the runners complaining.

The scenery of this race more than makes up for the terrain, boosting this event to the top of many runners' lists. They use words like *spectacular*, *breathtaking*, and *out of this world* in reviews of the marathon. And *Runner's World* magazine has named Mount Desert Island the most scenic marathon in the country.

LOCATION: Bar Harbor to Southwest Harbor, Maine
DATE: late October
DISTANCE: marathon, relay marathon (two or three runners)
FIELD SIZE: 1,000
WEBSITE: www.mdimarathon.org
RACE HIGHLIGHTS: run around Somes Sound, a body of water that cuts five miles into the island and is surrounded by granite; enjoy the solitude of a smaller race

The island itself is quintessential Maine, with a rocky coastline, quaint fishing villages, and the Acadia National Forest, home to Cadillac Mountain, the highest point along the immediate Atlantic seaboard. Adding to the beauty, the marathon is run in October, the peak time for viewing fall foliage (and perfect running weather—cool but not too cold).

The highly praised course starts in Bar Harbor, a small town that is a popular destination with tourists and Mainers alike. It swings south down Route 3 to Otter Creek, then Seal Harbor and Northeast Harbor. Much of the second half is spent circumnavigating Somes Sound, which is like a large bay that cuts five miles into Mount Desert Island and is bordered by granite rock.

The worst hill you'll encounter is a long one that comes at the worst possible time—from Miles 20 to 25—though the reward after that is a final descent toward the finish. Be sure to train for hills, and don't expect a personal record on this course.

The Mount Desert Island Marathon is a smaller race, with about 1,000 runners and few spectators, but you'll appreciate the solitude to enjoy the views.

There's no half marathon in this point-to-point course, but there are two- and three-person relay teams for those who don't want to run the full 26.2 miles.

MACKINAC ISLAND RUNS
Take a run back in time

LOCATION: Mackinac Island, Michigan
DATE: June/September/October
DISTANCE: 10K/8 miles/half marathon, 5.7 miles
FIELD SIZE: various
WEBSITE: www.runmackinac.com
RACE HIGHLIGHTS: step back into a simpler time with horse-drawn carriages and candy shops; run an island accessible only by ferry

Visiting Mackinac Island is like being transported to a simpler time. Horse-drawn carriages and bicycles are the preferred modes of transportation. Sounds of classical music, big band, and jazz fill the nightclubs. Downtown is filled with old-fashioned candy shops, and festivals with decades of history draw families from around the area.

Mackinac (pronounced Mackinaw) Island is a small island in Lake Huron in Michigan. Accessible only by ferry, the island is home to a large state park and some of the most beautiful scenery in the Midwest.

And each summer, you'll find one of Michigan's most historic and scenic road races here. The Mackinac Island Eight Mile Run and Walk started in September 1971 and annually marks the end of the busy summer season for the resort island.

The course follows the perimeter of the island clockwise, running through town, following the shore along the Straits of Mackinac, and ending on the lawn of Mission Point Resort.

Though the Eight Mile Run is the island's longest-running and most famous racing event, there are two other scenic races to enjoy on Mackinac.

A 10K Run/Walk each June celebrates the Mackinac Island Lilac Festival with a course through downtown and on paved roads through the wooded center of the island. And the Great Turtle Half Marathon and 5.7-Mile Run is a trail race in October, during the last weekend the island remains open before winter.

ST. GEORGE MARATHON
One of the top-rated marathons in the country

The accolades keep pouring in for the St. George Marathon.

So many, in fact, that it's difficult to list them all: most organized marathon, fastest fall marathon, and one of the 10 most scenic races from *Runner's World*. *Marathon & Beyond* named it the No. 4 marathon in North America.

LOCATION: St. George, Utah
DATE: early October
DISTANCE: marathon
FIELD SIZE: 7,600
WEBSITE: www.stgeorgemarathon.com
RACE HIGHLIGHTS: descend 2,600 feet overall; race touted as well organized, scenic, and fast

Besides the 2,600-foot overall descent and the great organization, runners love the St. George Marathon for the majestic Utah scenery.

The St. George Marathon starts in the Pine Valley mountains and descends to Worthen Park in St. George (though the downhill is mostly in the second half—there are some tough uphill sections in the first half). Its aid stations are well stocked, many of them with Gatorade, energy gels, and fruit.

The race is so popular it instituted a lottery registration process and only takes about 7,600 runners. Make sure to put in your entry by April if you want to make the cut.

Beloved by marathoners for its organization and majestic scenery, the St. George Marathon is held every October in Utah. Photo courtesy of Kelly J. Gardner

MARTHA'S VINEYARD 20 MILER
Run for the clam chowder

Martha's Vineyard is a favorite vacation spot of the rich, famous, and powerful (including several presidents), and for good reason: it is secluded, charming, and endlessly beautiful.

This Massachusetts island, about seven miles off Cape Cod and accessible by ferry boat, is quintessential New England, with rocky shores and beaches, lighthouses, and small fishing villages. The year-round population of only 20,000 swells to 100,000 in the summer.

LOCATION: Martha's Vineyard, Massachusetts
DATE: mid-February
DISTANCE: 20 miles
FIELD SIZE: 500
WEBSITE:
www.mvbgclub.org/mv20miler/
RACE HIGHLIGHTS: unique distance and course; clam chowder to help you warm up at the post-race party

No big surprise, then, that the Martha's Vineyard 20 Miler has been named to *New England Runner Magazine*'s top 100 races every year since it started in 1998. The 20-miler is an unusual distance, but it serves as a great tune-up leading to the Boston Marathon in April, or as a nice challenge for runners who are looking to up their mileage but aren't quite ready for a full 26.2.

Best of all, the course is mostly flat, with a few rolling hills. It starts at Vineyard Haven Harbor, then proceeds through the historic Copeland District, on a barrier beach road along Nantucket Sound, and across a state forest to Oak Bluffs. What the course lacks in challenge, though, the weather might make up for. This is New England in February, after all, so expect windy, cold conditions.

And the post-race party after you cross the finish line features a New England favorite—clam chowder—along with minestrone soup, fruit, and yogurt to promote recovery.

RACE REPORT

Big Island International Marathon
Don't let the humidity get to you!

. . . .

Kamiar Kouzekanani

The Hawaiian Islands consist of Ni'ihau (forbidden island), Kaua'i (Garden Isle), O'ahu (known for Waikiki beaches), Moloka'i (known for Moloka's bread), Lana'i (known for Manele Bay), Maui (Valley Isle), Kaho'olawe (used to be a Navy firing range), and Hawai'i (the Big Island).

Hilo, the second-largest city in the state (Honolulu is the largest), is located beneath Mauna Kea, the tallest peak in the Big Island. Its population is about 42,000. It is the southernmost as well as the wettest city (average annual rainfall is approximately 128 inches at the airport) in the United States. It is also vulnerable to tsunamis. Hawaiian Volcanoes National Park, 29 miles west of Hilo, and Waipio Valley, about 40 miles north of Hilo, are must-see places. I flew into Hilo on a Thursday afternoon in 2009 and stayed in the host hotel, Hilo Hawaiian.

LOCATION: Hilo, Hawaii
DATE: mid-March
DISTANCE: marathon, half marathon, 5K
FIELD SIZE: 700
WEBSITE: www.hilomarathon.org
RACE HIGHLIGHTS: scenery includes waterfall, exotic plants, and narrow bridges on Hawaii's big island

At 4:30 AM, buses began transporting the runners to the start line. The temperature was in the 70s. We had access to a community center before the race started at 6:00 AM. Although there was a net drop of 500 feet between Miles 0 and 10, there were several hills within the first eight miles, which was also the most scenic part of the route (waterfalls, exotic trees/plants, narrow bridges). Mile 10 to the finish was basically flat. We ran a large number of miles on slanted road shoulders which made the footing less than desirable. The route from shortly after Mile 17 to shortly after Mile 24 was out and back with our backs to the traffic, and I am one who does not like to run with his back to the traffic. Fortunately, there were not too many cars on the road. There were ample water/sports drinks stations. Wet sponges after Mile 18 were very much appreciated.

There was hardly any crowd support but race volunteers were cheerful. There were on-and-off rain showers, followed by in-and-out sunshine, which made it immensely humid.

There were more than enough recovery food items and drinks at the finish. Each finisher received a short-sleeved cotton T-shirt, medallion, and a bag of coffee. The run was not chip-timed, but individualized race-time reports were available a few minutes after crossing the finish line. High humidity made this a very challenging marathon.

There were 192 marathon finishers (120 males, 72 females) in an average time of 4:38:28. The winning times were 2:50:21 (overall male), 3:23:56 (overall female), 3:00:08 (masters male), and 3:38:39 (masters female). There was also a half marathon and a 5K.

My good friends, Al and Sandy Cumming, completed their quests to run marathons in all 50 states and the District of Columbia. My goal was to run with Sandy. We ran the half in 2:03:38 (9:26 pace), talked a lot, and had a good time. By Mile 17, I didn't think we could have done better than 4:10. I began to fade between Miles 18 and 19. I asked Sandy not to slow down for me. Up to Mile 22, I was fairly close to her. By Mile 23, I had run out of fuel.

I refused to walk and jogged to the finish. Sandy had finished in 4:11:11 (9:35 pace) and won her age group. I crossed the finish line in 4:16:54 (9:48 pace). Al finished in 4:31:34 (10:21 pace). We were three exhausted, yet happy, marathoners and agreed that humidity was the overall winner! I felt dizzy for several hours after the run. For me, it started as a pleasant running experience and ended as something quite humbling indeed!

005

RUN NAKED (OR CLOSE TO IT)

Starting more than 30 years ago with the Bare Buns Fun Run in Washington, nudist, or naturalist, colonies have been hosting clothing-optional races as a way to enjoy the outdoors and draw potential new members. The runs are all held on private property and take care to protect racers' privacy, usually posting results online with only a first name and last initial, or not posting them at all.

Once you get over the initial shock of baring yourself in front of complete strangers, the experience can actually be quite freeing. And you don't have to worry about tan lines!

This section also contains a few "undie runs" that usually are held in public and are fund-raisers for various causes. Check out one of those if you're not quite ready to go all the way.

CALIENTE BARE DARE 5K

National championship of nude racing

The Caliente Resort in Florida is in a class of its own among naturist resorts.

LOCATION: Land O' Lakes, Florida
DATE: first Sunday in May
DISTANCE: 5K
FIELD SIZE: 300
WEBSITE: www.nuderaces.com
RACE HIGHLIGHTS: paved path; one of the largest clothing-optional races

The 125-acre resort is fully developed, with paved roads, cart paths, and high-priced condos. The Caliente is in Pasco County and, with about a half dozen nudist resorts, is recognized as the unofficial nudist capital of the country.

Perhaps that's how the Caliente Bare Dare 5K manages to draw 300 runners from an average of 15 states each year, earning it the distinction of being declared the "National Championship of Nude Racing."

"We figured because it's such an incredible place that people would make a weekend out of it and travel here," race director Pete Williams said. "I think for the most part these people might be nudists for the day or this might be the one nude event they do a year. Of course, you have a ton of first-timers."

With so many themed races cropping up, Williams said the Bare Dare stands out even on the clothing-optional race circuit. First, it's along paved paths rather than trails, and Caliente throws an infamous all-day after-party featuring techno music and food. The race awards for the top 25 males and top 25 females are commemorative mini-bottles of wine customized with the race logo and date.

"I think 20 to 30 years from now, when people look back on their racing careers, this will be one that stands out," Williams said.

BARE BUNS FUN RUN
The original clothing-optional race

Thousands of runners have traveled to Washington state to experience the nude race that started them all: the Bare Buns Fun Run at Kaniksu Ranch Family Nudist Park.

LOCATION: Loon Lake, Washington
DATE: July
DISTANCE: 5K
FIELD SIZE: 350
WEBSITE: www.kaniksufamily.com
RACE HIGHLIGHTS: nude finisher T-shirts; a gorgeous Washington state course

The Bare Buns started three decades ago and each year draws hundreds of nudists and nude-curious to Loon Lake, about 30 miles north of Spokane. Of course, runners can wear clothing if they choose, but most in this race bare all.

If the thrill of running naked isn't incentive enough, do it for the T-shirt. Anyone wearing clothes receives a regular finisher's shirt, but those who strip down will receive a coveted "nude finisher" shirt sure to be prized, if maybe not worn in public.

The 5K has a split start on separate roads for the first one-eighth mile to accommodate all the runners, then merges onto a gravel road for an out-and-back course.

The Kaniksu offers camping for race weekend and a carbo-load dinner and dance the night before.

Skinnydipper Sun Run 5K
A clothing-optional cross-country race

Mike Davis

Everyone is born naked. Some people are born to run. But is everyone born to run naked?

This is something I had to find out for myself. So I signed up for a 5K on a naturist resort in Decatur, Texas, north of Fort Worth.

LOCATION: Decatur, Texas
DATE: late April
DISTANCE: 5K
FIELD SIZE: 200
WEBSITE: www.wildwoodnaturist.com
RACE HIGHLIGHTS: friendly, fun atmosphere; cross-country course with trails, ravines, and meadows

Upon arrival at the Wildwood Naturist's Resort, I was greeted by a sign notifying me that nudity may be encountered beyond this point. For the faint at heart, this sign may have harkened back to times when maps were labeled with "here be dragons" marking locations of unexplored territory. Immediately, I knew I was about to do something out of the ordinary and certainly out of my comfort zone.

Besides the actual race, as I later found out, the most difficult part of the event was removing my clothes and stepping out of the car wearing nothing but my running shoes. In the parking area, both sensical and nonsensical thoughts ran through my head. How was I going to look?

Was I going to stand out because I wasn't tanned? None of my thoughts centered on the run itself. Rather, I was worried about how I would fit in amongst a large group of naked individuals.

As I made my way toward the packet pickup, essentially every person I came across was also nude or partially nude. There were people of all shapes, sizes, and ages. Everyone was extremely welcoming and friendly, and by the time I was getting my race number applied to my chest by a topless woman with a marker—obviously there is no place to put an actual race bib—I was feeling pretty comfortable in my own skin.

As everyone gathered at the starting line, I started feeling my typical pre-race jitters.

I looked over the competition, trying to identify others who I may directly be competing against in my own age bracket. While this is a normal pre-race ritual for me, it certainly took on a different feel in a nudist race. Nonchalantly, of course, I also looked over many people's bodies and compared them to my own. I assume this is a natural reaction to being exposed to this kind of environment for the first time, or at least I hope it is.

As the gun sounded to start the race, I set off on a pace slightly quicker than normal. Any thoughts associated with being naked quickly dissipated as the course steered its way into the trail routes set around the resort. If there was any concern about being unclothed, it had little to do with modesty and more to do with safety, as there were many hills and turns on largely uneven ground.

I settled into a modest pace after the first mile and was greeted by people cheering us along at the first water station. The hills and terrain, however, began to take their toll on my legs shortly thereafter. About two and a half miles in, the course evened out and weaved through a field. Unfortunately, I was running out of energy fast and began to slow considerably.

At this point, I began to see more rear ends than anyone would care to see as I started getting passed in the final minutes of the race.

As I crossed the finish line, I was drenched in sweat. Thanks to the combination of the race and the hot Texas weather (the race starts at 1:00 PM on a late April Saturday), I looked like I had just stepped out of the shower. I was immediately given a cold towel and bottled water to help me cool off. The water tasted great but it was the cold towel that felt exhilarating. I talked with some other racers as I watched more people finish the race and then made my way into the cool air of the race registration building to check out the results and wait for the awards ceremony.

One of the rules of the resort is the use of towels whenever one sits on a chair, the floor, etc. I forgot to bring a towel, so I had to put my running shorts back on. In stark contrast to how I felt when I first arrived, I suddenly felt extremely out of place wearing clothes around a predominantly naked crowd of runners.

Knowing that I hadn't placed in my age group, I still was hoping to take home one of the door prizes, including the grand prize: a year's free membership at the resort. It is quite amazing that in a few short hours, I became so acclimated to the nude environment that I was disappointed I didn't walk away with this awesome prize. However, I did walk away with a completely unforgettable experience.

UNDIE AND SPEEDO RUNS

When you're not ready to go all the way

Start doing those sit-ups and pick out your most flattering skivvies so you can look your best for these events that call for baring *nearly* all.

Underwear and Speedo runs are popping up across the country and usually are more about fund-raising for a good cause than the actual run.

LOCATION: various
DATE: various
DISTANCE: usually around 1 mile
FIELD SIZE: various
WEBSITE: www.cupidsundierun.com, www.ssrunners.org, www.undierun.com
RACE HIGHLIGHTS: streak in your favorite underwear or swimwear; earn posh prizes through fund-raising for a good cause

Here are a few possibilities for those brave enough to show their underpants:

- The **Undie Run** pits college campuses against each other to raise money for various causes. In 2013, the charity beneficiary was Cancer for College, which helps send cancer survivors to school. Participants also can literally donate the clothes off their backs to charity. Since it was founded in 2006, the Undie Run has grown to 70 affiliated events and has donated more than 200,000 pounds of clothing to local service organizations.

  The run, declared by MTV to be the "sexiest charity work you can ever do," also offers fun merchandise for sale, like a "Keep calm and undie run" T-shirt.

  Sign up your school at www.undierun.com.

- **Cupid's Undie Run** is a "mile-ish" long run in cities across the country to benefit the Children's Tumor Foundation, which is researching treatments and potential cures for neurofibromatosis. The disease causes painful tumors to grow on nerves and can lead to blindness, deafness, and other chronic conditions.

  That's a serious cause, but the Cupid's Undie Run is anything but serious. Participants strip down to their best underwear, usually red or pink, and streak through the course on Valentine's Day weekend, meaning the weather in most locations is freezing.

  By 2013, the Undie Run had spread to 17 cities, such as St. Louis, Cincinnati, Detroit, Nashville, Orlando, and Austin.

  Participants are asked to raise money as individuals or as teams for the tumor foundation, with fun prizes as incentives. You can earn custom undies and personalized bathrobes, an engraved iPod, or even a romantic getaway. The 2013 edition raised nearly $1.2 million. See www.cupidsundierun.com for more information.

- **Santa Speedo Run** is an event that started in 2000 with a few friends streaking in their Speedos and Santa hats on a fun run in Boston. It has since caught on in other cities.

  The Boston Santa Speedo Run has raised more than $1 million for various children's charities, most recently the Play Ball Foundation, which helps kids learn teamwork and determination through sports. The one-mile jog now attracts about 500 participants a year and offers some primo prizes like iPads for top fund-raisers.

Santa Speedo Runs based on the original have spread to Chicago, Atlanta, Tampa, Annapolis, and Austin, benefitting causes from AIDS to diabetes.

Participants are asked to wear Speedos and any holiday flair they wish—just no thongs, please! Find out more at www.ssrunners.org.

BOUNCING BUNS 7K TRAIL RACE
Leave your clothes behind for a longer time

This race's slogan: "Race in anything from a snowmobile suit to your birthday suit."

About one-third of the runners in this clothing-optional race opt to be fully clothed. The rest are in varying stages of nakedness.

LOCATION: Palmerton, Pennsylvania
DATE: late June
DISTANCE: 7K
FIELD SIZE: 200
WEBSITE: www.pretzelcitysports.com
RACE HIGHLIGHTS: longer distance than most clothing-optional races; "cheeky" and fun attitude

"I've seen people run totally naked except for a necktie," said Ron Horn, president of the race's sponsor, Pretzel City Sports. "We've had people get naked to register and then put on clothes to race."

One woman, who ended up winning the race, thought she had discovered a clever way to give herself some "support" while still remaining exposed. The cling wrap she had wrapped around her chest proved to be too warm and unbreathable, though, and she ended up pulling it down around her waist like a belt.

Pretzel City Sports in Reading, Pennsylvania, took over the race from another company, gave it the Bouncing Buns name, and has since grown it from about 75 people to more than 200.

"You might say we've gotten them more exposure than they've ever gotten before," Horn said. "Every pun intended."

The race is a little longer than most nude races—a 7K instead of a 5K. Horn said the longer distance helps draw runners from a wider area around the Sunny Rest Resort in Palmerton, Pennsylvania.

"We tell people it doesn't matter what you're wearing," he said. "You'll still laugh more than you have at any other race."

TRAIL OF TEARS 5K RUN, WALK, CRAWL
Part of a nude racing series

Each May since the mid-1990s, Oaklake Trails Naturist Park in Oklahoma has opened its gates to the public and invited people in for a run.

Oaklake Trails is located between Tulsa and Oklahoma City, and features meadows, ponds, and rolling hills. The course shows off the 400-acre property, starting on a level gravel road, winding around the RV park, through a large meadow, downhill to a grotto and around a couple lakes, then back up to the main pavilion to finish.

LOCATION: Depew, Oklahoma
DATE: mid-May
DISTANCE: 5K
FIELD SIZE: about 80
WEBSITE: www.oaklaketrails.com (nrs. aanr-sw.org for racing series information)
RACE HIGHLIGHTS: challenging cross-country course; part of the southwest nude racing series

The fastest runners usually complete the "Trail of Tears" course in about 20 minutes, but the average time is usually closer to about 35 or 40 minutes, said Dennis Duncan, coordinator of the event.

"It's a challenging course," he said. "We have people who take advantage of the fresh air and walk the course as a way to get some exercise and enjoy the outdoors, and enjoy it clothes free."

The 5K is part of a five-event nude racing series in the Southwest Region of the American Association for Nude Recreation. Those completing at least three of the five races in the series are eligible for annual series awards.

The other races, all 5Ks, include:

- Skinnydipper Sun Run: Wildwood Naturist Resort in Decatur, Texas (see race report earlier in this chapter)

- Sahnoan Bare Buns Fun Run: Sahnoans at Star Ranch in McDade, Texas

- Roadkill Run: Armadillo Resort in Poolville, Texas

- Bare as You Dare: Bluebonnet Nudist Park in Alvord, Texas

Like the other races in the series, the Oaklake Trails run is "clothing optional," meaning you're welcome to go completely *au naturale*, though it's perfectly acceptable to wear underwear, a bra, or even a full outfit.

"What we've found is, this type of event gives people a little more incentive to come and visit our park," Duncan said. "We get some new members out of it, but mostly we make new friends."

006

CONNECT WITH NATURE

Getting back to nature is good for the soul.

These races, most of them on trails, will give you a chance to breathe some fresh air and come face to face with all kinds of wildlife, from squirrels to wild horses to moose.

Once you get a taste of the great outdoors and the relaxation brought on by such remote races, you just might not want to go back to those noisy, busy, big-city events.

The Big Wild Life Runs follow scenic coastal trails outside Anchorage, Alaska.

Photo courtesy of Rebecca Coolidge

BIG WILD LIFE RUNS

View coastal Alaska from the trails

A tip in case you see a moose along the trails of the Moose's Tooth Marathon: this is not necessarily a Kodak moment.

"Some people say, 'That's really cute, let's go take a picture.' But don't approach them," race director Sharron Fisherman said. "If you see them on the trail, you don't run near them. You kind of take a detour or go backward."

You're actually fairly likely to see a moose—or sandhill cranes, maybe even a bear—along the course. (If you do see a moose or bear, be sure to let a race official know so they can ensure everyone's safety.)

LOCATION: Anchorage, Alaska
DATE: mid-August
DISTANCE: marathon, half marathon, marathon relay, 5K
FIELD SIZE: 3,000
WEBSITE: www.bigwildliferuns.org
RACE HIGHLIGHTS: wildlife sightings; pre-race running clinic with Jeff Galloway and private running movie screening at Bear Tooth Theatrepub

The Moose's Tooth Marathon combines with the Bear Tooth Marathon Relay, the Skinny Raven Half Marathon, and the Snow City 5K to make up the Big Wild Life Runs in Anchorage. The races start and finish at Town Square Park in the city's downtown area.

"We have a fabulous trail system here," Fisherman said. "You start in downtown and within a mile you're on the trails along the inlets."

The courses wind along a coastal trail, past such landmarks as Westchester Lagoon, Earthquake Park, the Blue Ridge, and Goose Lake. The trails are all asphalt and mostly flat, though there are some rolling hills.

The Big Wild Life Runs are a revamped version of Humpy's Marathon, which started in the early 1990s. The event became the Anchorage Running Club's Wild Life Runs in 2008 and has grown by more than a third since then. Nearly one-fifth of the runners come from outside Alaska, and the race has become popular with the 50 States Marathon Club and Marathon Maniacs.

There's plenty to enjoy before the race, too. Olympian, author, and running coach Jeff Galloway has attended several Big Wild Life Runs and conducts a running clinic (registration required) the day before the races. And that night, the Bear Tooth Theatrepub is for runners only, with a private screening of a running-related movie.

Fisherman also recommends planning to get in some salmon fishing and other sightseeing during your trip to Anchorage.

"We've become a destination race because people want to see Alaska," Fisherman said. "Every year it seems like we grow a bit."

RUN WITH THE HORSES MARATHON
Let the wildlife be your guide

You might see more wild horses than other runners along the challenging and scenic Run with the Horses Marathon course.

Several herds of the gorgeous animals live in the high desert around Green River, Wyoming. With only 300 runners in all three event distances—100 of them in the marathon—the race can have a solitary feel, especially on the White Mountain plateau outside of town where there are few spectators.

You also might run across other wildlife, such as deer, quail, or badgers, but sightings are not guaranteed.

"You might not see wild horses, you might see them," race coordinator Ellen O'Neall said. "We've had runners say, 'I saw a ton of horse poop but no horses.'"

The course starts in Green River, on Expedition Island in the middle of town. Runners start on paved roads for the first two miles before turning onto Wild Horse Canyon Road, which turns into a graded dirt road that climbs from about 6,100 to 7,300 feet above sea level. The rest of the course runs along a plateau and has some rolling hills before turning back.

LOCATION: Green River, Wyoming
DATE: mid-August
DISTANCE: marathon, half marathon, 10K
FIELD SIZE: 300
WEBSITE:
www.runwiththehorsesmarathon.com
RACE HIGHLIGHTS: likely to see herds of wild horses; no time limit and aid available for even the last runner

Run with the Horses is one of only a handful of marathons in Wyoming, making it popular with the 50 States Marathon Club and Marathon Maniacs.

The event also attracts some slower runners because it has no time limit, O'Neall said.

"It's a relaxed race," she said. "Because there's no time limit, we have runners who will bring their cameras and even take group photos."

Volunteers will make sure everyone has course support; some have even driven back along the course to serve water to stragglers. And because of the isolation of the plateau, search and rescue crew patrols the course during the race.

"They always keep track of runners," O'Neall said. "Even if you're out there for nine hours, there's someone out there making sure you come in safe."

Someone will also be waiting at the finish line, because the course ends back at Expedition Island, where the River Festival is in full swing. The festival features a little bit of everything, and many runners like to take a cool dip in the river and stick around for concerts, a beer garden, kid-friendly games, dog competitions, and other events.

Avenue of the Giants Marathon
A relaxing run in the redwoods

Denise Malan

In the first mile of the Avenue of the Giants Marathon, I heard a runner joking that her neck would be the body part that was most sore after the race.

That turned out to be pretty close to the truth.

The Avenue is a 31-mile stretch of Old Highway 101 in Northern California known for the giant redwoods along the route and on hiking trails leading from the road. I spent a good portion of the 26.2-mile race craning my neck to look up toward the treetops or staring out into the forest.

LOCATION: Weott, California
DATE: early May
DISTANCE: marathon, half marathon, 10K
FIELD SIZE: 2,100
WEBSITE: www.theave.org
RACE HIGHLIGHTS: giant redwoods that are thousands of years old; cool Northern California weather and laid-back atmosphere

"The Ave" is nothing short of awe-inspiring. The redwood forest makes you feel both insignificant (the largest of the trees have been standing for thousands of years, reaching heights of more than 300 feet) and yet part of something larger.

The race has a strict no-music-player policy, mostly for insurance and safety reasons. Though many events have this rule, this was the first where I didn't see a single person breaking it. The fact that all couple thousand of us were running without distraction helped me enjoy the relaxing natural beauty of the course and had the added bonus of helping us chat and get to know each other.

There were long stretches where the only sounds were our breathing, feet pounding the pavement, and an occasional songbird high up in the

The awe-inspiring California redwoods are your companions during the Avenue of the Giants Marathon. Photo courtesy of Denise Malan

canopy or a bubbling creek. There were almost no spectators, just a few campers who stood along the course with their dogs to cheer.

The trees also provided a nice shady cover, keeping the temperature about 10 degrees cooler than it was in the sun, which did peek out here and there. Though the weather was perfect (starting in the mid-40s and reaching only to the 60s), those sunny patches toward the end did make me anxious to cool off afterward in the Eel River, along which much of the course snakes.

The marathon consists of two out-and-backs (the half marathon course uses one of these, and a 10K uses half of one). Normally I am not a fan of out-and-backs, but I liked the way the marathon was divided neatly into fourths, making it easy to pace oneself and eliminating some of the mental blocks from a marathon. The only downside was having to pass by the finish line at the halfway point.

The course is flat by Northern California standards. There was nothing too steep, but it seemed we were constantly going either slightly uphill or slightly downhill. One Marathon Maniac I met before the race told me he had driven the out-and-backs, and the race was downhill both ways.

This also turned out to be fairly accurate, though I'm not sure how.

On each of the runs out from the start/finish, I kept thinking how the downhill was nice but that I would pay for it on the way back. There were a few uphills, but nothing I couldn't handle. Then on the way back each time, I was surprised to again feel lots of downhill but only a few slight uphills. Maybe the downhill slopes were easier to feel than the uphills; maybe it was all in my head. Whatever made it seem this way, I was grateful.

I pushed to the finish, where most of the race's spectators were gathered. Afterward, I had enough left in my legs to walk a couple hundred yards from the finish to visit the Founders' Tree, which at 364 feet is the world's tallest known standing tree, according to the National Park Service.

After that I finally took that wade in the cool river and rinsed the sweat from my face and arms. It was a refreshing end to a surprisingly relaxing and revitalizing marathon.

I had run among the giants.

HAM RUN HALF MARATHON
Get away from the everyday hustle and bustle

There still exists a place to run where you can't get cell phone service, update your Facebook status, or even hear distant traffic.

That place is Superior National Forest in northeast Minnesota, home to the Ham Run Half Marathon. The race takes place miles from civilization, starting at the Gunflint Pines Resort and Campground, 43 miles, to be exact, from Grand Marais (population 1,362). It's even farther from the nearest large cities, Duluth and Thunder Bay, Ontario—about three hours to each, in opposite directions from the forest.

LOCATION: Superior National Forest, Minnesota
DATE: early May
DISTANCE: half marathon, 5K
FIELD SIZE: 200
WEBSITE: www.hamrunhalfmarathon.com
RACE HIGHLIGHTS: pristine wilderness along the Gunflint Trail in northeast Minnesota

Along the Gunflint Trail, runners enjoy views of granite outcroppings, ponds, creeks, and a river that runs along part of the course. It's not unusual to see moose, deer, beaver, grouse, and bald eagles along the trail. Race volunteers even saw a wolf when they were setting up one morning. The course is hilly and starts with about a mile uphill on a gravel trail before reaching the Gunflint Trail.

The Ham Run follows the same route the Ham Lake Fire scorched through the forest in 2007. The fire burned for more than a week and destroyed 75,000 acres of forest along the trail.

"There are various degrees of wildfire effects along the course," director Sue Prom said. "Some untouched areas, other areas that were burned to nothing, and some in between. It's interesting for runners to see the change each year and how much growth there is."

The Ham Run started the year after the fire and is a small race, with about 200 runners each year, about one-third of them from Canada.

The Gunflint Trail and the race end at the Way of the Wilderness Canoe Outfitters, where runners enjoy ham with all the fixings, massages, and door prizes.

It's only natural the Ham Run is one of the most environmentally friendly races as well, recognized by *Endurance* magazine as a "Race Without a Trace."

RACE REPORT

Deadwood Mickelson Trail Marathon
Like running on another planet

Scott Dunlap • www.atrailrunnersblog.com

My wife, Christi, and I are big fans of the HBO series *Deadwood*, so when the Deadwood Mickelson Trail Marathon was added to the Trail Runner Trophy Series, we signed up right away. The trip turned out to be more fun, mysterious, and magical than we ever could have imagined... and that's before the race even started.

LOCATION: Deadwood, South Dakota
DATE: early June
DISTANCE: marathon, half marathon, marathon relay (five runners), 5K
FIELD SIZE: 3,000
WEBSITE: www.deadwoodmickelsontrail marathon.com
RACE HIGHLIGHTS: supernatural beauty of the South Dakota Badlands; lots of attractions to check out before or after the race

Nothing could have prepared us for the supernatural world of the Badlands. As soon as we entered the Badlands National Park, the rental car screeched to a halt as we dropped our jaws and stared like zombies as the sun set over those painted, barren hills. The colors and texture seemed of another planet, both peaceful and frightening, stirring the soul at some deep, unknown level. So, of course, I strapped on my running shoes.

The Badlands were named so by the Lakota, who called it "mako sica," meaning "land that is difficult to cross." You certainly find out why as soon as you stray from the trails or road. I was surprised to find out that none of the park is off limits (just don't mess with the animals or fossils)—you can even run right up the moonrock mountain tops. If you can get there, that is.

I found the trails and roads suffice nicely. Running in the Badlands is amazing. The skies are still, the horizon seems limitless, and the colors shift every second as you run through prairies filled with wildflowers to infinite stretches of jagged red peaks. It is a land of extremes. As the sun set, we knew we would be back again before the trip was done, if only to suck up its mystery for a few more hours.

Deadwood is a thriving little town these days, thanks to a 1989 law that made low-stakes gambling legal again to help raise funds to rebuild the town (a recurring theme in the history of Deadwood). Our favorite spots were the Bullock Hotel, Saloon #10 (get a pint of Moosedrool—good stuff), the Deadwood Social Club restaurant (best choice for non-meat eaters or cheesecake lovers), and Jake's at the Midnight Star (Kevin Costner's "Me Wall" has three stories). And if $2.99 giant chicken fried steak is your game, you will have your choice of fare up and down Main Street.

The weather worked out perfectly for the Deadwood Mickelson Trail Marathon, with the canyon walls providing plenty of shade along the sunny course. The Mickelson Trail is a "rails-to-trails" location, meaning it's a former railroad covered with hard pack dirt to make a multi-purpose trail. This also means the course is fast and very road runner–friendly for a trail run. It also means the super-speedy road racers would be out in force.

On the bus ride out, I spoke with a couple from Chagrin Falls, Ohio. Both were working on their 50 marathons in 50 states, throwing in a few hundred-milers like Western States and Leadville along the way just for fun. Their eagerness and sense of adventure captured the spirit of most of the runners that morning who were excited to get started. We talked about the course a bit—13 miles of up, followed by 13 miles of down in a point-to-point section of the Mickelson Trail—and that the scenery was set to be epic.

As the gun went off, we ran about a half mile down the road to find the Mickelson Trail. I found a comfortable pace around 7:15 minutes per mile, which put me around eighth place. The three front-runners disappeared by the second mile, clocking well under a 6:40 mile up the hill. By the 14-mile point, I couldn't see anyone in front or in back of me, so I cranked up the tunes and leaned forward to let gravity help out as much as it could. The volunteers kept telling me I was in fourth place, so I had clearly been distracted by the gorgeous views and cheering spectators. But given the amount of space in front of and behind me, there was a pretty good chance this was going to be my finish place if I could hold it together.

It turns out it wasn't "all downhill" on the second half, and a few uphill and flat segments reminded me that although downhills seem easy, they do take their toll. Before too long, the mountain bike escorts picked me up around Mile 25 and guided me into downtown Deadwood for a 3:06 finish—good enough for fourth place.

As much as I wanted to hang around and cheer on the other finishers, we had to dash out to catch a flight back home (note to self for booking next year…the race is on Sunday, not Saturday). We were all smiles on the way back, recounting all of the activities we packed into a four-day trip.

LEAF PEEPERS HALF MARATHON
A stroll through famous New England fall foliage

When the Central Vermont Runners Club decided in the early 1980s to start a half marathon, the timing and the name were just natural choices.

LOCATION: Waterbury, Vermont
DATE: early October
DISTANCE: half marathon, 5K
FIELD SIZE: 1,000
WEBSITE: www.cvrunners.org
RACE HIGHLIGHTS: fall foliage in quaint rural Vermont

"That was actually pretty easy," said Darragh Ellerson, the race's first and longtime director. "People come here to leaf peep."

The Leaf Peepers Half Marathon in the early fall was conceived of as a way for Vermont to stand out in New England, which in those days was leading the country in road racing. For years, the 13.1-mile race was run partly on roads and partly on dirt trails, starting and ending in Waterbury but wandering through the countryside.

In 2013, organizers re-designed the course to stay in Waterbury and reduce some safety issues. The new course includes a two-mile, 500-foot climb on Perry Hill Road that rewards runners with a spectacular view from the top.

No matter the course, the Leaf Peeper will always feature beautiful fall foliage and rolling hills. ("You can't find a half marathon in Vermont that's flat," Ellerson says.)

The Leaf Peepers Half Marathon in Vermont is a great way to enjoy the colors of autumn. Photo courtesy of Jim Schley

WULFMAN'S CONTINENTAL DIVIDE TRAIL 14K
Honor one of Butte's favorite runners

LOCATION: Butte, Montana
DATE: late June
DISTANCE: 14K
FIELD SIZE: 240
WEBSITE:
www.buttespissandmoanrunners.com
RACE HIGHLIGHTS: single-track dirt trail along the crest of the Rocky Mountains; VIP registration available to skip to front of port-a-potty and food lines and pick your own starting seed

The website of the Butte's Piss & Moan Runners is full of tributes to John "the Wulfman" Wulf, the godfather of the running club who died of a heart attack in 2007.

"He had an unmatched zest for life and a magnetic personality that drew people to him," his obituary reads. "An avid skier, runner, hunter, and outdoorsman, he lived every day as if it were his last, managing to fit 14 days of activities into a seven-day week."

Around the time of the Wulfman's death, work was being completed on a new stretch of the Continental Divide National Scenic Trail, which runs along the crest of the Rocky Mountains, the line that divides the flow of water between the Pacific and Atlantic oceans.

Nicole and Ray Hunt used to hike the trail and decided it would be perfect for a race to honor the Wulfman, a huge proponent of the trail. They proposed the idea to the rest of the club, and the Wulfman's Continental Divide Trail 14K was officially founded.

The trail is a single-track dirt path that climbs up to 7,000 feet above sea level, though it shouldn't be too hard for someone acclimated to altitude, Nicole Hunt said.

"For Montana standards, I don't think it's very hard," she said. "If you've never done hills before, it is going to be tough."

The race is different every other year, though. In even-numbered years, it is run from north to south, from Homestake to Pipestone passes. But in odd-numbered years, the race goes from Pipestone to Homestake. Either way,

The Wulfman's Continental Divide 14K is a point-to-point run on a portion of Montana's Continental Divide Trail. Photo courtesy of Misty Oswald

you'll be treated to scenic views and stunning rock formations.

The race is run on Summer Solstice Saturday, the anniversary of the Wulfman's last group run. Race proceeds are used to help build and improve trails in southwest Montana.

Because the trail is single-track, all runners are required to submit their predicted times for a seeded start, with runners taking off every 10 seconds.

Everyone receives a race bib with his or her start time as the number. For example, someone seeded to take off five minutes and 10 seconds after the start time of 8:00 AM receives a race number of 80510.

At the end, the Piss & Moan Runners provide a homestyle picnic along with music and prize drawings for runners. For a $100 charity VIP registration, you can skip to the front of the food line, pick your own race start time, and be recognized at the award ceremony.

Along the course, don't miss some of the reminders of the Wulfman's presence.

"The Wulfman loved Miller Light in cans," Nicole Hunt said. "Our club will put Miller Light cans on the course to remember him."

Perhaps that will help you remember some of the Wulfman's favorite tips, such as, "It's all downhill except for the uphill" and "Start easy and taper off."

CATALINA ISLAND RACES
Explore a unique ecosystem

LOCATION: Catalina Island, California
DATE: January, March, September, November
DISTANCE: 50 miles, marathon, half marathon
FIELD SIZE: various
WEBSITE: www.runcatalina.com
RACE HIGHLIGHTS: challenging, rugged trails filled with wildlife; races benefit conservation causes

Catalina Island's 50 miles of coastline and 42,000 acres of wilderness offer eco tours, ziplines, scavenger hunts, wildlife cruises, and parasailing.

But save all that for after your race.

The island off the coast of Southern California is a trail runner's dream. In addition to the popular, long-running Catalina Island Conservancy Marathon, the area now offers a 50-mile race, a half marathon, and a second marathon throughout the year for runners to explore its wilderness.

The island's unique ecosystem is home to bald eagles, bison, deer, sea lions, seals, and rare plants.

The Conservancy Marathon and the Eco-Marathon benefit the Catalina Island Conservancy, a nonprofit dedicated to preserving the island's wildlife. The Avalon Benefit 50 Mile Run ultra marathon also raises money for the conservancy and other causes, including Avalon Hospital and high school scholarships.

The trip to the island adds a logistical step to this running adventure. It also provides some extra motivation to finish the race on Catalina's challenging, rugged trails.

"Most of the races on the mainland give you an escape clause. Drop out and you can catch a bus, hitchhike, or get a cab," runner Bob Babbitt wrote in *Competitor* magazine. "When you're on Catalina and you drop out in the middle of nowhere you become much more than a non-finisher: you become a resident."

BADLANDS TRAIL RUN
A taste of the Maah Daah Hey

The Maah Daah Hey Trail is a rugged 96-mile trip through North Dakota's Badlands, running from Sully Creek State Park north along the Little Missouri River and ending at the North Unit of the Theodore Roosevelt National Park.

LOCATION: Medora, North Dakota
DATE: mid-August
DISTANCE: 10K, 5K
FIELD SIZE: 150
WEBSITE: www.medora.com
RACE HIGHLIGHTS: explore portions of the nationally acclaimed Maah Daah Hey trail

Since it opened in 1999, the trail has received rave reviews from runners and mountain bikers for its scenic vistas, challenging hills, and wildlife. A couple runners reportedly have run the entire 96 miles at once, but you don't have to be an ultra trail runner to enjoy the Maah Daah Hey. You can experience a portion of it near Medora on the Badlands Trail Run 10K and 5K in August.

The Maah Daah Hey Trail is steeped in Native American culture. Its name comes from the Mandan Indian language and means "grandfather," and the trail's symbol of a turtle comes from the Lakota Indian's symbol for long life and patience, according to the North Dakota State parks and Recreation Department. Native Americans used the area for annual hunting trips, and it passes Theodore Roosevelt's Elkhorn ranch site on the Little Missouri.

The out-and-back trail run starts and ends in Medora at the Tjaden Terrace. All runners receive a complimentary lunch at Chuckwagon Buffet in downtown Medora after the race.

CAPULIN VOLCANO RUN
You versus the volcano

LOCATION: Folsom, New Mexico
DATE: late September
DISTANCE: half marathon, 10K, 5K
FIELD SIZE: 125
WEBSITE: www.capulinvolcanorun.com
RACE HIGHLIGHTS: run up and around the rim of the Capulin Volcano; see parts of at least four states from the top

Are you runner enough to take on a volcano?

The Capulin Volcano Run takes runners up the slope and around the rim of the national monument near Folsom, New Mexico.

The half marathon starts with a flat warm-up of about 1.3 miles to the visitor's center at the base of Capulin Volcano. Then the climb begins, about 1,000 feet over 2.15 miles on an asphalt road up the side of the formation, followed by another asphalt trail one mile long that winds 400 feet up into the crater and back down. Wheeee—time to descend the volcano again, then roll through moderate hills on the final half of the race into Folsom.

No need to worry about any sudden eruptions; the National Park Service says Capulin's volcanic rock is dated at between 56,000 and 62,000 years old, meaning it's been a while since this crater saw any volcanic action.

The view at the top is unbeatable. Some people claim to be able to see five states—New Mexico, Colorado, Oklahoma, Texas, and Kansas—from the highest point along the crater rim trail. The National Park Service says the Kansas claim might be a stretch because there are no high points in the western part of the state. Still, views of formations in four states is not too shabby.

The event also includes a 10K and a 5K, though those don't take runners onto the volcanic main attraction.

THE RUNNER'S BUCKET LIST

007

STAY INDOORS

Imagine running 150 or even 200 laps around an indoor track.

Now imagine that you're not bored.

If you think that's impossible, take a closer look at the races in this section. Indoor marathons and half marathons are gaining a small but very loyal following in frigid northern states where it can be a challenge to stage a race in the winter. These events get high marks for camaraderie, crowd support, and, of course, perfect and predictable weather.

But small tracks aren't the only places to stage an indoor race. A massive underground cave and the country's largest convention center also play host to some of the most unique races in the country.

Explore 1,200 acres of underground space in Kansas City at the Children's TLC Groundhog Run, held every year in late January. Photo courtesy of Mike Frazier

CHILDREN'S TLC GROUNDHOG RUN
Go underground for a good cause

One hundred feet under northeastern Kansas City, and unbeknownst to many residents, lies a 1,200-acre, manmade cave known as the SubTropolis. It is, according to its owner Hunt Midwest, the world's largest underground business complex.

The former limestone mine now is home to more than 50 warehouses and businesses, plus 6.5 miles of paved streets that once a year host one of the most unique races in the Midwest: the Children's TLC Groundhog Run.

LOCATION: Kansas City, Missouri
DATE: Saturday before Groundhog Day (usually last weekend in January)
DISTANCE: 10K, 5K
FIELD SIZE: 4,000
WEBSITE: www.groundhogrun.org
RACE HIGHLIGHTS: run in the world's largest underground business complex

(The race is held annually on the Saturday before Groundhog Day, naturally.)

The Groundhog Run started in 1982, the brainchild of a Children's Therapeutic Learning Center board member who had connections at Hunt Midwest, said Tracy Jones, who now manages the event for the center. The massive warehouse was at the time in its infancy and still being excavated.

"The run was sort of half-paved, half-gravel, and lit by lights they just sort of hung along the way," Jones said. "The people who ran that first year definitely have memories of dust and all sorts of things while they were running."

Still, the event was a hit, raising $8,000 for the center, which works with children who have developmental delays, disabilities, or medical conditions. The first running offered only a three-loop 10K and was limited to 1,500 runners because of the size of the SubTropolis.

As the cave grew, so did the Groundhog Run. By 1998, a 5K was added and capacity had increased to 2,200 runners. Just six years later, the race could hold 3,000 runners and the SubTropolis was large enough that the 10K became two laps instead of three.

Today, the race is limited to 4,000 runners and consistently sells out, raising more than $220,000 for the center. The cave's paved roads are closed to traffic for the event, and the temperature is always perfect for race day, at least compared to the Midwestern winter outside.

"We are lucky to have the partnership with Hunt Midwest that allows us to use their facility year after year, and they set up the course and provide security," Jones said.

Even among this unique set of indoor races, the Groundhog Run stands alone as a truly one-of-a-kind event.

ZOOM! YAH! YAH! INDOOR MARATHON
"The world's most prestigious indoor marathon"

The story behind the Zoom! Yah! Yah! Indoor Marathon starts the same way so many stories about other great races do: with running buddies joking over beers about starting their own race.

"We said, 'Well, we're spending a lot of money going to these races [in warmer climates]. We ought to have an indoor winter race here,'" said race director Dick Daymont. "It was sort of on a lark."

And that's about where the similarities with any other race end.

Fast-forward several years from that conversation, and the race held on the indoor track at St. Olaf College in Northfield, Minnesota, is billed as "the world's most prestigious indoor marathon," with a lottery system to win one of only 44 coveted spots each year.

It takes 150 laps on the indoor track to complete the 26.2-mile Zoom! Yah! Yah! (well, roughly 26.2 miles—more on that in a minute).

That's a lot to keep track of, so each runner is assigned a cross-country or track runner from St. Olaf to count every single lap. (Proceeds from the race benefit the collegiate team.) During the race, runners and their counters often form a special bond. Runners sometimes like to bring small gifts for their timers as a token of appreciation for cheering them on.

LOCATION: Northfield, Minnesota
DATE: early to mid-January
DISTANCE: marathon
FIELD SIZE: 44
WEBSITE: www.zoomyahyah.com
RACE HIGHLIGHTS: 150 laps and 600 aid stations; each runner is assigned one college cross-country runner to count his or her laps; their record of each lap becomes your finisher's certificate

"They are so much fun to have," Daymont said. "They are so cheerful, and the runners love them. You see these people 150 times."

At the end of the race, the timers' records—the elapsed time written at each lap, in six columns of 25 laps each—become finisher's certificates for each runner.

The Zoom! Yah! Yah! also boasts a record number of aid stations—600, to be exact—because each corner of the track has a table where runners can place their fuel and drink of choice.

This race has all the elements you need: plentiful hydration, constant cheering from the stands, peppy music on the loudspeakers, perfect weather (56 degrees, 0 mph wind), and no hills. So you would think this might be the perfect marathon to try for a personal record.

Not so fast.

You're actually likely to end up running more than 26.2 miles. The course is measured at the innermost lap, and not many runners will run the entire course there, especially the faster runners who will often pass the slower ones. Curves also slow you down a bit, and there's the matter of the course being just a smidge long. Technically, runners hit the 26.2-mile mark at about 149.5 laps, but it would be too complicated to stop there because the runners switch directions every 30 minutes to keep from putting too much wear on one side. (All of this contributes to the reason indoor marathon times are not accepted as Boston Marathon qualifying times.)

Even the race's name has an interesting story. The Yah! Yah! part was taken from the St. Olaf fight song, with its catchy chorus of "Um! Yah! Yah! Um! Yah! Yah!" The Zoom was added after Daymont's friend and fellow race founder Dennis Earley was looking for a race that starts with *Z* to complete his quest to run a marathon representing each letter of the alphabet.

The Zoom! Yah! Yah! receives almost universal praise on marathon review sites for its organization and intimate feel. The all-you-can-eat pre-race dinner the night before is served in a St. Olaf dining center, giving runners and timers a chance to get to know each other before the race. And there's no better way to get to know someone than running with them on a track for several hours.

"It will be, hands down, the most support you have ever received in a race," one runner from Virginia wrote on marathonguide.com. "It is the only race in America where it is impossible to go through a single minute without smiling."

MAPLE LEAF INDOOR MARATHON
Seven and a half laps per mile

It's mind numbing just thinking about the number of laps you need to run to complete the Maple Leaf Indoor Marathon: 204.

That's the highest number of laps, and thus the shortest track, of any indoor marathon I could find.

The Maple Leaf is run in Goshen, Indiana, on the 208-meter indoor track at the Roman Gingerich Recreation-Fitness Center on the campus of Goshen

College. Each running is limited to about 30 runners, but the race is run on two days, a Saturday and Sunday, to accommodate more runners. Several crazy racers even finish both.

The Maple Leaf uses chip timing and displays each runner's lap splits on a video board, so everyone can see their pace at least once a lap. And like many other indoor marathons, tables are provided at the four corners of the track for runners to place their fluids and snacks, and music is pumped through the loudspeakers for entertainment.

LOCATION: Goshen, Indiana
DATE: late February
DISTANCE: marathon
FIELD SIZE: 60 (two races of 30 each)
WEBSITE: www.mapleleafmarathon.com
RACE HIGHLIGHTS: chip timing for accurate lap counts; good running surface and small race for easier passing

RACE REPORT

Icebreaker Indoor Marathon or Heatbreaker Indoor Half Marathon
A perfect 55 degrees all year

Denise Malan

LOCATION: Milwaukee, Wisconsin
DATE: January (Icebreaker)/late July (Heatbreaker)
DISTANCE: marathon, half marathon, 5K, marathon relay (Icebreaker)/half marathon (Heatbreaker)
FIELD SIZE: 350 (Icebreaker)/300 (Heatbreaker)—in various heats
WEBSITE: www.indoormarathon.com
RACE HIGHLIGHTS: chip timing and lap counting; fun music and friendly volunteers to help occupy your time

How many times will I be lapped by the leaders? What if I hate the music they are playing? And most importantly, where can I blow my snot rockets?

These were actual anxieties I felt before trying the Heatbreaker Indoor Half Marathon, the summertime sister race to the more established winter Icebreaker

Indoor Marathon and Half Marathon at the Pettit National Ice Center in Milwaukee, Wisconsin.

The Pettit Center is no regular ice skating rink. It's an official training facility for the U.S. Olympic team (and happens to be where Dan Jansen trained for speed skating gold). Inside are two fenced-off ice rinks surrounded by a large, three-lane running track. One lap is 443 meters, slightly longer than the average outdoor track. The half marathon works out to be about 47.5 laps.

There actually wasn't much heat to break when I flew to Milwaukee for the Heatbreaker. Though it was late July, the temperature outside that morning was in the mid-50s, just barely warmer than the perfect racing conditions inside the ice center. I wore a tank top and running skirt, while many of the other racers donned long sleeves or pants. I was grateful for the jacket I brought as I set up before the race.

Each runner brings his or her own water bottle, which volunteers will fill with water. With the provided sticky labels, we all marked our bottles with our race numbers so the volunteers could find them for us as we ran. Anytime you felt like a drink, you yelled out your bib number on one lap, and your bottle would be ready in a volunteer's hand by the next lap—quite a handy system. You were also free to bring your own food, though the race provides some energy gels about halfway through. I had intended to bring some tissues to set on the table in case of a runny nose, but I forgot.

I had signed up for the first heat of three that day; each heat is limited to 125 runners. Some had registered for two or even all three heats to compete in the race's Two Alarm and Inferno challenges. Forty-eight laps on a track is enough for me, thanks!

We took our spot on the far side of the track, near a sign warning to watch for crossing Zambonis, to start the first half lap. The finish line would be on the straightaway closest to the entrance. Thanks to the indoor PA system, this was the first race I'd run where I actually heard all the pre-race announcements. The starting gun was shockingly loud.

The first heat also happens to be the required heat for those competing for overall prizes, so I knew I would be passed quite a few times by the leaders. I had planned to count how many times, partly out of curiosity and partly to keep my mind busy, but I abandoned that plan after two runners zoomed past me before I'd even completed two laps. This was going to be a long race!

Timing chips strapped to our ankles counted the laps each time we passed the finish line. A few steps past the line stood a video board that displays your name and lap number. It was interesting to look at the lap number of those around you. Normally in an outdoor race you run with people around your pace. But because we were spread out all over the track, the people surrounding you at any moment were usually faster or slower than you.

The fastest runners were given priority for the inside lane, and anyone was allowed to pass a slower runner on the left. I was usually in a comfortable spot in the middle lane, but occasionally I was forced to the outside. I don't know how much distance this added over the course of the race, but I think it was significant. At least, that's the excuse I'm using for not setting a personal record on the perfectly flat, climate-controlled course. (Spoiler alert: I missed a PR by two full minutes!)

By the second or third mile, I was glad I opted for the tank top and skirt. I was a bit nervous because of the forgotten tissues, but my usual race-day nose running didn't rear its head. Other runners didn't seem to have a problem acting like they were outside. I swear that one of the faster runners spit on the concrete to the inside of the track every time he passed me. Maybe it was just coincidence.

I had decided to break the race up into four sections of 12 laps (because of the extra half lap, our final tally would read 48 instead of 47), with three hydration stops. You could either grab your bottle from a volunteer and carry it once around the track and hand it back, or you could make a quick stop, take a drink, and leave your bottle at the table.

The strategy worked mentally, at least. My brain was constantly calculating the number of laps until my next drink, rather than worrying about the 40 or 30 or 20 total laps I had to go. The music piped through the PA system also helped pass the time. In the past, the Heatbreaker had accepted song requests from runners. This year, organizers picked the songs according to different themes for each heat. I was in the "rock" heat, which featured some great tunes by Metallica, Styx, and Journey. The next heat would be current pop songs, followed by 80s music in the final heat.

The time passed faster than I thought it would. I tried not to look down at the bright white lines on the track; those made me feel hypnotized and a bit dizzy. I was more than halfway through, down to about 20 laps to go, when the announcer's voice boomed through the speakers to announce the winner had crossed the finish line for the 48th time. I'm not going to lie; it was a bit depressing. It got even worse when the announcer started to tick off runners more and more frequently. He yelled a runner's name when he or she was down to five laps, a single lap, and at the finish. At one point, I worried I might be the last one on the track (an illogical worry because there was one walker in my heat and a few people I had passed, but not many).

Finally, I had taken my last drink and was down to the final quarter of the race. The laps felt like they started to count down faster now. By the time I was under 10 laps to go, I could see the light at the end of the track and stepped up my pace a bit. "Denise Malan, you have only five laps to go!" I heard over the speakers. I didn't really know the equivalent mileage I had left to go. I knew it was less than four laps to a mile, but because of the odd length of the track, I couldn't do the exact math in my head. I knew I was close to reaching my final mile and I still had enough energy to kick up my pace again.

Though I was a full two minutes off my personal best, the race went by much faster than I thought it would!

WARM YOUR HEART 5K
Escape the frigid Chicago winter

The average high temperature in Chicago in February is 36 degrees, with an average low of 22. Factor in an average eight inches of snowfall that month, and you're looking at some brutal running weather.

"Chicago has a big running community," said Bruce Buzil of Marathon

Media. "Around February is when people start to get cabin fever."

Thankfully, there is a race where the weather is a perfect 67 degrees and always dry.

The Warm Your Heart 5K is run inside McCormick Place, which, with four buildings and 2.6 million square feet of exhibit halls, is the largest convention center in North America. The most amazing thing about this race is that it's a single loop—all inside the convention center.

LOCATION: Chicago, Illinois
DATE: late February
DISTANCE: 5K
FIELD SIZE: 2,500
WEBSITE: www.warmyourheart5k.com
RACE HIGHLIGHTS: a single-loop 5K in the giant McCormick Place convention center; course includes skybridge with views of downtown

The course originally was run through two contiguous exhibit halls, but it was changed in 2013 to include two buildings connected by a skybridge over Lake Shore Drive. The change was popular and will likely remain every year, Buzil said.

The race is limited to 2,500 people all running in one heat, but the race could expand with more heats if its popularity continues to increase.

The Warm Your Heart benefits the Bluhm Cardiovascular Institute at Northwestern Memorial Hospital.

008

STUFF YOUR FACE

You're not going to burn enough calories in these races to make up for what you eat. But you can't worry about that, especially when you're running a race with a name like Fat Ass 5K or Jog 'n Hog. Just concentrate on keeping everything down while you run!

Pick your favorite food: a dozen doughnuts in five miles, six pepperoni balls in four miles, or seven fast-food items in 2.5 miles.

Then, like any challenge, take these races on one step— and one bite—at a time.

Racers can take a minute off their official race time for each Twinkie they manage to eat at the Twinkie Run each April Fool's Day in Ann Arbor, Michigan. Photo courtesy of Ann Arbor Active Against ALS

TWINKIE RUN
The Twinkie lives!

The recent apparent demise of the Twinkie was sad news for junk food lovers everywhere. Perhaps no one was worse off than the folks running the April Fool's Twinkie Run in Ann Arbor, Michigan.

"When Hostess was in bankruptcy status, we had to buy faux Twinkies from Canada," said Joel Dalton, a co-director of the race. "They weren't the same."

LOCATION: Ann Arbor, Michigan
DATE: April 1
DISTANCE: 5K
FIELD SIZE: 350
WEBSITE: www.a2a3.org
RACE HIGHLIGHTS: Twinkie-adjusted times; fun T-shirts and Twinkie prizes

That was in April 2013, when the world was Twinkie-less. Hostess, maker of the sweet treats, had gone bankrupt. But the Twinkie Run went on as scheduled that April Fool's Day, with the Canadian version of the treat and T-shirts proclaiming "Twinkie Lives."

By mid-year, the Twinkie had been rescued, brought back by a new manufacturer to much fanfare and the delight of the Ann Arbor Active Against ALS (A2A3) group that puts on the Twinkie Run every April Fool's Day. (If April 1 falls on a weekday, the race will be that evening.)

Twinkie Runners have the option to down one of the cream-filled goodies at the start and one in the middle of the 5K. They receive two official times: one chip-timed and a Twinkie-adjusted time where they receive one minute off for each Twinkie consumed.

"I think most people know what they're in for when they register," Dalton said. "Some people plan on not eating any Twinkies. They're just worried about barfing."

The sugary treats keep coming after the finish line. The race hosts a homemade Twinkie contest, and the entries can get pretty creative. There's Jamaican rum raisin cake Twinkies, espresso and chocolate Twinkies, vegan Twinkies, chocolate-dipped Twinkies, and on and on.

"Actually that's become my favorite part," Dalton said of the contest.

The race gives away Twinkie memorabilia for prizes, including a lunch box and pan to make "cream canoes," another name for the cream-filled sponge cakes.

The race has fun T-shirts, with three perfectly placed white dots on the back that look like the spots where cream is injected in the bottom of a Twinkie.

"When anybody's running, if they have the shirt, they really are kind of a Twinkie," Dalton said.

FAT ASS 5K
Leave the spandex at home

Paul Schafer liked to run 5Ks, but he was always intimidated by "the spandex people," as he calls them.

You know, the ones who jog two miles just to warm up for a 5K, or who finish and run back along the course as a cool down, trying to encourage the slower runners. They're usually wearing extremely tight clothing.

"I told my wife there ought to be a 5K for fat asses," Schaffer said. "That was always kind of a running joke."

On St. Patrick's Day 2008, Schaffer was sitting at the Celtic Mist Pub in downtown Springfield, Illinois, putting his idea to paper—actually, a bar napkin. Why not have a race with food and beer? The bar owner liked the idea so much, he agreed to provide the beer, and planning was underway for the first Fat Ass 5K.

The Fat Ass includes stops for ice cream, doughnut holes, corn dogs, and beer. Some years there are added bonus stops at a bacon-brownie vendor or a microbrewery, but those four are the staples every year. And if that sounds like a lot, get ready for seconds: this is a two-loop course, meaning you can make two stops at each station.

LOCATION: Springfield, Illinois
DATE: mid-May
DISTANCE: 5K
FIELD SIZE: 4,000
WEBSITE: www.fatass5k.com
RACE HIGHLIGHTS: beer, ice cream, doughnut, and corn dog stops; pig roast at the after-party

Even after all that, be sure to save room for the block party held after the race, complete with a pig roast and beer.

If you're a true Fat Ass and can't be bothered with the whole running part, this race still has something for you: the Fat Ass Detour.

"You go one-tenth of a mile, take a hard left straight into the Celtic Mist Pub, and you get a slab of bacon and a beer," Schafer said.

While the detour certainly is tempting, it's not as popular as you might think.

"There are a few people who do it just to say they did it," Schafer said. "There are some who just do one lap to check out the course. But most people do the full 5K."

The Fat Ass has grown from 400 that first year to 4,000 participants, thanks in part to the food but also its sense of humor and donations to charity. In its first few years, the event racked up more than $500,000 in checks to local and regional charities.

No doubt the race T-shirt is a draw for some participants as well. The "I Did the Fat Ass" shirt is sure to be a favorite in your collection.

Krispy Kreme Challenge
Philanthropy never tasted so sweet

Rusty Mau

Five miles, one hour, 12 doughnuts, and 2,400 calories—this is the Krispy Kreme Challenge. What started in December 2004 as a crazy collegiate dare between three North Carolina State University Park Scholars quickly turned into a nationally known phenomenon. The Krispy Kreme Challenge is more than a road race; it is a test of physical fitness and gastrointestinal fortitude, a North Carolina State University tradition, the largest annual timed running event in North Carolina, and the largest private contributor to the North Carolina Children's Hospital.

LOCATION: Raleigh, North Carolina
DATE: early February
DISTANCE: 5 miles
FIELD SIZE: 8,000
WEBSITE: www.krispykremechallenge.com
RACE HIGHLIGHTS: perfect your own doughnut-eating technique by downing 12 doughnuts and running five miles in under an hour

As the NC State Belltower chimed at 8:30 AM on race day, I was not sure what I had gotten myself into. Surrounded by 7,700 of my closest friends, I was about to engage in every child's fantasy: a chance to consume 12 Krispy Kreme Original Glazed Doughnuts in one sitting (well, not sitting, exactly). I was not nearly as excited about the five miles that lay ahead. After the horn sounded, my running partner and I sifted through the crowd of runners on Hillsborough Street as we tried to forget about the distance ahead.

The two-and-a-half-mile run to the Person Street Krispy Kreme Doughnut Shop was a blur. We passed Mr. and Mrs. Wuf, the official mascots of NC State, as well as a life-sized doughnut, a struggling Spartan phalanx, at least 50 ninjas, and a group of Raleigh police officers running in formation. The variety of costumes was better than Halloween. Whenever we passed someone in North Carolina blue, we

Costumes and plenty of doughnuts are the order of the day at the Krispy Kreme Challenge on the campus of North Carolina State University. The largest annual timed running event in the state, it raises funds for the North Carolina Children's Hospital.

Photos courtesy of Meera Venkataraman

started an obnoxious "Wolf-Pack" chant as if we were in the student section at an NC State basketball game. Before we knew it, about 20 minutes into the race, I could see the Hot sign at the Krispy Kreme ahead. Before my eyes lay the gauntlet: a tunnel of doughnuts.

More than 96,000 doughnuts lined Person Street and one dozen had my name on them. We grabbed our boxes, began chanting "U-S-A" with our fellow runners, and then put our training to the test.

Spectators cheered, and laughed, as I tore open my box. Unlike other runners before me, I had done my research. In true NC State fashion, I had used science to determine the most efficient doughnut-eating technique—the accordion, in which competitors smash three doughnuts together, forming four delicious super doughnuts. I dipped my first stack into water, shook of the excess liquid, and swallowed it whole.

This process continued as my consumption speed decreased with exponential decay. The first stack was delicious, the second was bad, the third was awful, and the fourth was painful. The last few doughnuts required excessive belching, small amounts of water, and extensive chewing. Although the process took 17 minutes from first bite to final gulp, I had done it. I proudly displayed my empty box to the race officials, slammed it onto the mound of empty boxes, let out another hefty belch, and sprinted through the gate. That's when it hit me: the 2.5 miles remaining.

My stomach churned and my legs slowed. A stranger yelled out encouragement to stand strong. This was a challenge but it would not defeat me. I glanced back and noticed the stranger was dressed in a full suit. He explained he was a businessman as I thanked him for his support and we exchanged the stickiest, least-professional handshake of my life.

We continued uphill and heard the heaves as novice runners experienced reversals. The only way to get through the gag was to persevere and pray. I started another "Wolf-Pack" chant as we summited St. Mary's Street and reached the start of the last mile. The pace began to increase. I knew my time would be close to one hour, but would I make it? The crowd of runners had thinned, but I continued to pick a target and make my move. Everyone was someone to beat. All I could think about was finishing in under one hour.

And then it appeared: the NC State Belltower. *Where is the clock, what is my time, and why did I do this?* I thought. The race clock was finally in sight, but I could not make out the numerals. The sugar was getting to me. The last few feet were the longest of the race, but I had done it—the clock above my head read 56:56.

As I passed the finish line, I knew I was a champion. I had conquered the challenge; I had done what no person should ever do.

The resulting feeling was the greatest yet worst feeling of my life. My doughnuts sunk to the pit of my stomach while I experienced the epitome of a runner's high. I felt like I could move a mountain at that moment, but all I wanted to do was sit down. I had completed my goal, I had overcome the challenge, and I had joined the ranks of the greatest athletes on Earth.

Completing the Krispy Kreme Challenge was one of the greatest and most insane feats I have accomplished. You cannot truly appreciate the atmosphere, understand the enormity of the crowd, or properly graduate from NC State until you have run in the Krispy Kreme Challenge. Even if you do not complete the Challenge there is a reason to feel special: your contribution helps support patients at the North Carolina Children's Hospital.

Since its inception in December 2004, the Krispy Kreme Challenge has donated $558,000 to the NC Children's Hospital. The event, entirely planned and executed by NC State Park Scholars and students, is a testament to the service-minded community of the NC State Wolfpack. The creators of the Krispy Kreme Challenge decided to meet at the NC State Belltower, run to Krispy Kreme, down a dozen doughnuts, and then run back, simply because they could. Who would have thought this finals-week procrastination tactic would turn into the sweetest philanthropic road race in the world?

Krispy Kreme Challenge co-founder Greg Mulholland, in an interview with ESPN, said, "I've talked to so many people who come back and feel like they're going to die. And yet every one of them feel like they're going to die with a smile on their face, and that's what's great about this event."

You won't regret your decision to attempt the Challenge, you won't regret your decision to support the NC Children's Hospital, and you will never regret eating warm Krispy Kreme Original Glazed Doughnuts.

JOG 'N HOG RACES
A gastronomical challenge

The Jog 'n Hog website has a section on nutritional info.

"Serving size: 1 race," it reads. "Calories: 570. Total fat: 12g."

And that's just the one in Erie, Pennsylvania, where racers down six four-ounce, doughy pepperoni balls from local Italian restaurant Stanganelli's.

You don't even want to know the calories in the other Jog 'n Hog race in

LOCATION: Yardley and Erie, Pennsylvania
DATE: June, July
DISTANCE: 4 miles
FIELD SIZE: 250 to 300
WEBSITE: www.jognhog.com
RACE HIGHLIGHTS: run two miles, eat a ton of food, and run two miles back; options for "Half Hoggers" to eat smaller portions

Yardley, outside Philadelphia, where runners eat a quart of Uncle Dave's ice cream.

Brothers Andy and Brian Smith ran the Krispy Kreme Challenge in North Carolina in 2010 and were awestruck by the popularity of the race.

"We looked around and saw thousands and thousands of people, and we thought there should be races in other cities with food," Andy Smith said.

So the Smiths, who grew up in Erie, devised a series of races in Erie and Yardley to celebrate some local food favorites. Each race is four miles, and participants must run two miles to the eating station, shove all that food in their mouths, then run the two miles back.

"I think a lot of people are just really entertained," Smith said. "People just love the eating area. You're all looking around at each other like, 'Are we really doing this?' Spectators love it, too."

Six pepperoni balls and a quart of ice cream proved to be a bit much for some runners the first year, so the Jog 'n Hog added a "Half Hogger" division for those who wanted smaller portions, specifically three pepperoni balls or a pint of ice cream.

The Jog 'n Hog added another element too: race the pig. A designated "Pace Pig" will run the race with the other participants, and even hang out for a while at the eating area to pose for photos. Then finishers will receive a sticker signifying whether they beat the pig or the pig beat them.

So do you think you can beat the pig? Sign up for a Jog 'n Hog and find out.

CORNDOG CLASSIC
An all-American race

State fairs are great places to have fun with the family, ride the Ferris wheel, play some games along the midway—and, of course, stuff your face.

From fried…well, pretty much anything, to cotton candy, fairs are known for their decadence and culinary creativity. That's what makes the Tulsa State Fair the perfect place to stage a foodie race with an all-American feel.

Racers at the Corndog Classic, held the week before the Tulsa State Fair each September, must eat three fair-food staples: cotton candy, lemonade (or beer for those over 21), and a mini corndog. Then at the end, if they're still hungry, racers are rewarded with a famous McKinney corn dog.

LOCATION: Tulsa, Oklahoma
DATE: late September
DISTANCE: 5K
FIELD SIZE: 2,000
WEBSITE: www.tulsastatefair.com/corndogclassic5k
RACE HIGHLIGHTS: cotton candy, lemonade or beer, and corn dog stops

"It's a fun race," fair manager Amanda Blair said. "It's timed and it's still serious, but it's family-friendly and reminds people of the fair."

More competitive runners can participate in a regular 5K without the food stops of the Corndog Challenge race.

The course itself is also unique, as it passes the Golden Driller, a 76-foot-tall statue of an oil worker, and along the interior loop of a horse track.

"It's definitely different than your average run-on-the-road 5K," Blair said. "It's a pretty unique environment that the runners get to experience."

NEW YORK CITY PIZZA RUN
Two New York favorites, together at last

Nothing is more New York than pizza. Or running. But what about pizza *and* running?

The New York City Pizza Run combines two of this city's biggest loves. You'll eat three slices of classic New York pizza while running four laps around Thompson Square Park, for a total of 2.25 miles.

Jason Feirman dreamed up the race in 2010 after writing his "I Dream of Pizza" blog for a couple years.

"I thought, *We're here in New York. People love pizza. What else do they love?*" Feirman said. "And I came up with running."

LOCATION: New York, New York
DATE: mid-September
DISTANCE: 2.25 miles
FIELD SIZE: 120
WEBSITE: www.nycpizzarun.com
RACE HIGHLIGHTS: eat three slices of NYC pizza; free beer at the after-party

He spent about six months planning and getting permits to run the event in the park.

"When I put tickets on sale. I thought I might be a little crazy and no one would come," Feirman said. "But it sold out within 24 hours. I don't think I spent a dollar on marketing."

It's true—this race practically sells itself. Now people look forward each year to the NYC Pizza Run, with its margherita pizza slices (mozzarella cheese, basil, and tomato sauce) provided by Pizza by Certé and its fun-filled post-race party with free beer.

"It's a wide range of participants," Feirman said. "There are definitely marathon runners who mark the race as part of their training calendar. Then there are other people who have never run in their lives."

Competitors at the NYC Pizza Run must scarf down three slices of margherita-style pizza in only 2.25 miles. Photo courtesy of NYC Pizza Run

Feirman said he's even heard of people who take the race pretty seriously and train for running and eating. But he sees finishing times everywhere from 16 minutes to 40 minutes.

"Some people finish at a slower pace than they started at," he said. "I think the third and fourth laps really start to wear on people. By lap four your mouth is dry and your stomach is full and you sort of kick it into last gear."

BRUNSWICK FAST FOOD CHALLENGE

A marathon's worth of calories in 2.5 miles

Just reading the list of items to eat at the Brunswick Fast Food Challenge might be enough to turn your stomach.

Here is what each runner must consume at each fast food stop, in this order:

- Pizza Hut: one slice of a large stuffed-crust pepperoni pizza
- Wendy's: one value-sized order of chicken nuggets
- McDonald's: small fries
- Taco Bell: one soft taco
- Fat Boy Drive-In: one Whoperburger—with mayo
- Burger King: one value-sized order of onion rings
- Cold Stone Creamery: one "like it"–sized order of chocolate ice cream

LOCATION: Brunswick, Maine
DATE: mid-August
DISTANCE: 2.5 miles
FIELD SIZE: 50
WEBSITE:
www.fastfoodchallenge.weebly.com
RACE HIGHLIGHTS: eat seven fast food items in 2.5 miles; two Twinkie "penalty lap" for those who toss their cookies

All of that—more than 2,000 calories worth of food—in only 2.5 miles of running.

And if you can't keep it all down, you'll only be forced to eat more. There is a "penalty lap" of two Twinkies for anyone who tosses their cookies.

"By and large, the reaction is, 'This is terrible; I can't believe I'm doing this,'" race creator Rob Gomez said. "It's a different kind of thing. I think in the end, people can say they did it, and they're actually pretty proud."

Gomez and his friend Jeff Sprague came up with the idea in 2009 as a way to combine their two favorite pastimes: running and eating. It's a low-key small event that attracts runners from around southern Maine.

Volunteers buy the fast food items before the race and have them ready at designated stops along the route. They also make sure runners have swallowed all of the food at one stop before taking off again. The logistics keep the race capped at 50 runners, and their entry fees are used to buy the food.

"No money goes to charity; there are no T-shirts," Gomez said. "All money goes solely to food. You can eat pretty well for 20 bucks."

Competition is hardly the point of the Fast Food Challenge, but the race has seen some pretty amazing times; the course record is an astonishing 22 minutes.

The winner receives a somewhat ironic prize: a gift certificate to Cold Stone Creamery, the final stop on the route.

"At that point, the last thing you want is ice cream," Gomez said.

The toughest part of the race, though, is likely the mayonnaise-laden burger from Fat Boy Drive In, a local institution.

"You take a big bite of that and it hits your stomach—you'll know right then and there if it's going to be your day," Gomez said.

HUNGRY MAN
As hungry as you want to be

The Hungry Man requires runners to eat an onion burger, a sushi roll, a burrito, and a cupcake.

At least in this race, you can have a little help.

The Hungry Man allows for two- or four-person teams to complete the course, with one person taking on a single food item and one leg of the 10K. Each person must swallow all the food before taking off to run their leg.

"You don't get just an easy appetizer," said Stacey Ninness, CEO of Neighborhood Services Organization, the nonprofit that puts on the race. "You have to have a good portion before you can tag up and run."

Or, if you're feeling really hungry, you can take it all on yourself.

"As long as you run all four legs of the race," Ninness said. "It's a fun race, so ideally we hope for four people."

The racers also love to compete in the Hungry Man costume contest. Teams have come dressed in everything from movie-inspired costumes to bunches of grapes.

"I think they get way more into the costumes than the actual race," Ninness said. "Once you get done it's fun to get everybody together and get pictures. I think they're glad they're done and they've finished. I think most of them are just glad they didn't throw up."

The Neighborhood Services Organization started the race as a fund-raiser at the suggestion of a creative board member, she said. Four local restaurants donate all the food.

"NSO is a 93-year-old nonprofit and we had never done a fund-raising event before," Ninness said. "So instead of doing the regular gala or golf tournament, he wanted to do something really unique."

009

CHUG-A-LUG

Chug it! Chug it! Chug it!

Run it! Run it! Run it!

Running and drinking go together well enough, just usually not at the same time. Most races save the partying for after the race is over.

The events in this section throw that silly notion out the window and make it an option—sometimes a requirement—to chug a few drinks along the course. Thankfully, none of the races are so long that you're likely to have a few too many and lose your way.

Featuring an aid station like few others, the Riverwest Beer Run in Milwaukee challenges runners to drink a pint of beer during its 1.8-mile course. Photo courtesy of Matt Baran

RIVERWEST BEER RUN
Chug as many beers as you can grab

How many beers can you drink in 1.8 miles?

Find out during the Riverwest Beer Run in Milwaukee. The run is a kickoff for the annual Locust Street Festival of Music and Arts.

LOCATION: Milwaukee, Wisconsin
DATE: mid-June
DISTANCE: 1.8 miles
FIELD SIZE: 900
WEBSITE: www.locust-street.com
RACE HIGHLIGHTS: four beer stops (mandatory for those competing for prizes); enjoy the Locust Street Festival after the race

Non-drinkers are welcome, but only those who make four beer stops along the 1.8-mile route will be eligible for prizes. The beers handed out are only four ounces each, making the total a pint along the entire course. But nothing's stopping runners from taking more than one at each stop.

"If they want more, they get more," said Linda Maslow, who directs the Locust Street Festival. "A lot of people drink four at each stop."

For those who are counting, that would be four pints of beer in 1.8 miles, a distance many people can run in 15 to 20 minutes. Maslow said not everyone takes the run seriously and tries to get a good time. Many are just enjoying themselves, and about a quarter of the field is made up of walkers, she said.

"Probably half the people are in some type of costume," Maslow said. "We've got people that run in inner tubes. We have people running with plungers on their heads. We have girls who run with angel costumes every year."

The streets of the Riverwest neighborhood are always lined with spectators who come early for the festival to watch the run. Likewise, many runners stick around for the festival, which includes about 20 bands on six stages, along with food, vendors, artists, and street performers.

RACE REPORT

James E. McNellie's Pub Run and Guinness Challenge
Gurgle and burp your way through four miles

Jeff Niese

You run, you chug, you may vomit, you will definitely burp. The James E. McNellie's Guinness Challenge in Tulsa, Oklahoma, has been giving Guinness lovers a reason to trade in the bar stool for running shoes each November since 2006. The run is as unique as the Irish stout by which it is inspired.

The four-mile run starts at Fleet Feet Sports in the Blue Dome district and winds through Tulsa's Deco, Brady, and downtown districts before finishing in front of James E. McNellie's Public House. But, as the name implies, the run is only part of the challenge. Runners must chug three 12-ounce glasses of Guinness, one at each of the three water stops.

The first Guinness stop is at approximately the 1.5-mile marker, the second at the 3-mile marker, and then runners must chug the third Guinness just before crossing the finish line.

As you will learn, the challenge is maintaining composure and pacing as Arthur Guinness' legendary stout fills up your stomach. I have run the race twice, and as they say, practice makes perfect. My love for Guinness and running goes back to college, but I never thought of mixing the two. As I found during the Guinness challenge, there is a very good reason for that.

LOCATION: Tulsa or Oklahoma City, Oklahoma
DATE: November, or an Oklahoma City version in May
DISTANCE: 4 miles
FIELD SIZE: 1,500
WEBSITE: www.mcnelliespubrun.com
RACE HIGHLIGHTS: chug three Guinness stouts in four miles, then try to stomach your two more free beers at the post-race party

The run itself is a fun little trek, starting in the Blue Dome district where restaurants and bars sit just on the outskirts of Tulsa's downtown. The race takes you over an overpass into the Brady District, where the first drops of Guinness wait for you in front of local bar, The Soundpony, and just south of historic Cain's Ballroom, the home of Bob Wills and western swing. I have found that this portion of the race, between the first and second pints, is the toughest. This is where the gurgling and burping begins. And the challenge is in full swing.

Most runners know what it's like to run through ankle, hip, or knee injuries, and that learned endurance will come in handy when running with a bellyful of Guinness. Just like a running injury, the Guinness Challenge is only met by bearing down and gutting out the miles, while ignoring the urge to toss whatever you had for breakfast.

The second Guinness break is in the Deco district, right in the heart of Tulsa's downtown that was built in the early 1900s when Tulsa was the Oil Capital of the World. As you can imagine, a race that features beer consumption typically brings out the most social and friendly of race participants who are easy to talk to as you run from Guinness stop to stop.

From downtown Tulsa, the race winds back to the Blue Dome district and to McNellie's Public House for the final pint of Guinness before crossing the finish line. Luckily, registration includes two additional drink tickets, so that pint doesn't have to be your last. With the Guinness Challenge met, the only thing left to do is to start the arduous task of preparing for next year!

LUNDI GRAS BAR-A-THON
If you get tired of running, just ride the float

There are few rules for the Lundi Gras Bar-A-Thon in Lafayette, Louisiana.

You will stop at six bars along the 3.2-mile route, and how much you drink depends on how fast you can chug. And if you get tired, you don't even have to run the whole route—just jump on the parade float that follows the runners.

LOCATION: Lafayette, Louisiana
DATE: Monday before Mardi Gras
DISTANCE: 5K
FIELD SIZE: about 70
WEBSITE: www.latrail.org (registration on www.active.com)
RACE HIGHLIGHTS: six bar stops in 3.1 miles; parade float follows the race carrying ice chests, music, and tired runners

Lundi Gras, French for "Fat Monday," is the day before Mardi Gras and has become nearly as popular for partying.

A group of triathletes in Lafayette, about 135 miles west of New Orleans, wanted to start a Mardi Gras–themed race. They put something together for Lundi Gras and made it a fund-raiser for TRAIL, or Transportation Recreational Alternatives in Louisiana, a group that supports construction of parks and trails.

The first race, in 2005, had about 30 runners and was six miles long with five bar stops, plus a vodka shot station at the home of one of the runners. That year also brought about the tradition of the decorated float filled with ice chests and blaring music that follows the runners.

"The first year, somebody's wife wanted to go but she was pregnant and couldn't run, so we got the float," said Scott Schilling, president of TRAIL.

"Then we had so many people jumping on because they didn't want to do the whole six miles, so we just made the float a part of the race."

In later years, the race moved to downtown Lafayette and was shortened to a little more than a 5K starting at Marley's Sports Bar, then cycling through The Filling Station, Bisbano's Cellar Door, Krooked Nickel Dockside Tavern, Blue Moon Saloon, and returning to Marley's. Each stop has beers ready for the runners, and drinks are included in your race registration (quite a bargain at $50; the fee also covers the cost of your T-shirt).

There's no rush to get through the beer stops. The whole race usually takes about 90 minutes, leaving time for some runners to chug a couple beers at each bar. The event isn't timed, and the runners usually stick together from bar to bar.

"Your metabolism is running really high," Schilling said. "Even though you're drinking six to 12 beers in an hour and a half, it will burn off a lot more quickly than you think."

The Bar-A-Thon wraps up just in time for the runners to watch the Queens Parade, Lafayette's Lundi Gras parade celebrating the women's krewes, roll past Marley's.

HANGOVER RUN 3K AND BEER MILE
Start the new year off right with…another drink!

Run Wild Adventures, a trail-racing company in the Northwest, calls the Hangover Run on New Year's Day its "puke and rally event of the year."

LOCATION: Salem, Oregon
DATE: New Year's Day
DISTANCE: 3K, 1 mile
FIELD SIZE: limit 30 for beer mile
WEBSITE: www.runwildadventures.com
RACE HIGHLIGHTS: adult beverage stop; beer mile challenge event after the 3K

The Hangover Run is fast, flat, and short enough to run even if you're actually hung over—only a 3K, or 1.86 miles. Plus, it starts at noon, so you can sleep in after your partying the night before and still make it to the race.

If you can stomach it, there's an adult beverage stop along the route, which is a combination of gravel, grass, and dirt trails. And afterward, if you still have some more energy left, you can compete in a "beer mile" event.

The beer mile is a challenge that involves drinking four full beers (12 ounces each) in just a mile. The race is run on a quarter-mile track, and competitors must chug one beer at the beginning of each lap.

Anyone who can't hold their liquor must run a penalty lap (though don't worry, no additional beer is required for that one).

TAP 'N' RUN
Responsible drinking and running

LOCATION: various
DATE: various
DISTANCE: 2.5 miles
FIELD SIZE: various
WEBSITE: www.tapnrun.com
RACE HIGHLIGHTS: multiple beer stops in 2.5 miles; finisher's medal that doubles as a bottle opener

Tap 'N' Run events, held across the country, invite participants to wear costumes as they enjoy their favorite beers and compete for whimsical awards. Photo courtesy of Nedra McDaniel/ adventuremomblog.com

You'll have to chug a beer before you even start the Tap 'N' Run.

The race series, which travels to various cities, features beers at the start, finish, and several stops in between on a short race route of 2.5 miles. Those ounces can really add up! Every runner also receives a finisher's medal that doubles as a bottle opener.

Racers are chip-timed, but many participants are just at the Tap 'N' Run to have fun (or even to Tap 'N' Walk). To add to the experience, many runners dress up in costumes or compete for the ridiculous extracurricular awards, such as Best 'Stache, Hot Mess, Walk of Shame, or even Best Belcher. (What else would you expect from a beer-chugging race?)

The Tap 'N' Run tour has visited cities such as Dallas, Cincinnati, St. Louis, Nashville, and Jacksonville. You can request the tour come to your city on the Tap 'N' Run website.

The race also promotes responsible drinking and running: any staff member will help you get a safe ride home if you forget to designate a driver.

TCHOUPITOULAS BARATHON
A classic New Orleans party

The formula for the Tchoupitoulas Barathon is simple: six bars, six beers, six miles. It's been successful enough for the race to keep running for more than 30 years, since 1983.

Maybe runners keep coming back for the coveted finisher's koozie. Or the Barathon T-shirts and posters.

Probably, though, it's the chance to down six beers in about an hour while partying with 1,000 of their running brethren.

LOCATION: New Orleans, Louisiana
DATE: mid-May
DISTANCE: 6 miles
FIELD SIZE: 1,000
WEBSITE: www.facebook.com/TheBarathon
RACE HIGHLIGHTS: six miles, six bars, six beers

The Barathon starts at Le Bon Temps Roule on Magazine Street, then stops at five other bars, with each runner receiving a free beer at each stop. Some are canned and some are draft, but all are local favorite Abita.

The race stays in Uptown New Orleans, and the bars are a collection of neighborhood restaurants and dive bars. You won't find any of the big name, French Quarter, touristy bars on this list. The final two stops are on Tchoupitoulas Street, which lends the Barathon its name.

Afterward, racers party with a band, food trucks, and beer specials, just in case six beers weren't enough for them. And as the race organizers say, "Go home when you're no longer any fun."

THE RUNNER'S BUCKET LIST

010

TOUR WINE COUNTRY

It's hard to pinpoint the biggest incentive for running these wine country destination races.

Is it the picturesque scenery? The perfect running weather? The wine tastings at the finish line?

No, wait, it's definitely the wine.

Though these races are beautiful, you'll no doubt be looking forward to the finish line for the wine tastings and food samplings awaiting you.

Whether you prefer a fine pinot noir from Oregon, a classic Napa Valley variety, or an up-and-coming North Carolina wine, there is likely to be a wine country destination perfect for you.

Wind your way through some of Oregon's most acclaimed vineyards at the Fueled by Fine Wine One-Half Marathon. Photo courtesy of Bethany Burgee

Fueled by Fine Wine One-Half Marathon

A fine reward for running all those hills

Amber Tafoya

LOCATION: Dundee, Oregon
DATE: mid-July
DISTANCE: half marathon
FIELD SIZE: 1,200
WEBSITE: www.fueledbyfinewine.com
RACE HIGHLIGHTS: amazing views of the Dundee Hills in Oregon; post-race wine tasting, pastries, and fruit

The Fueled by Fine Wine One-Half Marathon is all about the hills, the views, and the wine.

Set in the wine country of Dundee, Oregon, a small town 30 miles south of Portland, this race enticed me with the promises of beautiful scenery and a post-race party where I could sample local wines.

But first I had to earn that wine. This was my second half marathon and, with a total elevation gain of 839.9 feet, it may be one of the toughest I'll ever run. Dotted with stacks of rolling hills, breathtaking views, and close encounters with local vineyards and wineries, this was a challenging and beautiful way to run 13.1 miles.

The course winds through an area known as the Dundee Hills, which includes more than 1,264 acres of vineyards. About 1,200 runners stood behind the starting line at 7:00 AM, and the relatively small group was intimidating. As a rookie racer I was happy to sit in the back of the pack, but I did not want to be left completely behind as I made my way through the hills.

And the hills hit us fast. Within the first few steps of the race I made my way up the first one in the small neighborhood near the starting line. I had prepared for this by training on the hills in my neighborhood, and steadily pumped my way up and was quickly rewarded with a downhill through the first field of grapevines as the neighborhood gave way to the countryside. Much of the race is like this: you run up a few hills and received a quick relief of a downhill run before making your way up again.

The day before the race an organizer eased my concerns and said many choose to walk and lightly jog through the course to enjoy the views. She was right. As we pushed higher in the hills the views forced me to take in the scenery. I could see vineyards, large beautiful buildings of the wineries, and to the east a clear view of Mt. Hood. The steepness and height of each hill varied. Some were gradual while others felt like I was heading up a roller coaster track.

By Mile 4 I accepted that I was going to have a tough time later in the race if I ran up all the hills, so I opted to walk some of them. And when you add in the distracting views, it's easy to let go of the competitive aspect of the race and just enjoy yourself. With such a scenic backdrop, some runners made stops mid-run to take group photos in front of green vineyards and the surrounding hills. The volunteers along the course were helpful and happy to take photos.

The volunteers also provided a great service by simply being on the course, which at times felt like a remote mountain trail as it transitioned from pavement to dirt to gravel paths and winded through fields. This made the race exciting but lacking in the energy spectators often bring to the sidelines. About every two miles volunteers handed me water, cheered me on, and answered my questions, mainly "How many hills left?" The answer was always, "One more."

The last leg of the race was a welcomed relief of easy downhill running. I headed into my last three miles and noticed that I was finally making my way back down the hillside. Yes! Soon after passing the last winery I saw the finish line and pumped my legs to finish strong.

After finishing I was awarded a light-blue-and-black medal and refueled at a food station filled with croissants, pastries, and bananas.

But all I really wanted was the wine. I grabbed my keepsake glass and headed to a large white tent where runners were tasting wine from the vineyards they just ran through. The pinot noir, which is what Dundee Hills wineries are known for, ruled the selections. The tent was packed but full of satisfied energy as people drank a variety of local pinot noirs, blushes, and zinfandels and chatted about their accomplishment. I asked a vendor to fill my glass with a pinot and found a shady tree to sip and savor.

NAPA VALLEY MARATHON
This is the good life

The Napa Valley Marathon is perhaps one of the most lauded races in the country.

In more than three decades of running, the marathon has been named one of the top 10 marathons worth traveling for by Forbes Travel Guide, and one of the top 10 marathons to ensure your first 26.2 is memorable by *Runner's World*, among numerous other accolades.

"Napa offers runners the good life," *Runner's World* says.

LOCATION: Calistoga to Napa, California
DATE: early March
DISTANCE: marathon, 5K
FIELD SIZE: 2,300
WEBSITE: www.napavalleymarathon.org
RACE HIGHLIGHTS: tour the Silverado Trail, a scenic highway in the eastern Napa Valley; get a taste of luxury from the expo and pasta dinners to the finish line celebration

It's easy to see why.

From wine at the expo to a great swag bag and soup, showers, and massage therapists at the finish line, the Napa Valley Marathon gives runners a taste of luxury at every step. And let's not forget to mention the scenery; the route runs from Calistoga at the northern end of the valley down the famous Silverado Trail to Napa.

Nearly all of the course is rural, winding, and, best of all, has a net downhill elevation change (though don't be surprised when there are some uphills). Also a favorite ride among cyclists, the Silverado Trail travels along the eastern side of Napa Valley, past vineyard after vineyard, with unbeatable views of grapevine-filled hillsides and the lush valley.

As you're running, you can plan your wine trail trip for the rest of the week. The marathon is in March, a less-busy season in the valley and a great time to visit.

Traditionally about one-third of the field in the Napa Valley Marathon are first-time marathoners, though the race is popular among veterans, too. Entries are limited to 2,300 runners.

DESTINATION RACES
Find the perfect destination for you

There may be no better destination for a race than wine country—whichever wine country that may be.

A company called Destination Races had the brilliant idea to mix the ever-popular half marathon distance with the ever popular wine country vacation, ending up with a series of races through major wine growing regions in the United States and Canada.

With sophisticated wine tasting at post-race parties, gorgeous scenery, typically ideal racing weather—and did I mention the wine?—these races frequently sell out. Destination Races keeps the events small (the largest has a cap of 3,500) to ensure a boutique race feel. The tour stops include:

LOCATION: various
DATE: various
DISTANCE: half marathon; some offer shorter alternate distances or relays
FIELD SIZE: 2,000 to 3,500
WEBSITE: www.destinationraces.com
RACE HIGHLIGHTS: wine and music festival post-race parties; beautiful scenery and typically ideal racing conditions

- Santa Barbara Wine Country Half Marathon (May; Santa Ynez, California)

- Virginia Wine Country Half Marathon (June; Hillsboro, Virginia)

- Napa-to-Sonoma Wine Country Half Marathon (July; Napa, California)

- Oregon Wine Country Half Marathon (September; Willamette Valley, Oregon)

- Kelowna Wine Country Half Marathon (September; Kelowna, British Columbia)

- Healdsburg Wine Country Half Marathon (October; Geyserville, California)

LEELANAU PENINSULA VINTNERS HARVEST STOMPEDE

A little bit of romance, a lot of wine

The Leelanau Peninsula, north of Traverse City in Michigan, is known for cool-weather varieties of wine grapes like pinot grigio, riesling, and chardonnay.

Each fall, as the grapes are nearly ready for picking, the Leelanau wineries host the Harvest Stompede, a scenic

LOCATION: Leelanau Peninsula, Michigan
DATE: early September
DISTANCE: 7 miles, 5K
FIELD SIZE: 900
WEBSITE: www.lpwines.com/harvest
RACE HIGHLIGHTS: run through rows of grapes before they are harvested; enjoy a weekend-long winery tour afterward

and challenging vineyard race followed by a weekend of winery tours, special pours, and food pairings.

"The whole concept was to create an event that would give people a different way to experience wine country," said Andy McFarlane of the Leelanau Peninsula Vintners Association.

Runners and walkers can choose from the seven-mile or 5K courses through Michigan vineyards, starting at the Ciccone Vineyard and Winery in Suttons Bay. The seven-mile race goes from Ciccone to L. Mawby sparkling wine makers, through Black Star Farms, and then back to Ciccone. The 5K runs from Ciccone to Mawby.

The Leelanau Peninsula Harvest Stompede is a great excuse to tour some of Michigan's most beautiful vineyards. Photo courtesy of Kathleen Swinehart

The course is challenging, through rows of grapes, over hills, and through unsure footing. But it also is extremely beautiful.

"I see a lot of couples do the race," McFarlane said. "It's kind of got that little bit of romance to it."

A separate ticket allows you to tour the 23 wineries in the Leelanau Peninsula Vintners Association during the entire weekend.

"It does have a competitive race, but it also has that nice recreational feel," McFarlane said. "So people feel like they can go out, have a nice run or walk, and then go and enjoy the wine tour."

VINEYARD STOMP 5K SERIES
Four unique wineries and races

The Vineyard Stomp has to be one of the best deals in racing.

Register for four cross-country 5K races in five months, and at each one you'll receive a T-shirt, wine tasting, and bottle of wine (for those over 21). Plus, you'll be eligible for series awards and receive a technical race series T-shirt. All for under a hundred bucks.

The racing series was the brainchild of Kari Heerdt and her husband, Ken Gulaian, who own Round Peak Vineyards in Surry County in the Yadkin Valley, North Carolina's wine country. Both are recreational runners who decided to host a cross-country 5K through their scenic vineyard in the shadow of the Blue Ridge Mountains.

LOCATION: Surry County, North Carolina
DATE: June through October
DISTANCE: 5K
FIELD SIZE: 80 to 110 per race (40 in series)
WEBSITE: www.roundpeak.com
RACE HIGHLIGHTS: perks include a bottle of wine and wine tasting at each race (for those over 21); four cross-country courses through vineyards with unique histories and scenery

"We thought, *Wouldn't it be fun to host a race, a 5K, right here in the vineyard?*" Heerdt said. "There are very few that are cross-country, and even fewer that go through wineries, that I know of."

After two successful races in 2011, the couple pitched the idea to other Surry County wineries, and the Vineyard Stomp 5K series started the next year. The series includes four races, each with a unique character. Of course, they all have one thing in common: good Yadkin Valley wine, which typically includes dry varieties of French and Italian wines.

You can register for races separately, but to be eligible for series prizes, you must run at least three. The four races are:

- **Stony Knoll Vineyards (June, Dobson):** Stony Knoll is what's known in North Carolina as a Century Farm, or one that has been in the same family for more than 100 years. The former tobacco farm now hosts a vineyard and other crops. The course circles around old farm buildings that date back to the 1800s and a couple drainage ponds.

- **Olde Mill Winery & Vineyards (August, Mt. Airy):** One of the valley's newer wineries is found on a series of farms owned by the Mosley and Brown families. The 5K runs through the various connected properties and over rolling hills along a creek that runs between them.

- **Grassy Creek Vineyard and Winery (September, Elkin):** The historic site known locally as the Klondike Farm now is a corporate retreat with a rustic inn and surrounding cabins. The run starts and ends in the vineyard, but much of it runs through the woods and near a lake on the property.

- **Round Peak Vineyards:** This run is entirely through the 13 acres of grapes planted on the 32-acre property in the foothills of the Blue Ridge Mountains. Runners have spectacular views of the mountains, and spectators can see the entire two-loop course from the tasting room, which sits on a high ridge of the property.

GREAT ARIZONA GRAPE STOMP
Four autumn 5Ks through Arizona's desert wineries

Arizona's wine country is a hidden gem—even some people in nearby Phoenix are not aware that the high country is a great place to grow grapes. But the Arizona Wine Growers Association is out to change that, and a series of 5K races is helping them.

LOCATION: Willcox, Sonoita, Verde Valley, and Fountain Hills, Arizona
DATE: September, October, November
DISTANCE: 5K
FIELD SIZE: 40 to 200
WEBSITE: www.arizonawine.org
RACE HIGHLIGHTS: experience four different grape growing areas of Arizona; stomp some grapes after the race

"Growing wine grapes and producing wine isn't about alcohol consumption—it's about the art of making wine," said Patti King, executive director of the association. "We wanted to bring families to the region so they could understand that this is your hands in the dirt, working to produce the best type of grape you can."

The association came up with four races in different wine-growing areas, each with its own unique course. The races are in the fall, generally after the harvest each year, and the Arizona high country typically is 20 to 30 degrees cooler than it is in Phoenix, making these races a great excuse to get out of the city and explore Arizona wine country.

At each race, you can even experience a real grape stomp.

- **Willcox:** This race is the farthest from Phoenix and generally the smallest, with about 40 participants. It takes place at Zarpara Vineyard in Willcox, a small town on Interstate 10 near the New Mexico border.

- **Sonoita:** Sonoita, about an hour south of Tucson, is host to a strong group of vineyards, including the popular Flying Leap Vineyards. The 5K runs along a scenic road and attracts 200 runners.

- **Verde Valley:** This race doesn't go through the vineyards in Verde Valley, nearly two hours north of Phoenix, but at the end, runners can experience all the wines.

- **Fountain Hills:** The only urban race, this 5K is in the Phoenix suburb of Fountain Hills and features a mini wine garden with tasting from all the vineyards.

SPICEWOOD VINEYARDS HALF MARATHON AND 10K

Enjoy Texas Hill Country

This small race lets runners experience the charm of Texas Hill Country on scenic farm roads through Burnet County.

Spicewood Vineyards is located in the heart of the Texas Wine Trail, about 40 minutes west of Austin and 90 minutes north of San Antonio. Spicewood was founded in 1992.

LOCATION: Spicewood, Texas
DATE: early December
DISTANCE: half marathon, 10K
FIELD SIZE: 375
WEBSITE: www.runintexas.com/spicewood
RACE HIGHLIGHTS: souvenir wine glass; challenging course in Texas Hill Country

The weather in December is just about perfect for a run in the Hill Country, an area of Texas known as much for its scenery as for its wines. In a place named Hill Country, it's no surprise there are several significant climbs on the out-and-back course.

The after-party includes wine, of course, plus grapes, crackers, cheese, and hors d'oeuvres to complement the tasting. And all runners receive a souvenir wine glass to commemorate the race.

011

FEEL THE SAND
BENEATH YOUR TOES

Leave the hard, unforgiving asphalt behind for these races where sand cushions your every step.

Beach races can be found coast to coast, from Sea Isle, New Jersey, to Humboldt, California, and the Gulf Coast in between.

Some of these are run completely on the beach, others just for a portion. One lets you splash through the water at the mouth of a river. Another brings you up close and personal with a sea turtle. There's even a championship of beach racing.

So give one a try, and you'll enjoy the soft sand, sea breezes, and the rolling waves as you mark another race off your bucket list!

Runners at the
Long Beach Marathon
enjoy beautiful ocean
views as they head for
the downhill finish.
Photo courtesy of Nancy Yoshioka

LONG BEACH MARATHON
A beautiful ocean view

Don't let the urban start and finish fool you—about 80 percent of the Long Beach International Marathon takes runners within view of the Pacific Ocean, with a couple miles along the beach itself.

LOCATION: Long Beach, California
DATE: mid-October
DISTANCE: marathon, half marathon, 5K
FIELD SIZE: 20,000
WEBSITE: www.runlongbeach.com
RACE HIGHLIGHTS: most of the course has a view of the ocean; few hills, with highest elevation 45 feet

Long Beach can truly hold its own with its more famous neighbor to the north, Los Angeles, for a scenic and fun marathon course. This one starts in downtown Long Beach on Shoreline Drive. It circles around the Aquarium of the Pacific, the Lighthouse at Rainbow Harbor, and Shoreline Village before heading down a concrete path along the beach for a couple miles.

Around the halfway mark is Marine Stadium, which was dredged from an estuary in 1925 and was the site of the 1932 Olympic rowing competition and the 1968 Olympic trials.

After running past the stadium, the course heads to the campus of California State University–Long Beach, where students take pride in forming a loud and rowdy cheer zone. The course then heads back downtown from Ocean Boulevard onto Shoreline Drive for the downhill finish.

Like many coastal courses, this one is also relatively flat and fast. There are a couple bridges and a few hills, with the highest elevation at 45 feet.

BEACH RUNNING WORLD CHAMPIONSHIPS
Barefoot on the beach

Mitch Varnes founded the Beach Running World Championships almost tongue-in-cheek. He had wanted to start a beach race in Cocoa Beach, Florida, where running on the sand is popular. When he found out there wasn't a championship race, he figured, why not have one in Cocoa Beach?

Varnes got the half marathon sanctioned by USA Track and Field and found out pretty quickly the championship moniker was a great marketing tool.

"It's become an extremely popular event," Varnes said. "Last year we had runners from 22 states and six countries."

LOCATION: Cocoa Beach, Florida
DATE: October
DISTANCE: half marathon, 10K
FIELD SIZE: 300
WEBSITE: www.runonthebeach.com
RACE HIGHLIGHTS: compete for title of beach racing champion; enter a special barefoot division

The race has two divisions—regular and barefoot—plus a 10K for those not ready for the half marathon.

Of all the events Varnes puts on with his company, Smooth Running, including the Melbourne Music Marathon, he said the beach championship is the race where the runners are happiest. Even a timing snafu one year didn't faze them, he said.

"We watch the sun come up, there are birds, there are waves slapping the shore," Varnes said. "It just changes the mood of the whole race."

RACE REPORT

Surfside Beach Marathon
All 26.2 miles on the beach

Kamiar Kouzekanani

Surfside Beach is a small coastal town on the Gulf of Mexico, west of Galveston Island and south of Houston.

LOCATION: Surfside Beach, Texas
DATE: late February
DISTANCE: marathon, half marathon
FIELD SIZE: 550
WEBSITE:
thedriven.net/surfsidemarathon
RACE HIGHLIGHTS: well organized, great swag, and generous after-party; run all 26.2 miles on the beach in a small Gulf Coast community

We all knew that it would be raining hard the day of the Surfside Beach Marathon, resulting in a tough marathon to run. The wind, blowing rain, and resulting streams of water had washed out beach sands, making it quite challenging and rather unpleasant. Nevertheless, I was glad that the run was not canceled. Surprisingly, the race organizers offered refunds to those who had decided not to show up!

The packet pickup on Friday afternoon/evening was very efficient. Each runner received a long-sleeved technical shirt, a ceramic tile with the name and logo of the event on it, and a personalized bib number. This was my first time running the Surfside Beach Marathon; thus, I was given a nice duffle bag, too.

Race morning temperature was in the 60s. We ran on the beach for 26.2 miles. We first ran an out-and-back for about five miles toward the south/southwest and then the longer out-and-back toward the north/northeast. I thanked the volunteers for staying out there in the heavy rain, staffing the aid stations, and remaining cheerful and encouraging throughout.

The finisher's medal was nice. There were plenty of recovery food items and drinks awaiting the finishers inside the community center at Stahlman Park (barbecue, breakfast tacos, smoothies, cookies, oranges, soft drinks, and bottled water). It was a well-organized running event and it was obvious that the race organizers had done everything they could to make it a runner-friendly event. If the weather cooperates, it can be a nice marathon to run.

TRINIDAD TO CLAM BEACH RUN
Ditch your shoes on a West Coast beach

Nearly 300 miles north of San Francisco lies Trinidad, one of California's smallest cities and a former whaling village.

The Trinidad to Clam Beach Run originally was a winter training race for track runners at nearby Humboldt State University. Now it's a nationally known race with nearly 1,000 runners.

The event includes three peculiar race distances: 8.75 miles, 5.75 miles, and 3 miles. The original and most popular distance, the 8.75-mile run, starts at Trinidad and ends at Clam Beach. The 5.75-miler joins that course three miles in, near the finish for the three-mile race. Thus, the only true "Trinidad to Clam Beach Run" is the longest distance.

LOCATION: Trinidad, California
DATE: late January or early February
DISTANCE: 8.75 miles, 5.75 miles, 3 miles
FIELD SIZE: 1,000
WEBSITE: www.trinidadtoclambeach.com
RACE HIGHLIGHTS: cross the Little River at low tide; finish on the beach with a bonfire

However, both the 8.75-mile and the 5.75-mile courses feature the race's most unique attribute: a river crossing and finish on the beach.

The course crosses the Little River at Moonstone Beach. Because runners need to cross at low tide, the time and date of the race are determined by the tide patterns on the Saturdays in either late January or early February. Though the water depth is usually low, there are ropes and Coast Guard Rescue Swimmers available to help runners cross the river.

Many runners like to ditch their shoes at the river and run the rest of the way on the beach barefoot. Volunteers will bring their shoes back to the finish line.

The final leg of the run is on Clam Beach, with a bonfire and chili awaiting at the finish to warm up the runners.

TYBEE TURTLE TROT
Run the beach and meet a turtle

The Tybee Turtle Trot is your chance to feel the sand beneath your toes and get an up-close look at a real sea turtle.

Tammy Smith, coordinator of the Tybee Island Marine Science Center sea turtle program, and another volunteer came up with the idea of a Turtle Trot 5K to draw visitors to the island and raise awareness—not to mention some money—for the sea turtle program.

Almost 70 volunteers patrol Tybee Island's five miles of beaches during loggerhead turtle nesting season from May through October. Each morning they look for fresh tracks that could indicate new nests. Any nests are marked and monitored through the incubation period to give hatchlings the best chance at survival.

The Turtle Trot 5K takes place on the last weekend of April, just before nesting season begins. The course is an out-and-back all along the Tybee Island beach, followed by a festival with educational exhibitors and the grand finale—the release of a rehabilitated turtle back into the wild.

LOCATION: Tybee Island, Georgia
DATE: late April
DISTANCE: 5K
FIELD SIZE: 650
WEBSITE:
   www.tybeemarinescience.org/turtle-trot
RACE HIGHLIGHTS: kick off loggerhead turtle nesting season; watch a loggerhead be released into the wild

In 2013, the Marine Science Center released two loggerhead turtles: Chatham, named for the local county; and Silas, named for a Georgia boy who is battling liver cancer and has a passion for sea turtles. Silas helped attract 650 people to that year's 5K.

Smith uses the opportunity to teach people to keep their lights off at night—they can disorient female turtles and even discourage them from leaving the water to lay eggs—and to be extra careful on the beach during nesting season.

"It's a good way to kick off nesting season and remind people to turn off their lights and keep the beaches clean," Smith said.

CAPTAIN BILL GALLAGHER 10-MILE ISLAND RUN
An oceanfront race on the Jersey Shore

This long-running 10-mile New Jersey beach race started neither as a 10-miler nor a beach run.

In 1970, the race was a 14.7-mile contest only for ocean lifeguards, drawing a couple dozen competitors. It ran on city roads from inlet to inlet, along a favorite training route of one of the guards, a collegiate runner.

Four years later, Bill Gallagher, the Sea Isle Beach Patrol captain at the time, opened the race to the public. As the race grew, running it on the streets became hazardous because of traffic. A scuffle one year between a runner and a drunk passerby was the final straw, and Gallagher decided to move the race to the oceanfront, said Renny Steele, the current captain, who has worked at beach patrol since 1968.

LOCATION: Sea Isle City, New Jersey
DATE: early August
DISTANCE: 10 miles
FIELD SIZE: 1,200
WEBSITE: www.sicbp.com
RACE HIGHLIGHTS: evening beach race; about two and a half miles on paved boardwalk, the rest on the beach

The move to the beach coincided with a change in the race length to the standard half marathon. But in the late 1980s, construction of jetties and groins chopped the race again to 10 miles, the length it remains today. About two and a half miles are on a paved boardwalk, and the rest of the race takes place on the beach.

The Gallagher beach run has another unique aspect: it starts in the evening, at 5:30 PM, and does not allow walkers to ensure that everyone is off the course by nighttime. That also allows for a couple good running hours during low tide, so racers can take advantage of the harder-packed sand near the waterline.

The timing works perfectly for spectators, too.

"The whole way you always had people cheering you on," said Steele, who has run the race many times himself. "You were never in a desolate area. People like to take their dinner down to the beach and watch runners."

012

BRAVE THE ELEMENTS

Though Mother Nature is never totally predictable, many races, especially marathons, try their hardest to set their events during ideal racing season, when the temperature ranges from the 40s to the 60s, with low humidity and winds.

The organizers of the races in this chapter do exactly the opposite.

They've built their events' reputations on being either incredibly hot (even into the 100s), cold (think single digits), snowy, or otherwise adverse.

You'll want to make sure you're trained to handle these extreme temperatures, especially the ones on the hot side. At least at the colder races you can pile on more clothes, though you might require some special equipment to run on the snow or ice.

If you're especially daring, choose one race to conquer from each side of the temperature scale.

The Delaware Special Olympics holds a chilly 5K the day before its Polar Plunge as part of a weekend of festivities. Photo courtesy of Special Olympics Delaware

POLAR BEAR PLUNGE 5K
A very cool cooldown

Doesn't a dip in the water sound nice after a good run?

LOCATION: various
DATE: various
DISTANCE: usually 5K
FIELD SIZE: various
WEBSITE: various
RACE HIGHLIGHTS: dunk in the frigid water after you run; most runs are affiliated with Special Olympics Polar Plunges

Be careful what you ask for.

If you do a Polar Bear "Run to the Plunge" you could be dunking yourself in an ice-cold lake, ocean, or pool in the dead of winter.

It's all for a good cause, though. The frigid plunges are held around the country, from California to Minnesota to Delaware, often as fund-raisers for the Special Olympics. More and more Polar Plunges are adding running events as a way to raise more money and interest in their events. Some people even choose just to do the chilly run but skip the dunk.

"It's a really good opportunity to brave the elements but not have to jump in the ocean," said Lisa Smith with Special Olympics Delaware, which hosts a Run to the Plunge at Rehoboth Beach every February. "Not everybody will do that."

The Rehoboth 5K is actually the day before the plunge, making the plunge a weekend event for families to enjoy, Smith said. Other chapters have their runs just before the plunge, making the dip a nice cooldown—make that an extreme cooldown—after the race.

While the Polar Plunges are a signature fund-raising event for the Special Olympics, some plunge races aren't affiliated with the nonprofit.

Tatur's Polar Bear Plunge in Tulsa, Oklahoma, features three swimming pool dunks in only two miles on New Year's Day. Runners are offered "liquid courage" liquor shots at the start and must retrieve their giant finisher's medals from the bottom of the third pool.

No matter where you live, there's bound to be a polar run and plunge near you.

WEE-CHI-TAH TRAIL RACE
Brave the Texas Panhandle heat

LOCATION: Wichita Falls, Texas
DATE: late August
DISTANCE: half marathon, 10K
FIELD SIZE: 400 (trial runs), 175 (Triple Threat)
WEBSITE: www.hh100.org
RACE HIGHLIGHTS: temperatures usually over 100; trail race in a natural oasis in the middle of Wichita Falls

How hot does it get in northwest Texas, near the Panhandle, in August?

Ask anyone who's done the Hotter 'N Hell Hundred races in Wichita Falls.

"Well over 100—we are very accurate with our name," said Sandy Monson, race director for the Wee-Chi-Tah trail races. "It was really cool last year—it was only 93."

The Hotter 'N Hell Hundred originally was just a 100-mile cycling race on a

Saturday in August in Wichita Falls. Then organizers added a mountain bike race on the Wee-Chi-Tah Trail the Friday before the endurance ride, and finally, in 2005, the Triple Threat was completed with a half marathon and 10K running races added the Sunday after.

Attempting all three events in the Triple Threat has become increasingly popular, but you can also just run one of the trail races. And in this heat, that should be challenge enough!

"Running a half marathon on a trail is not really that large of an accomplishment," Monson said. "But running one where the starting temperature is in the 80s is an accomplishment."

To combat the high temperatures, the race provides plenty of rest stops and encourages runners to bring their own water. Local firemen cruise around on four-wheelers on the lookout for anyone with heat-related illness.

The Wee-Chi-Tah Trail is a 13-mile, natural-surface trail so named because it runs along the banks of the Wichita River. It's an oasis inside the city of about 100,000 people.

"You can hear [Interstate] 44 but you're in the woods, and there are deer and squirrels and opossums," Monson said. "Wichita Falls is very fortunate that we have that little pocket of nature in the middle of town."

RACE REPORT

Snow Joke Half Marathon
No wimps allowed at this wintery Montana event

Stuart S. White

The inaugural Snow Joke Half Marathon was run the first weekend in March back in 1980. Unfortunately for race management, the weather was on the balmy side, so the race was moved back into February in hopes of finding weather more appropriate for a Montana winter running experience.

"Organized quirkiness" is how colorful race director Pat Caffrey describes the underlying philosophy of the Cheetah Herders Athletic

Club, which conducts the race in the mountain hamlet of Seeley Lake. It is that philosophy, embodied by Caffrey, that is largely responsible for the growth of the race from the 32 hardy pioneers who ran in 1980 to the 595 who completed the 34th annual Snow Joke in 2013. (That total doesn't include the 39 dogs that competed in the canine division; a soup bone is formally presented to the winner at the awards ceremony).

LOCATION: Seeley Lake, Montana
DATE: mid-February
DISTANCE: half marathon
FIELD SIZE: 650
WEBSITE: www.cheetahherders.com
RACE HIGHLIGHTS: freezing temperatures, icy and snowy roads; canine division for those who bring their dogs (with a soup bone to the winning dog)

It was my good fortune to hear of the original race through the grapevine. The novelty of a half marathon on snow and ice piqued my sense of adventure, and I became a "joker" for life. I have run every Snow Joke except for 1990, when I was out of the country. For a while it afforded me the illusion of small-time celebrity; in the early 1980s the three-mile pie-plate-on-a-stick mile marker read, "Stu White 24 Furlong Mark." In 1989 I received a trophy as the only runner who had completed all 10 previous Snow Jokes.

Winter weather in Montana is nothing if not fickle and unpredictable. It's always a challenge to guess how best to dress for the event, particularly when you're leaving home in the dark, on the other side of the Continental Divide, as I used to do. For my first 31 Snow Jokes I lived in Great Falls, 125 miles east of Seeley Lake. In 2011 we moved to Portland, Oregon, turning a half-day jaunt into a pilgrimage of several days.

Several years ago while driving to Seeley Lake, I watched in near-panic as the dashboard thermometer began to drop, finally registering an outside temperature of minus-11 degrees. I was prepared to run in the cold, but not that cold. Fortunately, in the relatively protected Seeley-Swan Valley, the temperature rose to the low teens by race time and I didn't have to test my survival skills. On the other end of the spectrum, one of the early races was held on an unseasonably balmy day, allowing me to run in shorts and a singlet.

Runners must brave snow, ice, and freezing temperatures to complete the annual Snow Joke Half Marathon in Seeley Lake, Montana. Photo courtesy of Megan Gustafson

Race information describes the course as simply as possible: one lap around Seeley Lake. Start and finish is outside the elementary school. It's part of the joke that the colder the temperature, the longer Caffrey's pre-race instructions become. After a couple of blocks of icy backstreets, the course turns north on Seeley's main street and the highway to Glacier National Park. The first five-plus miles are on plowed pavement, sometimes wet, sometimes dusted with the previous night's new snow. It's a good chance for the field to space out and make good time.

Then the work begins. A left turn onto Boy Scout Road puts runners on the backside of the course and presents them with, depending on the year, either horrible running conditions or merely terrible running conditions. The road is plowed by the county and is accessible to cars, pickups, and snowmobiles. Snowmobiles are common; a couple of popular trails cross the course. Typically there is a base of ice, often rutted. In a good year, an inch or two of fresh snow covers the ice and offers a bit of traction. In a bad year, it's just ice and snowpack. In a *really* bad year, the temperature warms up enough and allows the ice to start melting. Slippery doesn't even begin to describe the footing.

Some runners carry a pair of slip-on traction devices with them, or have a spouse or non-running friend bring a pair of spikes to change into, but the running surface tends to be so unpredictable that I've always regarded the advantage as marginal.

Covering the seven miles of the backside becomes an exercise in route-finding. I weave back and forth across the road in hopes of finding a bit more traction. Inevitably, by the time I reach dry pavement again my quads and hamstrings are trashed and I can only make a determined hobble the last half mile to the finish.

The awards ceremony is an induction into the Royal Order of Cheetah Rangers. Division winners are invested with faux-cheetah-fur sashes and made to affirm, among other things, that they will never step on a cheetah's tail. In keeping with the race organizers' motif, the divisions are Pygmy (age 15 and under), Bushman (16 to 39), and Zulu (40 and over).

In spite of the race's substantial ration of whimsy I've always considered it a hard-core race—racing 13 miles in Montana in February doesn't fit the normal definition of a fun run. Having participated through parts of four decades I've never come close to induction into the Cheetah Rangers.

I quote from the official course description on the Cheetah Herders website: "Between 6 and 10 miles is the 'Charlie Cheetah Preserve.' You and the rest of your tribe are running over the Serengeti Plain, which is so bright and shimmering under the hot African sun it appears white as snow. You are effortlessly rounding up cheetahs at full sprint and herding them to your village corrals because, well, because you can. All you need is a little endorphin and a really twisted imagination."

SHOWSHOE THE BEAR
Get out of the gym and into the snow

Have you ever run in sand wearing swim flippers on your feet?

That might give you a preview of what it's like to run in snowshoes.

"I would say it's a little bit like running in sand where you don't always get your full traction and your full stride," said Karen Lundgren, race director for Snowshoe the Bear. "It's not hard, but you just imagine that you can't have your feet always where you want them."

LOCATION: Big Bear Lake, California
DATE: late February
DISTANCE: 5K, 10K
FIELD SIZE: 300
WEBSITE: www.openairbigbear.com
RACE HIGHLIGHTS: try your luck racing with snowshoes; enjoy the mountain trails near California's famous Big Bear Lake

Snowshoe the Bear is a 5K and 10K race on trails near California's Big Bear Lake, an area known for its endless outdoor activities, about 100 miles northeast of Los Angeles. Lundgren and her friends love to snowshoe during the winter, even taking on trails during the night.

"There are a lot of people who live in Big Bear who have never experienced that," Lundgren said. "In the wintertime they just go to the gym."

So the group decided the area needed a winter event and started Snowshoe the Bear in 2008.

As the name of the event implies, snowshoes are required most years, but the weather doesn't always cooperate with a fresh layer of deep snow.

"We've had years of pouring rain," Lundgren said. "We've had years where there's hardly any snow on the trail and it just becomes kind of a mudfest. We're committed to making the race happen every year, no matter what. We've had every kind of weather imaginable."

In years where there is good snow, the race is perfect for snowshoe newbies. It is short enough that you can put the snowshoes on over your regular running shoes rather than wearing bulky boots. Your feet might get a little wet, but you'll still be more comfortable.

Just be prepared for your normal running time to be doubled or more.

"Everyone is laughing, and I see so many people smiling and just enjoying the silliness of it," Lundgren said. "I think it makes it a little bit less serious than standing at the starting line of a 5K and everybody is going to go as hard as they can."

RUN ON WATER
Anything goes to make it across the "ice road"

This is your chance to walk on water.

Or run, or ski, or skate, or snowshoe—whatever you have to do to get across frozen, snowy, and slick Lake Superior.

LOCATION: Bayfield, Wisconsin
DATE: late February or early March
DISTANCE: 4.2 miles
FIELD SIZE: 100
WEBSITE: www.bayfieldwinterfestival.com
RACE HIGHLIGHTS: run across the frozen "ice road" across Lake Superior; use any kind of gear (including snowshoes or skis)

"People can run it, ski it, skate it, any human-powered way—or even dog-powered, if they think that's the funnest thing to do," race director Scott Armstrong said. "We leave that completely wide open for people to enjoy."

The runners, skiers, and snowshoers race along the famous "ice road" between Bayfield and Madeline Island in northern Wisconsin. Each winter, when the freshwater lake freezes, the ferry between the mainland and the island stops running, and a six-lane "ice road" is cleared from the snow and marked with small evergreen trees.

Because the ice road is not your normal street, the route you take across the lake is up to you, as is the proper footwear and technique to make it 2.1 miles to the island and back again.

"You might have to make a decision where you want to put your feet," Armstrong said. "Do you want to be on ice or snow?"

The temperature is typically around freezing in the late winter for the Run on Water, but it's ranged from 15 degrees with a strong wind all the way up to 50 degrees with a sunny sky.

There have only been a couple recent years in which the winter was too mild for the lake to freeze. The race, part of the Bayfield Winter Festival, is still run in those years, Armstrong said, but it draws a much smaller field, about 25 racers compared to the normal 100.

"People want to run on ice," Armstrong said. "It's highly weather dependent."

FROZEN SASQUATCH TRAIL 50K/25K
Too cold even for Bigfoot

You'll want to dress warmly for the Frozen Sasquatch Trail races—but not too warmly.

Race director Mike Dolin has seen racing outfits on the extreme ends of the spectrum, from one man wearing shorts and minimalist shoes, to people who can barely move in their layers of clothing. Somewhere in the middle is probably best.

LOCATION: Kanawha State Forest, West Virginia
DATE: early January
DISTANCE: 50K, 25K
FIELD SIZE: 200
WEBSITE: www.wvmtr.org
RACE HIGHLIGHTS: challenging mountain trail; hot chocolate at rest stops and post-race party

"If you can stand outside before you run and you're comfortable, you're probably overdressed," Dolin said.

Temperatures are usually in the low 20s or upper teens, though Dolin said it can be "freakishly warm" for that time of year, up to around 60 degrees. For a couple years, there's even been a fresh layer of snow the morning of the race.

"Pretty much, we're not going to cancel it," Dolin said. "Anything goes."

The race is either one or two times around a 15.8-mile loop that combines some of the best trails in Kanawha State Forest. Dolin's favorite, Middle Ridge Trail, is a rolling forest trail about 3.5 miles long in the middle of the loop.

Each loop features three major hill climbs: one of 685 feet, one of 400, and another of 650. Some of the terrain can be rough. The first climb of one mile

Temperatures can be in the single digits for the Frozen Sasquatch 25K/50K trail run in West Virginia. Photo courtesy of West Virginia Mountain Trail Runners

is so steep, some runners ascend on their hands and knees.

"I'm sure even the track record-holder doesn't run up the whole thing," Dolin said. "It's pretty brutal."

The final descent on Teaberry Trail is a 620-foot drop over one mile; one runner broke an ankle there the first year of the Frozen Sasquatch. (He's been back every year since, though, Dolin said.)

There are four aid stations per loop, featuring some unconventional race food like hot chocolate and warm broth to keep the runners warm.

"All aid stations have a fire going and can warm them up," Dolin said. "We just hope they don't get too comfortable and drop out."

HOTTER THAN HELL MARATHON
Nothing informal about this heat

Six runners were training for a marathon in September 2001 when at Mile 20 one of them wisecracked about just going ahead and finishing a whole marathon. That 26.2-mile training run morphed into the informal Hotter Than Hell Marathon, run in early July in New Orleans.

When the race organizers say "informal," they mean it.

LOCATION: New Orleans, Louisiana
DATE: Sunday closest to July 4
DISTANCE: marathon
FIELD SIZE: 160
WEBSITE: search "Hotter Than Hell Marathon" on Facebook
RACE HIGHLIGHTS: sock-wringing heat and Gulf Coast humidity; keep track of your laps (all 13) on a white dry-erase board

Each runner is responsible for his or her own supplies, including coolers, ice, water, and food for refueling. Luckily, the race is run in laps, so it's fairly easy to provide your own race support.

The laps—13 times around a 2.015-mile lap surrounding Audubon Park—are counted on a white dry-erase board with hash marks next to each runner's name. And everyone starts any time he or she chooses, after midnight, so they can finish in time for the 9:00 AM awards presentation (the race isn't too informal for T-shirts, medals, and awards).

The race founders also meant it when they named the race "Hotter Than Hell." New Orleans in July, even in the dead of night, is hot and, worst of all, muggy. The average high for the city in July is 91 with an average low of 75, though it no doubt feels much hotter thanks to the Gulf Coast humidity. One runner commented that he had to stop and wring sweat out of his socks after every lap.

The Hotter Than Hell doesn't have an official entry fee, though donations are encouraged to benefit RaceMD, a foundation that helps children with the genetic degenerative disease Duchenne Muscular Dystrophy.

BLISTER IN THE SUN MARATHON
A course designed for complaints

The first few lines of the waiver you have to sign for the Blister in the Sun should be enough to scare you away:

> I acknowledge that participating in running the Blister in the Sun Marathon is foolish and make this choice on my own free will. I understand that marathon running imposes harm to the body and will not hold the race director responsible for any injuries or deaths that I may sustain during this event.

LOCATION: Cookeville, Tennessee
DATE: first Sunday in August
DISTANCE: marathon
FIELD SIZE: 100
WEBSITE:
www.flyingmonkeymarathon.com/blister
RACE HIGHLIGHTS: tongue-in-cheek ribbing from the race director; personalized bibs with drawings instead of names

If that doesn't do it, race director Josh "the Sadist" Hite will try to scare you away himself.

"Please go and update your will," he says in an email to runners a couple days before the race. "Show your family that you really do care."

But somehow, people keep choosing to run this marathon.

Hite started the race in 2009 because he wanted to finish 12 marathons in 12 months and he needed an August race, a rarity in the South, with good reason. The temperature is typically in the upper 90s by late summer, and the Blister course has only minimal shade.

The race is run on five, 5.26-mile loops of Cane Creek Park in Cookeville, Tennessee. Basically, it's a course made for complaining.

"I knew that people complain about repeating," Hite said. "I knew people complain about the heat, they complain about the sun, the complain about the hills, humidity, everything. I thought, *This is perfect.*"

To make matters worse, the course is essentially a figure 8, meaning you'll have to pass the starting point—and the parking lot, your car, a way out, and spectators having a good time drinking beer—nine times before you finish.

"I didn't want to make it as physically challenging as possible, but mentally it really messes with you," Hite said. "It's so easy to quit."

Many runners carry water bottles to stay hydrated during the Blister in the Sun Marathon in Tennessee. Photo courtesy of Elly Foster.

Runners know that going in, so Hite said the race has a surprisingly small number of people, maybe one a year, who do not finish. Most will take a long time relative to their personal records, though. One of Hite's friends can run a 2:30 marathon but takes four hours to finish the Blister in the Sun. Most people finish within eight hours.

The race is limited to 100 people so the park doesn't get overcrowded and so the race can keep its small, intimate feel. Instead of race numbers on their bibs, each runner receives a personalized picture depicting their name or nickname—a toilet for a man named John, for example—hand-drawn by Hite's wife and her friends. Instead of the typical race T-shirt, runners get race shorts.

After all, it's probably too hot to wear a shirt anyway.

BADWATER ULTRAMARATHON
The ultimate endurance test

LOCATION: Death Valley to Mount Whitney, California
DATE: mid-July
DISTANCE: 135 miles
FIELD SIZE: 100
WEBSITE: www.badwater.com
RACE HIGHLIGHTS: 135 miles from the world's hottest spot to a mountain in California; small, invitation-only field

Only the baddest of the bad runners take on the Badwater Ultramarathon.

After all, it is run in the hottest spot on the planet: Death Valley, California. In July, when temperatures can reach 130 degrees. And it's a grueling 135 miles to Mount Whitney.

Badwater Basin in Death Valley, where the race starts, sits at the lowest elevation in the Western Hemisphere at 280 feet below sea level. It finishes at Mount Whitney, the highest point in the contiguous United States, though not at the summit (because that would be a little *too* crazy, apparently).

So, how hot is it? It's so hot that a runner who finished the route in 1986 (before the official race was founded) described in an interview with *Northern California Sport* going through six pairs of shoes because the soles melted.

Before Badwater was an official event, the allure of running or hiking from the world's hottest place in Death Valley to the cool breezes of Mount Whitney drew individual adventure seekers. Between 1974 and 1986, runners made 70 attempts to complete the route, though only four succeeded, according to the Badwater website. The first to finish was Al Arnold in 1977—it took him 84 hours. The first official Badwater was run 10 years later with five competitors.

The race now is legendary, not only for the heat and distance, but also the hills.

By the time runners have reached the finish line at the trailhead to the Mount Whitney summit, they have crossed three mountain ranges for a total ascent of 13,000 feet (nearly 2.5 miles!) and descent of 4,700 feet.

No wonder the race has a time limit of 48 hours (or a 21:20 pace) and a strict apply-for-invitation policy that accepts only the cream of the running crop. Just to apply to Badwater, runners must have either finished a previous Badwater; finished at least three 100-mile races; or finished the Brazil 135, plus another 100-mile race. You can round out your application with other races such as 24-hour races, Ironman triathlons, or ultra bicycle races (more than 500 miles).

The race invites only 100 runners from its many applications each year. Of those, usually about 95 start the race, and usually 80 to 90 finish. On the list of finishers are some of the world's greatest ultra runners, Dean Karnazes and Scott Jurek among them.

Despite the heat, hills, and what many of us would describe as torture, Badwater still tops the bucket list for many ultra marathon runners who want to tackle the ultimate challenge.

013

PARTY HARDY

Some races feel like they are only a prelude to the main event: the after-party! You just have to get through the miles to make it to the beer, music, and camaraderie at the end.

A few of these races have classic party settings, like the French Quarter in New Orleans, parades, or New Year's Eve celebrations, while others make their own party atmosphere, like the Boilermaker in Utica, New York, where the whole town throws race parties. Some are even family-friendly shindigs, like a Richmond, Virginia, race with 10 bands per mile.

So crack open a beer, start swapping exaggerated stories with your running buddies, and relax. You deserve it!

The Crescent City Classic, which bills itself as the first party race, tours part of New Orleans' French Quarter. Photo courtesy of Michael Zamora

Crescent City Classic
The original party race

· ·

Denise Malan

The real challenge of the Crescent City Classic lies in saving the partying for *after* the race.

LOCATION: New Orleans, Louisiana
DATE: late March
DISTANCE: 10K
FIELD SIZE: 20,000
WEBSITE: www.ccc10k.com
RACE HIGHLIGHTS: free drinks and food at the expo and after-party; scenery including the French Quarter, French Market, and City Park

New Orleans' classic 10K road race, which started in 1979, claims to have invented the party race that has become ubiquitous today. The race brochure says the CCC was the first to have live music during the race and a post-race party where the food and drinks flow freely.

I don't doubt their claim. The Classic is the only race I've seen with free and unlimited beer, plus red beans and rice, at the expo the day before. As if that wasn't tempting enough, you'll also have to resist the lure of New Orleans' French Quarter, famous signature drinks such as the Hurricane or Hand Grenade, and a host of rich, fried, and creamy foods that could haunt you on race day.

I fared pretty well, limiting myself to one drink at the expo, but I saw some other runners carrying around an awful lot of empty cups. I did splurge on a shrimp po-boy but only ate about half.

I was feeling good as I took to the starting corrals on Poydras Street near the Superdome. The corrals were crowded with 20,000 runners, from elites on down to the walkers and parents pushing baby strollers. No one heeded the race announcer's calls for each corral to let the one in front of it clear for three minutes before taking off. Everyone just went.

Perhaps we should have stuck with the plan.

The streets, which are narrow in downtown New Orleans, were congested for most of the race. I saw several runners fall, forced onto curbs or tripping on rough roads. And I'm embarrassed to say I took a tough spill myself, tripping on an inch-tall median on South Peters Street before even hitting the first mile marker.

I popped back up and limped right back into the race, trying not to wince so I would look tough. My right knee was skinned and bleeding, but I knew the left knee was worse and would begin swelling soon.

I was so paranoid about falling again that I missed much of the scenery. I know we ran through the French Market area on Decatur Street and took a left on Esplanade Avenue. Most of the race was a straightaway on this divided street.

The race provided water stops every mile, but more fun were the unofficial beer stops—at least two along Esplanade. "Beer free! Gatorade five dollars!" one man yelled as he handed beer cups to passing runners. At another stop, a couple runners were chugging through a beer bong as I ran past.

The final two miles of the Crescent City Classic wind through City Park, a large, beautiful green space that also is home to the infamous race after-party.

Somehow, I finished in personal record time, and it was not until I crossed the finish line that I became aware of the pain in both my knees. I visited the medical tent to get my skinned knee cleaned and bandaged, and one of the EMTs told me there had been an unusually high number of falls that day. I was only slightly comforted knowing I wasn't the only klutz out there.

The after-party also took my mind off my banged-up knees. The Michelob Ultra flowed from kegs around the party, and I enjoyed a small cup (okay, two cups) of jambalaya. Live bands played jazz and blues from the stage, interrupted only by an awards ceremony for the winning runners.

I left the party and headed back toward my car just in time to see the final finishers crossing the line—towing a beer cooler in a wagon, no less.

The original party race definitely lived up to its reputation.

HOLYOKE ST. PATRICK'S ROAD RACE

A "miniature Boston Marathon" with a great St. Paddy's Day party

I don't have to convince anyone that Holyoke, Massachusetts, can throw a great St. Patrick's Day party.

The annual parade in Holyoke started in 1952 and is continually ranked among the best parades celebrating Ireland's patron saint. It certainly is one of the largest, with 25,000 participants and 400,000 rowdy spectators in this small city just north of Springfield.

LOCATION: Holyoke, Massachusetts
DATE: mid-March
DISTANCE: 10K
FIELD SIZE: 6,000
WEBSITE:
    www.holyokestpatricksroadrace.org
RACE HIGHLIGHTS: pre-race tailgating and concert; stay for the infamous Holyoke St. Patrick's Parade

The St. Patrick's Road Race is the day before the parade, but no less of a party. The race draws nearly 6,000 runners, everyone from Olympians Alistair Cragg and Amy Hastings—who won the men's and women's division in 2013—to casual runners and walkers who think nothing of tailgating before the race.

The race even has a pre-race party with a concert starting about an hour before the 1:00 PM starting gun.

RACE REPORT

Bay to Breakers
Only in San Francisco

Scott Dunlap • www.atrailrunnersblog.com

Every May in San Francisco, the Bay to Breakers 12K takes over the city streets with enough beer, nudity, and costumed craziness to rival Mardi Gras. The year 2011 marked the 100th running (my sixth), and despite more constrictive rules and the doubling of police to curtail the Bacchanalia, it was as crazy as ever. Let those freak flags fly, my brothers and sisters!

LOCATION: San Francisco, California
DATE: mid-May
DISTANCE: 12K
FIELD SIZE: 23,000
WEBSITE: www.baytobreakers.com
RACE HIGHLIGHTS: a true racing spectacle with drinking (though alcohol laws are enforced), nudity, and costumes; one of the oldest road races in the country, started in 1912

I had originally planned to take my daughter Sophie the whole way in our new running rickshaw, but found out the day before the race that no parade floats or wheeled vehicles would be allowed that year, including baby strollers. Oops! That put us in a tough spot, since four-year-old Sophie isn't quite old enough to walk 7.5 miles in forecast wind and rain, but she's heavy enough that a three-hour piggy-back ride was out of the question.

So with no costume and no rickshaw, I picked up a seeded number (just bring a copy of a fast finish time, and you can get one, too) and decided to just run the damn thing for once. I didn't bring the camera due to projected rain, but grabbed my iPhone when the morning weather broke enough for a dry start. I made my way to the front, thrilled to warm up alongside Olympic medalist Meb Keflezighi (promoting his new book); Boston Marathon winner Deriba Merga; local Olympian Magdalena Lewy-Boulet; Mario Mendoza (fresh off his third-place finish at the 15k national championships the day before, here to run in the Asics Aggies centipede); a dozen Kenyan and Ethiopian gazelles; and the usual mix of costumed characters such as the ape, the busy bees, and some naked dudes in racing flats. Now *that's* a starting line!

Despite clocking 5:28 for the first mile, I was at least 100 people back. The speed of the centipedes in particular was simply amazing, given that they were all hooked together with less than four feet between them. By the time we turned onto Hayes Street, they were already heading up the hill nearly a mile ahead! That was easily a sub-five-minute-mile pace. It was odd for me to go through this section of the course without seeing tens of thousands of people around me—the salmon people going in the other direction—and I think it made Hayes Hill even more ominous. No problem—I just tucked in behind San Francisco Giants pitcher Tim Lincecum (a guy in a costume, that is) and tried not to red-line.

After we got over the hill, I tucked into a small group with Lincecum, Waldo (of *Where's Waldo?* fame), a guy running barefoot in a sequined tunic, and a Japanese runner singing karaoke out loud. We had good momentum (5:50 pace) for a group of misfits and were making ground on the next group of runners which included the towering 6'6" naked guy and a guy dressed as a Raggedy Anne doll. Spectators were out in force, also in full costume, cheering us on. Did I say this race was awesome?

We entered Golden Gate Park (Mile 4), where the downhills spread us out. I checked my watch—25:30—surprised at how much Hayes Hill had slowed us down, but also astounded that this race would be over before 8:00 AM. Do they still serve beer at the finish that early? I hoped so.

As we glided through the final downhill section (Mile 7), we all realized a sub-six-minute average was within reach if we kept at it. I got passed running straight into the headwind, but I drafted enough to cross the finish line in 44:34, roughly 132nd place (14th master), just behind Waldo and a naked guy.

Phew! That was fun, but tiring.

I did the cooldown walk, making friends with Dusty from San Luis Obispo as we became the first to enter the beer tent. Beer for breakfast? Absolutely! As the sun warmed us up, I met a lot of great people, including Reggie and Lisa from New Jersey, a couple from the Russian River Valley tackling their first B2B, and many others who trekked far and wide to be a part of this event. There's no doubt that Bay to Breakers is a "must do" race for a lot of people. Once I got a few beers in me, I walked the course backward to take in the revelry—ain't nothing like it!

EMERALD NUTS MIDNIGHT RUN
An alternative to Times Square

LOCATION: New York, New York
DATE: December 31/January 1
DISTANCE: 4 miles
FIELD SIZE: thousands
WEBSITE: www.nyrr.org
RACE HIGHLIGHTS: fireworks display, costume contest, and dance party

Is there a better way to ring in New Year's Day than with champagne, fireworks—and a four-mile run?

The Emerald Nuts Midnight Run has been a tradition since 1979 in New York's Central Park. Hosted by the New York Road Runners, this party starts at 10:00 PM with music and dancing, followed by a costume contest at 11:00.

Then, as it gets close to midnight, the runners will count down to the new year and then take off when the clock strikes 12:00, just as the fireworks light up the sky over Central Park.

The Central Park location and the party atmosphere make it easier for race "bandits"—those who don't register for the race but join anyway—to jump

Get the new year off on the right foot with the Emerald Nuts Midnight Run, held every New Year's Eve in New York's Central Park. Photo courtesy of Kari Geltemeyer

in. But take my advice and pay for the race—the Road Runners deserve the support, plus you'll want your own festive foam headgear provided by longtime sponsor Emerald Nuts.

Runners can stop midway for a toast of champagne—well, sparkling non-alcoholic cider. Aside from a few elites, the run is not scored, so you can take it easy, enjoy the 20-minute fireworks display, and go to bed knowing you will wake up feeling a lot better than the millions of partygoers down the road in Times Square.

VOLKSLÄUFE
The People's Race

The town of Frankenmuth, known as "Michigan's Little Bavaria," hosts all kinds of festivals throughout the year to boast its German heritage—Bavarian fests, music fests, Oktoberfests, and one of the state's most beloved road races, Volksläufe.

Pronounced "volk-slōy-fay," German for "the People's Race," Volksläufe got its name when in the late 1970s organizers wanted to give the race its own identity and tie it to the community's heritage. Frankenmuth, about 15 miles southwest of Saginaw, had been settled by immigrants from the Bavarian kingdom in the 1840s.

LOCATION: Frankenmuth, Michigan
DATE: July 4
DISTANCE: 20K, 10K, 5K
FIELD SIZE: 2,500
WEBSITE: www.volkslaufe.org
RACE HIGHLIGHTS: great community spirit and fun at the "People's Race"; enjoy a race-eve party and lots of entertainment on the course

The course entertainment includes Bavarian dancers and an accordion player, and the race weekend kicks off with a race-eve party with a beer garden.

The first race in Frankenmuth was organized for July 4, 1976, to honor the 200th birthday of the United States. That year, it was a seven-mile race with 180 participants, according to a history of the race on the Volksläufe website. A 15-miler was added in the next couple years, along with T-shirts for runners and a big marketing push.

That's when the three organizers visited other races across the country to get ideas. They changed the race's name, switched the distances to 10K and 20K, and brought in the Frankentrost Band, all traditions that continue today.

FIESTA FANDANGO
Be part of the parade

Fiesta San Antonio is the city's 10-day celebration of its heritage and unique place in Texas history. Fiesta dates to 1891, when residents decided to honor the men who fought at the Alamo and at San Jacinto, both pivotal battles in Texas' fight for independence.

The first Fiesta event was a Battle of Flowers Parade, which still runs today. The celebration has grown to include numerous parties, festivals, food tastings, and the granddaddy of all Fiesta parades, the Fiesta Flambeau, the nation's largest illuminated night parade. (Flambeau is French for "torch." In the parade's early days, four-men brigades literally carried torches in between each of the units. Today, Boy Scouts carry safety flares.)

The dazzling lighted floats, marching bands, and dancers make the Flambeau quite a spectacle for the 700,000 people who gather to watch it each year.

It's along the route of this parade, just before the main attraction kicks off, that the San Antonio Roadrunners host the Fiesta Fandango.

The 1,500 to 2,000 runners in the race dress in flashy costumes that match the theme of that year's parade. Themes from past years have included rock stars, movies, and "holiday magic," race director Debra Acosta said.

Acosta says racers are always creative with the costumes. For the holiday theme, one group had a man dressed as a doctor running with several pregnant women. For the rock star theme, a group of about 20 runners dressed as zombies from Michael Jackson's "Thriller" and acted out the video along the route.

LOCATION: San Antonio, Texas
DATE: late April
DISTANCE: 2.6 miles
FIELD SIZE: 1,500 to 2,000
WEBSITE:
www.iaapweb.com/fandangorun
RACE HIGHLIGHTS: feel like you're part of the country's largest illuminated night parade; pass out candy and toys to children waiting for the parade

The race has other traditions, too. The first 1,000 runners get a Fiesta Fandango medal, and the runners like to throw prizes to the children and crowd awaiting the parade.

"It's become tradition that some people carry bags of beads, some carry candy," Acosta said. "I ride in the lead truck, and we roll up the shirts we have left over from other races and toss them into the crowd."

PHILADELPHIA NEW YEAR'S EVE MIDNIGHT RUN & PARTY

Be healthy "for at least the first few minutes of the new year"

You know when a race puts the word *party* in its name, it's got to be good.

The Philadelphia New Year's Eve Midnight Run & Party really puts the emphasis on having fun.

LOCATION: Philadelphia, Pennsylvania
DATE: New Year's Eve
DISTANCE: 5K
FIELD SIZE: 75
WEBSITE: www.runbucks.com
RACE HIGHLIGHTS: competition for fastest runners in formal wear; after-party at Dave & Buster's with limited open bar; light food and $5 Power Cards for each runner

The scenery might not be the most exciting—the course is a mall parking lot, starting and ending at a Dave & Buster's (which provides a lit setting, plus the parking lot is cleared of snow). But there is a limited open bar (it opens two hours before the race), each runner receives a $5 card to play arcade games, and there are cash prizes for the top man and woman wearing formal wear.

That way, you're already dressed up for the after-party when you finish the race!

All racers also receive a race sweatshirt, a step up from the usual T-shirt.

The race goes off at midnight, so you can start the year off right, as the race says, and keep your resolution for at least the first half hour or so of the new year. Then, after the race, you can fulfill your resolution to have more fun.

BOILERMAKER
A town full of parties

The Boilermaker is Utica's Super Bowl.

The entire town parties for this famous 15K, which now sells out months in advance, even with a generous cap of 14,000 runners in the 15K and 4,500 in the companion 5K. The race is something this small town of about 62,000 people in the foothills of the Adirondack Mountains looks forward to all year.

"All of central New York becomes decorated in Boilermaker," race spokeswoman Mary MacEnroe said. "The race course gets lined with banners, along with homes and businesses alike. Runners and non-runners put on their best Boilermaker shirts to show their pride."

And the best part—even after the official post-race party at Matt Brewing Company with Saranac beer, a band, and a flyover—is that there's still more partying to be done.

After the race, residents all around town host Boilermaker parties to grill burgers, drink more beer, and swap stories about their favorite race moments.

Chris and Joanne Midlam, Boilermaker veterans who now help with the race's training program, host a get-together every year with their daughters, friends, and family—usually about 30 people.

"Everybody just hangs out and talks about their different Boilermaker experiences," Chris said.

Some people party-hop after the race and try to make it to as many parties as possible. That increases your chances of seeing some of the most famous faces in the running world, many of whom come to run the Boilermaker or to attend the induction ceremony for the National Distance Running Hall of Fame, which is held every other year the night before the Boilermaker. About 1,500 runners usually attend the induction. (Previous inductees include Steve Prefontaine, Kathrine Switzer, Fred Lebow, and Alberto Salazar.)

"Can you think of a better way to prep for the big race than hearing stories about the runners who made the sport great?" MacEnroe said. "Many of the inductees have overcome physical challenges to become

LOCATION: Utica, New York
DATE: early to mid-July
DISTANCE: 15K, 5K
FIELD SIZE: 18,500
WEBSITE: www.boilermaker.com
RACE HIGHLIGHTS: induction ceremony for National Distance Running Hall of Fame; parties all around town to celebrate the race

The entire city of Utica, New York, celebrates the Boilermaker 15K, with many residents throwing their own parties. Photo courtesy of Boilermaker

some of the best runners in the world."

Bill Rodgers, one of the most famous runners of all time, actually helped elevate the race to elite status after winning in 1983, only five years after the event was founded by Earl C. Reed as a way to give back to the community that supported his business, Utica Boilers.

Thirty years later, you name the honor, this race has won it. The Boilermaker has been ranked as the world's most competitive 15K, one of the top 20 races of any distance by the Road Runners Club of America, Road Race of the Year by *New England Runner*, and a "must-run" race by *Runner's World*.

MONUMENT AVENUE 10K
Take over one of America's greatest streets

LOCATION: Richmond, Virginia
DATE: mid-April
DISTANCE: 10K
FIELD SIZE: 38,000
WEBSITE: www.sportsbackers.org
RACE HIGHLIGHTS: 30 bands in three miles; neighborhood block party feel

Monument Avenue in Richmond, Virginia, is listed on the National Register of Historic Places and has been named one of the 10 greatest streets in America.

Its grassy median is dotted with monuments to Civil War history and local heroes such as tennis great Arthur Ashe, and the street is lined with beautiful turn-of-the-century churches, houses, and apartments.

It's also the perfect setting for a block party!

That's exactly what the Monument Avenue 10K has done. The race is an out-and-back along a 3.1-mile stretch of Monument Avenue. In that relatively short course, organizers pack in 30 bands, four party stops, and as many screaming spectators as they can.

"This race is different because it is along a residential street that stands behind the event," said Jackie Stoneburner, PR manager with race owner Sports Backers. "Neighbors throw porch parties and cheer on the participants. They set up lawn chains in the front yards and watch the sea of participants go by. This is truly a day that Richmonders look forward to."

The Monument Avenue 10K in Richmond, Virginia, is the eighth-largest race in the country. Photo courtesy of Jesse Peters/Sports Backers

The fun atmosphere and historic course helped the Monument Avenue 10K grow to 40,000 participants, making it the eighth-largest race in the country, only a dozen years after its first running in 2000.

And this party happens to be family-friendly. Sports Backers offers prizes for elementary children as they train for the race, and area schools compete for the honor of having the most students in the event.

"Yes, it's a party. Yes, it's a good time," Stoneburner said. "But it is also a way to celebrate an active lifestyle. People take pride in the fact they participate."

So round up the family, brush up on your Civil War history, and help make this block party rock!

014

DRESS UP

Looking good trumps running well in this group of highly spirited costume runs.

Much in the same way people let go of their inhibitions on Halloween, runners at costume races aren't bashful about having a good time. Many of these events have excellent after-parties with drinks and food, and the crowds tend to cheer even more loudly for the costume contest than actual race winners.

Your getup can be as simple as a wig or a kilt. Or it could require six friends, a theme, and rope to tie you all together.

However far you take your costume, make sure your ensemble is run-tested and race-approved. You don't want to find out in Mile 10 why more people don't run in squirrel outfits!

Competitors in the Kilted Run in Seattle make kilts from skirts, fabric, and even tablecloths. Photo courtesy of Pro-Motion Events, Seattle

GREAT KILTED RUN
Channel your inner Braveheart

The Great Kilted Run starts with hundreds of kilted runners charging up a steep hill, *Braveheart* style.

"The run up Kite Hill is definitely one of the tougher starts to a 5K," said Garett Slettebak, marketing director for race owner Pro-Motion Events. "But it's on grass, and with the fact that the bulk of the participants are wearing kilts and getting into character, they seem to enjoy the uniqueness of it. We even have a bagpipe performer playing music at the top of the hill."

LOCATION: Seattle, Washington
DATE: mid-August
DISTANCE: 5K
FIELD SIZE: 400
WEBSITE: www.promotionevents.com
RACE HIGHLIGHTS: wear a kilt and get into the Scottish theme

Pro-Motion revived the Great Kilted Run in 2009 after a hiatus under previous ownership. The run takes place in Seattle's

Magnuson Park and typically has about 400 participants, about 85 percent of whom wear kilts.

"We see a lot of people in plaid boxers," Slettebak said. "More creative are those who use cut up tartan picnic blankets or bed sheets. We have an inventory of 200 or so Velcro 'running kilts' that we rent to those who desire."

He said the smaller race feel, combined with the costume aspect, make the Great Kilted Run one of the friendliest and most fun races in the area.

"Of all of the running events our company produces throughout the year, the Great Kilted Run event is typically the friendliest," Slettebak said. "Peoples' guards are down and they are much more likely to smile at each other if they are all wearing kilts."

RACE REPORT

Cincinnati Gorilla Run
How much fun can you have in a gorilla suit?

Denise Malan

As soon as I got my gorilla suit in the mail, I knew I was going to need a costume for my costume at the Cincinnati Gorilla Run.

LOCATION: Cincinnati, Denver, Austin, and Edmonton (Canada)
DATE: various
DISTANCE: 5K
FIELD SIZE: hundreds
WEBSITE: www.gorillaevents.com
RACE HIGHLIGHTS: get a gorilla suit to keep; compete in best individual or group costume contests for most creative gorillas

Sure, running in a gorilla suit is unique and fun, but you don't want to look like every other gorilla out there. Judging from the pictures of previous Gorilla Runs, I needed to dress up my suit. I'd seen photos of gorillas dressed like the rock band Kiss (complete with painted gorilla faces), geisha gorillas, and even a gorilla paying homage to the *Where's Waldo?* books.

I didn't want to spend much more on another outfit. Race registration is relatively expensive—$85 for early registration—but you get to keep the gorilla suit, and it's for a good cause, supporting the Mountain Gorilla Conservation Fund. (The fund is based in Denver, where it started the first Gorilla Run, which spread to Cincinnati and now other cities.)

I dug through my closet and found the perfect old Halloween costume: the Karate Kid. The large karate outfit would fit over the gorilla fur and not be too constraining.

The day of the race in Cincinnati was cold, about 35 degrees, with a mixture of snow and sleet falling. I was actually hopeful that the temperature would keep us cool in our gorilla suits, but I could have done without the precipitation.

The couple hundred gorillas gathered before the race at the host restaurant Montgomery Inn at the Boathouse on the Ohio River. I stayed in street clothes for a while and enjoyed watching as other participants arrived. There were a group of 1980s rapper gorillas complete with a boom box, a group of guys wearing thrift-store suits, and one gorilla in a shower cap with a towel wrapped around her waist munching on a pre-race banana.

The Gorilla Run allows any kind of human-powered wheels, such as bikes, skateboards, and roller skates. One gorilla on a scooter was even pulling another on roller skates. The wheeled-division competitors took off a couple minutes before the runners.

Taking off from the Boathouse, my goal was to leave the mask on as long as possible, to get the complete gorilla experience. That lasted about 10 seconds. The eye holes are too small, and every step caused the mask to move around to the point that I could barely see. Other gorillas had cut out larger eyeholes; they either had much more foresight than I, or they had run the race before.

The course sticks to downtown Cincinnati, running by the stadiums for the NFL's Bengals and MLB's Reds before heading back in a riverfront park. I was startled to see a President Obama gorilla sitting on a park bench flanked by two stoic Secret Service gorillas. I laughed and waved as I passed, but they remained motionless.

With sleet and snow pelting my face and my gorilla suit getting soggy and heavy, I was relieved the race was only a 5K. I crossed the finish line and grabbed my camera to capture some of the other runners. There were lots of tutus, sports jerseys, and swimwear (which provided a chuckle on such a cold day).

The post-race meal from Montgomery Inn was rich and warming: a barbecue sandwich, homemade chips, and creamy mac and cheese, topped off with free beer. I enjoyed the meal while watching the results of the costume contests. The individual winner was "Baby Got Silverback," a woman in a coconut bra and tiny skirt that lifts to reveal the silver buns on her backside.

Some gorillas were still enjoying the music and drinks when I left to return to my hotel. I needed to warm up—and blow dry the gorilla suit so it could make the trip back home and be stowed away for next year.

ELVIS PRESLEY 5K
The King is alive—and he is running a 5K!

Each year, friends, family, and fans of Elvis Presley flock to Memphis to celebrate the King of Rock 'n' Roll with gospel services, concerts, impersonator contests, and Elvis trivia—so why not a road race?

LOCATION: Memphis, Tennessee
DATE: mid-August
DISTANCE: 5K
FIELD SIZE: 1,200
WEBSITE: www.elvispresleyrunandwalk.com
RACE HIGHLIGHTS: compete in Elvis and Priscilla Presley costume contests; start at the gates of Graceland

A tradition going on more than 30 years, the Elvis Presley 5K starts at the gates of Graceland and runs around the neighborhoods near Elvis Presley Boulevard.

The race has a large local following but even attracts international fans in town for Elvis Week, said Kelly Burrow, executive director of Livitup Inc., a charity that works to empower people with disabilities and receives donations from the race. (Elvis used to donate to the charity, which then was called United Cerebral Palsy.)

Runners are encouraged to dress up (though not all do because of the August heat), and the race hosts Elvis and Priscilla Presley costume contests. Some runners just wear Elvis-style sunglasses, while others go all out with white jumpsuits and bouffant black wigs. One family came with Dad dressed as Elvis in a jumpsuit, Mom as Priscilla in a gold sequined gown, and their young daughter as Lisa Marie.

Burrow said the race likes to stick to the Elvis theme, serving doughnuts—a favorite of the King—and inviting food vendors from around Elvis Presley Boulevard. (Though, sadly, one of Elvis' favorite treats, peanut butter and banana sandwiches, aren't available at the race because of copyright issues, Burrow said.)

The race also gives out Elvis-themed medals and T-shirts.

"Every year people start calling me in September to ask what the shirt will look like for the next year," Burrow said. "People love the race shirt. It has a following of its own!"

SUPERHERO HALF
Your chance to be a hero

We've all dreamed of being a superhero. Now you have your chance at the Superhero Half in Morris and Harding townships in New Jersey.

The Superhero Half encourages all participants to dress up like any superhero—Superman, Batman, Wonder Woman, Wolverine, it doesn't matter. The first race in 2010 supported the Christopher & Dana Reeve Foundation for spinal cord injury research, so organizers decided the superhero theme would best honor the man who was Superman. The theme stuck, although subsequent runnings have supported other charities.

LOCATION: Morris, New Jersey
DATE: mid-May
DISTANCE: half marathon, half marathon relay (two runners)
FIELD SIZE: 2,000
WEBSITE: www.superherohalf.com
RACE HIGHLIGHTS: dress like your favorite superhero

Race organizers aim big—in 2012 they attempted to set the world record for most superheroes at one event. Co-founder Heather Gardiner estimates that about 75 percent of runners dress up to help the cause.

"There have been several scantily clad Catwomen, an Iron Man, and pretty much every other superhero," Gardiner said. "There was also a guy who wore a Clark Kent outfit for half the race and Superman for the other half."

The race is on a flat, two-loop course through Morris and Harding townships, fast for runners and perfect for spectators to watch runners. All finishers receive a Superhero logo medal—proof of the superhuman feat they've just completed.

WICKED 10K
Some serious—and seriously fun—costume competition

LOCATION: Virginia Beach, Virginia
DATE: late October
DISTANCE: 10K
FIELD SIZE: 10,000
WEBSITE: www.wicked10k.com
RACE HIGHLIGHTS: highly competitive costume contests; relaxed party atmosphere

The costume competition is fierce at the Wicked 10K.

One runner dressed as a centaur—half man, half horse—and when one of his horse legs fell off, he carried it to the finish line so he'd have a complete costume.

Despite the effort, he only got second place. (The winner that year was a squirrel chasing a nut—a man in a squirrel costume with a nut dangling out in front of him.)

Organizers Jerry and Amy Frostick started the Wicked 10K on the weekend near Halloween to fill a void in fall races and help bring people to Virginia Beach in the tourism off-season. The first year, they signed up 5,000 runners and promoted wearing costumes, but they weren't sure what to expect. It turned out those who didn't dress up were the ones who felt out of place.

"We were really hoping there would be costumes," Jerry Frostick said. "We had no idea. It went out of control that first year. Probably 80 percent of people dressed up in crazy costumes."

The race has now grown to 10,000 runners with costume contests for individuals, couples, and groups. With so much creativity to choose from,

The Wicked 10K in Virginia features creative running attire and a fierce costume contest. Photo courtesy of Brightroom Photography

judges tend to reward those who make their own costumes and live out their characters (like a dead ringer for exercise guru Richard Simmons who gave the spectators some attitude).

Past winners include a group cheeseburger costume, where each person dressed like a different piece of the burger—patty, bun, cheese, pickle, and onion. After crossing the finish line, then the runners all piled on top of each other to form the complete sandwich.

Two men dressed as Clark Kent and Superman in a phone booth, with one of them running backward. And one woman won with her hamster-in-a-wheel costume.

"I don't know how she managed to run in that thing," Frostick said.

The street is lined with spectators angling to see the costumes, and after the 10K, kids can join the fun with a one-mile costumed race of their own.

While you're waiting for the costume contest and awards to be handed out, you can enjoy a hearty meal of chili in bread bowls and wash it down with a beer at the after-party.

RED DRESS RUNS
A hasher tradition since 1988

It started in 1987 with one woman making a simple statement in a red dress and heels. The Red Dress Run is now one of the most cherished traditions of the Hash House Harriers' worldwide running organization (see the "Seek Adventure" chapter for more on the hashers).

That was the year that the Lady in Red, as she would become known, flew to San Diego to visit a friend, her luggage lost in the process. Though she was still wearing the red dress and heels she had traveled in, the friend introduced her to the local kennel of hashers.

As the story goes, according to the hashers at RedDressRuns.org, "One member, noting her gender and attire, urged that she 'just wait in the truck' until her host returned. With that goading, she ran into history sporting her red dress and heels."

The hashers so loved that first run that they took up a collection for a plane ticket to bring the Lady in Red back the next year for an official Red Dress Run in which everyone—men and women alike—donned a red dress. The phenomenon has since spread to other Hash House Harrier kennels across the country and even the world, and benefits various charities.

The New Orleans Red Dress Run attracts several thousand runners each year. Beer starts at 9:30 AM, and the run is at 11:00. Remember, these are hashes, not races, so they are noncompetitive and usually involve beer.

LOCATION: various
DATE: various
DISTANCE: various
FIELD SIZE: various
WEBSITE: www.reddressruns.org
RACE HIGHLIGHTS: never a dull moment with the Hash House Harriers; women and men dolled up in red dresses for charity

The website RedDressRuns.org collects information on official affiliated runs that are held throughout the year.

BAYOU CITY CLASSIC
Take team running to a whole new level

Roger Boak has seen it all.

As the organizer of judges for the costume contest at the Bayou City Classic 10K and 5K in Houston, Texas, Boak can tell the best stories of runners dressed as port-a-potties linked together by toilet paper, or a group of naughty schoolgirls being chased by a nun.

LOCATION: Houston, Texas
DATE: early March
DISTANCE: 10K, 5K
FIELD SIZE: about 2,000
WEBSITE: www.bayoucityclassic.org
RACE HIGHLIGHTS: costume contests, including prizes for centipedes (chains of at least six runners in a cohesive costume)

The Bayou City Classic has a costume contest for individuals, but what really sets the race apart is the special division for "centipedes," teams of runners wearing costumes and linked together.

There are few rules for centipedes: groups must have at least six runners and be linked somehow (though the method is only limited to their imaginations); and those competing for the fastest centipede title must race in the 10K. That's it.

Technically, the award categories for centipedes are fastest, longest, loudest, best current event, best movie, best Texas theme, best corporate, best club, best media, and best school teams. But those categories are flexible, and the judges always find some way to bend the rules so that every centipede wins something.

"We've never had a centipede go without an award," Boak said. "The one category that cannot be changed is the fastest. We changed it one year to something else and they were furious."

Many centipedes play off current events or movies. One of the largest centipedes Boak remembers was inspired by the movie *27 Dresses* and involved 27 runners in truly horrible bridesmaid dresses. Another *Get Smart* centipede was so large it broke into three separate centipedes during the race so one of them could go for the title of fastest centipede.

Of course, running in a centipede presents its own set of challenges. Before race day, you'll want to practice running in the individual portion of your costume, as well as linked together. Try refueling at water stops, turning, and stopping. Otherwise, you might be unpleasantly surprised by your performance.

The first year of the centipede contest, Boak remembers a costume of six runners dressed as a six pack of St. Arnolds beer, complete with paper plates for bottle tops. Though it looked great, the bottle costumes proved too restrictive for the runners, and they struggled to shuffle down the street. The team fell behind all the other runners and ended up taking off their costumes to make up some ground when no one was looking.

"Just make sure you can run with it and make sure it's colorful," Boak said. "That's the main thing."

MULLET HAUL
It's not a hairstyle—it's a lifestyle

There are glam rocker mullets, country singer mullets, redneck mullets, and even femullets for the ladies.

LOCATION: Johns Island, South Carolina
DATE: early March
DISTANCE: 10 miles, 5 miles
FIELD SIZE: about 200
WEBSITE: www.ccprc.com/mullethaul
RACE HIGHLIGHTS: runners sporting mullet wigs and costumes; country-themed meal and party after the race

Pick your favorite mullet and try it on for the Mullet Haul trail race on Johns Island, South Carolina. The race is your chance to sport the hairstyle that's "business in the front, party in the back." Though runners are encouraged to wear mullet wigs (or for the truly dedicated, to sport your own mullet) and dress up, costumes are not required.

The five- and 10-mile races were inspired by Mullet Hall Equestrian Center on the island. Named after the family that used to own the land, the center normally is open only to horse owners who use the live-oak-lined, moss-draped trails for horseback riding, and for horse shows that are open to the public, said Sarah Reynolds, publicity coordinator for the Charleston County

South Carolina's Mullet Haul 5- and 10-Mile Trail Run was inspired by an equestrian center named Mullet Hall in Charleston County Parks. Photo courtesy of Amie Grace Photography

Park and Recreation Commission, which puts on the race.

"We wanted to do a themed race at Mullet Hall, and the theme sort of created itself based off the name and the growing popularity of costume races," Reynolds said.

About two-thirds of runners don costumes, organizers estimate, and they don't stop at the wigs. If you're wearing a mullet, after all, you might as well go the full nine yards.

"We had some really great costumes, running the gamut from rocker-style 1980s mullet wigs to more 1990s country-style mullet wigs and costumes à la Billy Ray Cyrus," Reynolds said. "A lot of people went all out with their costumes—a real challenge when you're running, too!"

After completing the off-road race, you can compete in the costume contest, jam to local band Unkle Funkle, partake in beer from a local brewery, and eat a good country meal—vegan chili, cornbread, and collard greens.

THE RUNNER'S BUCKET LIST

015

HONOR OUR COUNTRY'S HEROES

Many races across the country honor members of the military in their own ways, through fund-raising and run-for-a-soldier programs. But these races make it their sole mission to honor servicemen and women, first-responders, and people who lost their lives in tragic events.

These events offer a solemn reminder of the sacrifices made by average people, every day, in the service of our country. Make it your mission to attend one of these runs and show your support.

Founded by the family of a firefighter who gave his live to save others on 9/11, the Tunnel to Towers run in New York City pays tribute to all of those affected by the 2001 terrorist attacks. Photo courtesy of Asterio Tecson

TUNNEL TO TOWERS
Follow in the footsteps of a hero
. . . .

September 11, 2001, was one of the darkest days in United States history.

LOCATION: various
DATE: September
DISTANCE: about 3.5 miles (New York), various
FIELD SIZE: various
WEBSITE: www.t2trun.org
RACE HIGHLIGHTS: remember those who died in the 9/11 attacks by supporting veterans' causes; in the New York City event, retrace the footsteps of hero firefighter Stephen Siller

But that day in New York started clear and bright. Firefighter Stephen Siller had just worked a late shift at his station in Brooklyn and was headed to play a round of golf with his brothers. He heard the news about the first plane hitting the World Trade Center on his scanner.

A father of five, Siller called his

wife to let her know he'd be late, and then drove toward the Twin Towers.

Siller found the Brooklyn Battery Tunnel into lower Manhattan had been closed. Carrying 60 pounds of gear, he abandoned his truck and took off on foot toward the World Trade Center. Like 342 other firefighters, Siller didn't make it back.

Siller's family founded the Tunnel to Towers Foundation that now donates to causes such as building homes for severely injured veterans, supporting hospital burn centers, and giving scholarships to children who lost a parent in the wars in Iraq and Afghanistan.

The original Tunnel to Towers Run/Walk is in New York City every September, with a course that traces Siller's footsteps from the tunnel to Ground Zero. The foundation also has approved Tunnel to Towers events in other cities, such as Savannah, San Antonio, Orlando, and Nashville. Check the website for information about each year's runs, usually held on the weekend closest to September 11.

RACE REPORT

Bataan Memorial Death March
A touching tribute

Kamiar Kouzekanani

LOCATION: White Sands Missile Range, New Mexico
DATE: late March
DISTANCE: marathon, 14.2 miles
FIELD SIZE: 5,000 to 6,000
WEBSITE: www.bataanmarch.com
RACE HIGHLIGHTS: tributes to those serving in the Armed Forces; division for runners/marchers carrying at least 35 pounds

In 1942, during WWII, more than 75,000 soldiers (67,000 Filipino, 1,000 Chinese Filipino, and 11,796 American) were forced to march for days in the scorching heat through jungles in the Philippines. Thousands died. The survivors became prisoners of war.

The 60-mile march occurred after the three-month Battle of Bataan. It was the largest American surrender since the American Revolution. The march was accounted as a Japanese war crime.

To honor the survivors of the Bataan, the Army ROTC Department at New Mexico State University began sponsoring the Memorial March in 1989. In 1992, White Sands Missile Range and the New Mexico National Guard joined in the sponsorship, and the event was moved to the Missile Range. In 2003, for the only time in its history, the March was canceled because of Operation Iraqi Freedom. Since its inception, the March has grown from about 100 participants to thousands of marchers from across the United States and several foreign countries. While primarily a military event, many civilians choose to take the challenge.

The March offers two routes: a 26.2-mile marathon run or a 14.2-mile run. The marathon categories are military and civilian individual light; military and civilian individual heavy (carrying a minimum of 35 pounds in rucksacks/backpacks throughout the run); team military; and team civilian. Each team consists of five members, and each runner has to cross the finish line within 20 seconds of each other.

The event was very well-organized. Each marcher received a short-sleeved cotton T-shirt, a dog tag, and an individualized multi-colored certificate of participation. The pre-race pasta buffet dinner on Saturday was very good and cost only $10.

The morning of the race was chilly. I was dressed like an onion, in layers! The temperature ranged from the high 30s to mid-60s. It was sunny and there was hardly any wind, which pleasantly surprised us, as the blowing sands would have made the run really tough (it was quite windy on Friday and Saturday). There were nearly 5,700 runners and marchers.

The start time was at 7:05 AM. We had been asked to report to the Missile Range by no later than 4:30. There was a continental breakfast at no charge. The opening ceremony started at 6:35 and included playing of the national anthem, reveille, invocation, remarks, and a moving roll call. Two F22s flew over at the end of the ceremony. A few WWII survivors were present. I shook their hands as I was walking to the start line; in a few years, there will not be any survivors.

The course, as expected, was quite challenging. There were hills. The sandy portions of the terrain made running energy-consuming. In short, this marathon is not for the timid. The elevation range was from 4,100 to 5,300 feet. It was mainly on trails. Between Miles 9 and 10, we began a 3.5-mile climb on a paved road to the HTA (Hazard Test Area). At the HTA, we made a left turn and began running on a scenic trail, circling a mountain, before returning to the paved road (about Mile 19). As we were running down the road, hundreds of marchers were on their way up. I found myself more of a spectator than a runner. It was an amazing sight. I made several stops to take photos.

The last 10K was on a trail. The infamous "Sand Pit" (ankle-deep soft sand) is around Mile 21 and I found it to be the hardest part of the course.

I had a great time running the marathon. I did not walk any of the hills. I ran the last 10K with a German runner who had moved to New Mexico 20 years ago. She was having serious calf problems. We talked a lot, which helped us mentally. She gave me a high-five at the finish. I should have asked for a hug!

This turned out to be an amazing running experience. I highly recommend the Bataan Memorial Death March Marathon.

MARINE CORPS MARATHON
"A truly American marathon"

Sid Busch of Charleston, South Carolina, tries not to miss a Marine Corps Marathon.

The retired Navy man has run more than a dozen since 1996, and each time he sees something that touches his heart. A rehabilitated soldier running on prosthetic legs. A man carrying a picture of his fallen soldier son.

"A lot of people carry flags," Busch said. "Almost everyone running is wearing a shirt they had made up dedicated to a fallen member of the military. There also are a lot of active duty."

Perhaps the most powerful tribute he has seen was a row of pictures of fallen soldiers lining a portion of the course.

"I get emotional talking about it," he said. "A lot of us, we couldn't run past it. I walked that half mile just looking at the pictures."

Now the fourth-largest marathon in the country, the Marine Corps Marathon in Washington, D.C., started in 1976 with fewer than 1,200 runners. It was the brainchild of Col. Jim Fowler, who convinced the Marine Corps to start the race as a way to promote positive feelings toward the military after the Vietnam War, and also to give local Marines a chance to qualify for the prestigious Boston Marathon.

LOCATION: Washington, D.C.
DATE: late October
DISTANCE: marathon, 10K
FIELD SIZE: 40,000
WEBSITE: www.marinemarathon.com
RACE HIGHLIGHTS: pay tribute to fallen military members; receive medal from a Marine officer at the finish line

The first few races were organized by the Marine Corps Reserve, but as the event grew, planning duties were passed to active duty Marines. To this day the race receives high praise for its organization.

The course is a tour of Washington points of interest, starting in Arlington, Virginia, near the Pentagon and ending close by, at the U.S. Marine Corps War Memorial, the famous statue of Marines raising the flag at Iwo Jima. In between, runners cross the Potomac River into D.C. and pass Georgetown University, the Lincoln Memorial and Reflecting Pool, the National Mall, and the U.S. Capitol.

At the finish line, Marine officers present each runner with a medal.

Because it is the largest marathon in the world that does not offer prize money, the Marine Corps Marathon also is known as "The People's Marathon."

The race has grown rapidly over the years and even received a boost from celebrity runner Oprah Winfrey in 1994. By 2012, the race had opened 30,000 slots that sold out in less than three hours. A 10K that joins the last 6.2 miles of the marathon also runs at capacity of 10,000 runners. The marathon has a long list of charity partners, with guaranteed entries for runners who raise money.

If you don't make it into the Marine Corps Marathon, take a look at other events now included in the Marine Corps racing series, including a mud run in June and the Historic Half in May.

"Anyone who runs a marathon has to run the Marine Corps at least once," Busch said. "It's a truly American marathon."

ARMY TEN-MILER
Hooah!

LOCATION: Washington, D.C.
DATE: October
DISTANCE: 10 miles
FIELD SIZE: 30,000
WEBSITE: www.armytenmiler.com
RACE HIGHLIGHTS: highly competitive race with teams from various military installations vying for the Commanders Cup; scenic Washington, D.C., course

The Army Ten-Miler is the Army's premier running event and a grand tradition since 1985.

The race, organized by the U.S. Army District of Washington at Fort Lesley J. McNair, starts and ends at the Pentagon, with a flat and fast course through Washington, D.C.

The Army's Golden Knights parachute team starts the race morning with aerial precision jumping demonstrations, and the Wounded Warriors (active duty amputees and blinded or visually impaired soldiers) and wheelchair athletes start five minutes before the rest of the field, an inspiration to all the runners.

Military athletes have a great history of competition at the Ten-Miler, though it wasn't until 1995 that a military man, Ronnie Harris of the U.S. Navy, won the race, according to a history of the event written by George Banker. (The first military person to win actually was a female Russian Army sergeant, Olga Markova, in 1990.)

Teams from military installations have competed to win the coveted Commanders Cup, a tradition since 1987, with a female division added 10 years later. Teams from Fort Bragg, Fort Carson, Fort Hood, and the National Guard have won bragging rights. The host team, the Army District of Washington, won the first two Commanders Cups but haven't had much luck since.

The 30,000 registered runners in Washington aren't the only ones running the race. In 2012, nearly 20 "shadow runs" took place at military bases around the world, mostly in the Middle East, as a way for military personnel to show solidarity and participate in the fun.

After the race, be sure to hit the HOOAH Tent Zone, where another much-coveted award, Hank the Hooah Bird, is awarded to the military command tent that best exemplifies the Army theme, "Relevant and Ready."

Much like the Marine Corps Marathon, also in D.C., the Army Ten-Miler is a huge race and sells out quickly—30,000 runners registered in about nine hours in 2012. Both races follow a similar course.

Proceeds from the Army Ten-Miler go to a worthy cause: the Army Morale, Welfare, and Recreation programs, which support leisure services to enhance the lives of soldiers and their families.

MEMORIAL DAY RUNS
A great way to remember

On the last Monday in May, the entire nation takes a day off and pauses to remember loved ones and to honor sacrifices made by fallen military members and law enforcement officers.

LOCATION: various
DATE: Memorial Day
DISTANCE: various
FIELD SIZE: various
WEBSITE: various
RACE HIGHLIGHTS: runners dressed in red, white, and blue; veterans carrying military flags on the run; military tributes

Across the country, Memorial Day races help runners and their communities fulfill that promise to remember. Many events have storied histories of their own and have been run for decades.

- **BolderBOULDER 10K (Boulder, Colorado):** With an amazing 50,000 participants, the BolderBOULDER 10K has grown into many things—a party and entertainment festival, a scenic tour of Boulder, and a fitness challenge for the community. But at its heart, it will always be a Memorial Day race. The grand finale to the day's activities is a show with skydivers carrying flags from each military branch, a military jet flyover, and a ceremony honoring local military heroes. (www.bolderboulder.com)

- **University City Memorial Day 10K (University City, Missouri):** This St. Louis suburb hosts a 10K and 5K that claims the title "Oldest Continuously Run 10K West of the Mississippi." (www.ucitymemorialdayrun.com)

- **Boys Town Memorial Day Run (Boys Town, Nebraska):** The Boys Town National Research Hospital near Omaha hosts this annual five-mile race, with companion one-mile and kids races. The event raises money for the hospital's center for deaf and visually impaired children. (www.memorialdayrun.com)

- **Cotton Row Run (Huntsville, Alabama):** One of Huntsville's classic races, the Cotton Row Run encourages runners to wear red, white, and blue. Retired or active duty military members are invited to carry their military flag or the American flag throughout the 10K, 5K, or one-mile fun run. (www.huntsvilletrackclub.org)

OKLAHOMA CITY MEMORIAL MARATHON

"A step toward a better future"

LOCATION: Oklahoma City, Oklahoma
DATE: late April
DISTANCE: marathon, half marathon, marathon relay (five runners), 5K
FIELD SIZE: 23,000
WEBSITE: www.okcmarathon.com
RACE HIGHLIGHTS: a touching start with a moment of silence at the Oklahoma City National Memorial and Museum; raise money for the memorial

The nation's worst attack of homegrown terrorism struck right at the Heartland. One hundred sixty-eight people, including 19 children, died, and hundreds more were wounded when the Alfred P. Murrah Federal Building was bombed in downtown Oklahoma City in 1995.

The conspirators were captured, but Oklahoma City will never fully heal from the wounds suffered that day.

Founded six years after the bombing of the Alfred P. Murrah Federal Building, the Oklahoma City Memorial Marathon raises money for the Oklahoma City National Memorial and Museum. Photo courtesy of Jerry X Shea

The Oklahoma City National Memorial and Museum, built on the spot where the Murrah Building once stood, is a sobering and touching tribute to the victims, survivors, and their families.

Outside the museum, 168 empty chairs stand in a field along a reflecting pool, one chair for each victim of the attack.

Along this heart-wrenching backdrop is the starting line of the Oklahoma City Memorial Marathon. Before the runners take off, they pause for 168 seconds of silence.

"We run to give to the Memorial," the website says. "We run to involve the community, the nation, and perhaps the world in the continuing process of coping with the tragedy of the past. We run as a step toward a better future."

Two Oklahoma City businessmen were out on a morning run when they conceived the idea of a memorial marathon. The first race was in 2001, and its reputation has grown along with the event. It gets high marks for supportive crowds, scenic neighborhoods, and for being a superb tribute to victims and all affected by the bombings.

As the website so eloquently says, "The Memorial Marathon is not about running, it is about life."

PAT'S RUN
From Sun Devil to national hero

Pat Tillman was a hero to many before he enlisted in the Army.

At Arizona State University, he was a decorated football player and led the Sun Devils to an undefeated season and the Rose Bowl in 1997. He was drafted by the Arizona Cardinals and became their starting safety, even breaking the team record for tackles in 2000. He also was an avid runner, competing in a marathon and a half Ironman triathlon.

LOCATION: Tempe, Arizona
DATE: late April
DISTANCE: 4.2 miles
FIELD SIZE: 35,000
WEBSITE: www.pattillmanfoundation.org
RACE HIGHLIGHTS: raise money for the Tillman Military Scholars program; finish inside Arizona State University's football stadium

But 9/11 changed all that for Tillman. The terror attacks inspired Pat and his brother Kevin to enlist in the Army, and to call for others to help serve their country. Walking away from a multimillion-dollar NFL contract made Tillman a household name and a symbol of selflessness and service.

The Tillman brothers served in Iraq and Afghanistan with the 75th Ranger Regiment based at Fort Lewis, Washington.

Pat Tillman was killed by friendly fire in April 2004 while serving with the regiment in Afghanistan.

His friends and family established the Pat Tillman Foundation to honor his legacy, with the first major donation creating a scholarship program at the Arizona State University business school. The foundation changed its mission in 2008 to give scholarships to military veterans and their spouses.

The foundation's signature fund-raising event is Pat's Run, a 4.2-mile run and walk that ends at the 42-yard line in Sun Devil Stadium. The mileage and yard number are symbolic of the No. 42 jersey Tillman wore while he played for the Sun Devils. The race has become one of the largest among the shorter-distance events, attracting 35,000 runners in Tempe and a couple dozen shadow runs across the country and at military bases around the world.

016

SET A PR

You deserve a break.

After pushing yourself in other challenging races, the races in this section are perfect to let yourself relax a bit. From flat and fast, to downhill and fast, these courses are designed to help you achieve your personal record, or PR, at several distances. Many of them are also top Boston Marathon qualifying races, as ranked by Marathonguide.com.

So set the cruise control and enjoy the ride.

Great weather and a flat course have helped make the Carlsbad 5000 in California the World's Fastest 5K. Photo courtesy of John Bryant

CARLSBAD 5000
World's Fastest 5K

An unbelievable 16 world records have been set at the Carlsbad 5000, earning this California race the title of World's Fastest 5K.

The elite men's and women's invitational races are highly competitive, with large prize purses and $10,000 bonuses for a world record, or $5,000 for an American record. If you've dreamed of watching someone run a 13-minute road 5K, this is the place.

LOCATION: Carlsbad, California
DATE: late March
DISTANCE: 5K (with a special 25K challenge)
FIELD SIZE: 7,000
WEBSITE: carlsbad.competitor.com
RACE HIGHLIGHTS: flat, fast course that has seen 16 world records set; main event with highly competitive elite races

We mere mortals can run the race too, with seven "people's races" taking off at intervals starting at 7:00 AM and leading up to the main event. The people's races are divided into age group categories: Masters Men, Masters Women, Men 30-39, Women 30-39, Men and Women 29 & Under, People's 5K Walk, and Wheelchair Invitational.

Runners can choose to run any of the open races, though they are only eligible for prizes in their correct age division race.

The course is, obviously, flat and fast, with the first two miles along the Pacific Ocean and a finish in downtown Carlsbad. The race is run by San Diego–based Competitor Group, the same company that organizes the Rock 'n' Roll Marathon events across the country and internationally.

If you're not interested in running one blazing 5K but want a challenge with more distance, try the All Day 25K. This means running all five of the Carlsbad open races: Masters Men, Masters Women, Men 30-39, Women 30-39, and Men and Women 29 & Under.

Runners in the All Day 25K get access to an exclusive lounge with seating and refreshments while they wait for the next race, although some of the turnarounds are fairly quick, with race starts periodically from 7:00 AM to 11:30 AM. Finishers receive a special medal, but the challenge is not competitive. (Runners are still eligible for awards in their appropriate age group 5K race.)

POTOMAC RIVER RUN MARATHON
"The easiest marathon in America"

There are a host of races claiming to be the toughest marathon in the country.

One bills itself as the easiest: the Potomac River Run Marathon each May along the Chesapeake & Ohio Canal Towpath in Washington, D.C.

The Potomac River Run is so flat, the elevation chart on the race's website looks like this:

- - - - - - - - - - - - -

In reality, the course is only slightly more hilly than that, with an elevation ranging from 12 to 44 feet above sea level. To top that off, it's also shaded and scenic, the perfect recipe for a personal best.

Many runners choose the River Run for their first marathon or to try for a PR or Boston Qualifier. In 2013, more than one in five runners qualified for Boston.

The race is two out-and-backs along the towpath, a sandy path on the C&O Canal, which for nearly 100 years transported goods from communities along the canal to market. Now the canal is a 185-mile-long national park.

LOCATION: Carderock, Maryland
DATE: early May
DISTANCE: marathon, half marathon
FIELD SIZE: 300
WEBSITE:
www.safetyandhealthfoundation.org/marathon/
RACE HIGHLIGHTS: flat, sandy, shaded course; two out-and-back loops that break up the run

SLACKER HALF MARATHON
It's okay to slack off once in a while

Though you have a good chance at one, a PR might not even be your favorite souvenir at the Slacker Half.

More on that in a minute.

First, let's talk about the reason it's known as the Slacker Half Marathon.

The half marathon is run on the BTL trail near Georgetown, Colorado, with a net elevation loss of more than 2,200 feet. But it's not all hard-pounding, flat-out descents. The trail has a nice, rolling downhill that shouldn't be too hard on the legs, race director Beth Luther said. Those who worry about the toll on their knees can run on dirt shoulders to minimize impact.

There is one major downhill with a couple tricky sections from Miles 10 to 12.

LOCATION: Georgetown, Colorado
DATE: June
DISTANCE: half marathon, half marathon relay (three runners), 4 miles
FIELD SIZE: 1,700
WEBSITE: www.slackerhalfmarathon.com
RACE HIGHLIGHTS: net elevation loss of more than 2,200 feet over rolling hills and traveling over a rolling hill descent to 8,400 feet

"We give people a heads-up about that," Luther said. "Don't open up that stride too much. There are two switchbacks, and you don't want to get there and have to put on the brakes."

The Slacker Half name came naturally when Luther and a group of friends were running the course one day.

"My friend Tom said, 'You know, this is a real slacker half marathon,'" Luther remembers. "And I said, 'That's it. That's the perfect name.'"

The name has attracted a lot of first-time half-marathoners and walkers who find the course relatively nonthreatening. The event also offers two three-person relay divisions: one for any three people, and an ADA relay in which the second of the three participants is physically disabled. (The second leg of the relay is safest for wheelchairs.)

The race does harbor one little surprise at the end.

"The last mile is pretty flat, and that can kind of take you by surprise," Luther said. "You've got to really propel yourself instead of gravity propelling you."

That's an improvement, though, from the earliest version of the course, in which there was a small hill right at the end.

"Boy, I got beat up for that," Luther said with a laugh.

Now, for the souvenir. The Slacker Half offers some of the most unique door prizes around: solar-powered, light-up garden gnomes with "Slacker" painted on it by a local artist. The gnomes even earned the race a mention in *Runner's World* for best post-race swag.

SUGARLOAF MARATHON AND 15K
Enjoy the Maine Scenic Highway

The Sugarloaf Mountain area sees skiers and snowboarders in the winter, and campers, hikers, and golfers in the summer. And each May it hosts the Sugarloaf Marathon.

Don't let the mountainous terrain of western Maine fool you; the Sugarloaf Marathon actually is consistently ranked among the fastest marathons in the country.

That's because most of the course is downhill—and thankfully none of it is actually on Sugarloaf Mountain itself.

The point-to-point course starts in Eustis near Flagstaff Lake and follows Route 27, the Maine Scenic Highway, down to Kingfield. The first five miles are flat, with rolling hills between Miles 5 and 10 (including a two-mile climb at Mile 8). But then the reward is a nice downhill for the last 16 miles.

LOCATION: Eustis to Kingfield, Maine
DATE: mid-May
DISTANCE: marathon, 15K
FIELD SIZE: 1,600
WEBSITE: www.sugarloaf.com
RACE HIGHLIGHTS: gorgeous scenery in the mountains of Western Maine; mostly downhill course, especially in the second half

For an even faster experience, skip all those pesky hills and run the 15K instead, the last part of the marathon course that has a small net loss in elevation and no uphills.

RACE REPORT

Houston Marathon
Full-crowd support

Denise Malan

LOCATION: Houston, Texas
DATE: mid-January
DISTANCE: marathon, half marathon, 5K
FIELD SIZE: 24,000
WEBSITE: www.houstonmarathon.com
RACE HIGHLIGHTS: consistently among events with the highest number of Boston Marathon qualifiers; big-city race feel and constant crowd support

My favorite part of the expo at the Chevron Houston Marathon: a huge white banner with the words "I run because…" at the top and a cupful of markers waiting for runners to add their personal touches.

The answers ranged from the inspirational ("I run because I'm alive!!!") to the funny ("My freedom from five kids!") to the absurd ("My mom dared me to when I was drunk!").

I'm glad I stopped to read the banner, because I needed all the inspiration I could muster the next morning as I stood at the starting line in a steady, 40-degree rain. The weather report called for only a 30 percent chance of rain, so I had taken my chances by not wearing a jacket or poncho. Most other runners were smarter than me and had at least brought trash bags to keep dry. Only the day before, Houston was 80 degrees and muggy, and I hadn't quite expected how much the temperature change would affect me. I was also too cheap to buy a $10 disposable jacket at the expo. Standing and shivering at the starting line, I would have paid someone $50 for one.

Finally, 17 minutes after the starting gun, I was crossing the starting line outside Minute Maid Park, home of the Houston Astros. Almost immediately, the steady rain turned into a downpour. The weather made me worry a little about meeting my goal of setting a personal record on the course, which is known for being flat, fast, and runner-friendly. In 2012, the course hosted the U.S. Olympic Marathon Trials, which became two of the fastest trials ever, with Shalane Flanagan leading five women under 2:30 and Meb Keflezighi leading four men under 2:10 for the first time in trials history.

The elevation chart shows a few inclines, but nothing more than 25 feet. Many are nice, gradual downhill slopes.

After leaving downtown Houston, the course winds through the Heights neighborhood and then south into Montrose, known as the city's funkiest and most diverse area. The rain had stopped after the first couple miles and only started up again for a few minutes in the first half. I started to dry out and felt a little better about the weather.

Marathon and half marathon runners stayed together from the starting line through Mile 9, making the course a little crowded. (Houston is a large race; the event is capped at about 13,000 for the marathon and 11,000 for the half.) But after the half runners turned and started back toward downtown, I was able to relax a little more.

The middle of the course tours the most upscale parts of Houston—Rice University and the shopping Mecca the Galleria. It also has some nice, long, and very slight downhills that helped me run my best splits from Miles 9 to 18. And, this being Houston, the commuter capital of the country, there's no way to escape the freeways completely. The least scenic, and thankfully shortest, portion of the course runs along a freeway feeder road into the Galleria area.

By the time I reached Memorial Park, home of the city's best running trails and the loudest crowd support on the course, I was feeling pretty good. Volunteers were pumping the music and handing out plenty of energy gels, water, and even beer to help runners make it through "the wall." I started to feel thankful that the temperature hadn't risen above 45 degrees and that the clouds had stuck around after the rain.

We made it back into downtown Houston, with a strong wind at our backs and a downhill slope into the finish line. I made my PR by two minutes, not a disappointing achievement at all, especially considering my sloshy shoes and rain-soaked clothes. I can only imagine what my PR would have been without the rain.

LIGHT AT THE END OF THE TUNNEL MARATHON
Just like having a good day

The Light at the End of the Tunnel Marathon sold out in just seven hours in 2013, which organizers said on their website took them by surprise, because the previous year took a month to sell out.

There's a reason runners are clamoring to get one of the 400 spots in this race. Its easy-going, 23-mile, 2,000-foot drop is perfect for setting a personal best.

As the name implies, there is also a tunnel involved, lending the marathon another unique trait. The race starts about 50

LOCATION: Snoqualmie Pass to North Bend, Washington
DATE: mid-July
DISTANCE: marathon
FIELD SIZE: 400
WEBSITE: www.littlemarathon.com
RACE HIGHLIGHTS: gentle, 23-mile downhill grade that is easy on the legs; first couple of miles in a dark, cool tunnel

miles east of Seattle, Washington, near Snoqualmie Pass, with a half-mile warm up before entering the cool, damp, and unlit Hyak Tunnel. Shortly after entering the darkness, runners should be able to see a small point of light ahead—the literal light at the end of the tunnel—although it's still two miles away. A flashlight is recommended for the tunnel.

After runners emerge from the Hyak Tunnel, the gravel trail starts descending on a nice, gentle slope. The scenery is gorgeous to boot, with four high trestle bridges and wooded trails. The trails for the course, the John Wayne Pioneer Trail and Snoqualmie Valley Trail, are former railroad grades turned into gravel paths.

"It's never steep enough to be uncomfortable," the race website says. "You just feel like you're having a good day."

Marathoners in online reviews report setting PRs of 13 or even 20 minutes by running the Light at the End of the Tunnel. The race is also popular among the Marathon Maniacs and 50 States Marathon Club.

For those who don't get into the race, there's also a "lite" version scheduled each September with less course support and no starting and finishing arches, but the same sloping course that offers a last chance to get that Boston qualifying time.

CHARLESTON DISTANCE RUN
A 15-miler PR

LOCATION: Charleston, West Virginia
DATE: late August
DISTANCE: 15 miles, three-person relay, 5K run, 10K and 5K walks
FIELD SIZE: 1,300
WEBSITE: www.charlestondistancerun.com
RACE HIGHLIGHTS: unique race distance; scenic Charleston course

Unless you've run it before, you're guaranteed a PR at the Charleston Distance Run.

That's because it is one of America's very few 15-mile races, and certainly the most well known.

Is that cheating? Maybe a bit, but a PR is a PR, and the scenery in the race makes it worth it besides.

The Charleston Distance Run started in 1973, just before the huge running boom, so there weren't many marathons and barely any half marathons in the country. It has kept its unique distance through the years, except for some years that have been affected by construction. (In 2010, the race director at the time made a move to change the race to the increasingly popular half marathon, though he was outvoted by the race committee, according to a history of the race written by longtime Charleston runner Gary Smith.)

The event has drawn some big names in racing to either run or speak, including Steve Prefontaine, George Sheehan, Hal Higdon, Bill Rodgers, and Jeff Galloway, Smith wrote. Today it still draws elites from around the world.

The course starts at the West Virginia State Capitol, then makes its way through downtown, hillside neighborhoods, and the scenic riverfront.

The Distance Run has added some shorter courses, including a 5K and 10K, but those common distances don't necessarily guarantee a personal best!

RACE REPORT

Steamtown Marathon
It's all downhill from here (for 23 miles, at least)
. . . .

Julie McAllister

LOCATION: Scranton, Pennsylvania
DATE: mid-October
DISTANCE: marathon
FIELD SIZE: 2,000
WEBSITE:
www.steamtownmarathon.com
RACE HIGHLIGHTS: point-to-point, net downhill course with scenic fall foliage; small and well-organized race

My husband, John, and I run two destination marathons each year, one in the spring and one in the fall. In October 2012 we choose to run the Steamtown Marathon in Pennsylvania.

We chose this marathon because it is a point-to-point, net downhill marathon, and several of our friends were going. The weather was another big consideration in our decision to go to

Scranton. Training for fall marathons in Corpus Christi, Texas, means the peak of the training schedule comes in the midst of the hottest and most humid part of the season. Late summer and early fall in Corpus Christi can bring 90 percent humidity and temperatures above 90 degrees for weeks on end. We reason (lie) to ourselves by saying that training in the heat and high humidity will give us an edge over the locals who train in the cool, dry climate. (We have to justify the insanity of it all, right?)

The expo, held at Scranton High School, was small and well organized. We picked up our packets and orange tech shirts with no waiting. The weather was damp and cool as we ran to and from the car, a great respite from the South Texas double H (heat and humidity).

The marathon hotels were about one mile or less from the start, so on the morning of the race, most runners drove to the downtown location where the school buses were lined up to take us to the starting line.

The 45-minute bus ride to Forest City was comfortable. We were greeted with cheers by many of the Forest City high school students as we exited the bus. The students escorted us to the gymnasium and even more students offered us coffee, water, Gatorade, and snacks as we walked through the halls. I was amazed by how many students were present at that time of the morning. I asked a few of them if they were given extra credit for volunteering. Their response was generally, "No, we just like doing this." I can't say enough about how helpful and polite the kids from that school were. It is also a testament to the parents and faculty of that school. Kudos!

We were allowed to stay inside the gymnasium before the start to keep warm. The starting line was just outside the building, so we had very little time to stand and get cold (38 degrees at the start, with very little wind). There were plenty of port-a-potties outside so the lines went quickly.

The course is beautiful throughout the whole distance. Each town we ran through had its own distinctive character, and many of the residents were out to support the runners. We ran along a creek for many miles and the sound of it was very calming. At about Mile 14 the course followed a path through a picturesque fall-leaf-lined path. The scenery along the course was ever-changing and beautiful. Being from South Texas, where we have no "real" trees or change of seasons, I was in awe of the brilliant fall colors. The weather stayed mild throughout the entire race.

The net downhill of the course was a bit rough on the quads but very manageable. The last three miles of the course are not as kind as the previous 23. There is a course elevation chart on the website dedicated just to the last three miles. The crowd support as we finished Mile 23 was very encouraging; they knew what we were in for. There was a guy dressed as the devil at Mile 25, saying, "Slow down, walk, you are almost finished, don't hurry." It took a few seconds for me to register what he was saying. It made me laugh.

I am an average runner, and I finished seventh in my age group in 4:19.

THE RUNNER'S BUCKET LIST

017

INDULGE YOUR INNER SPORTS NUT

Which sport do you go nuts for? Football, baseball, NASCAR, or even horse racing? This chapter has all the bases covered.

Get out of the bleachers and into these races that make you feel like you're part of the action. You can make a Lambeau Leap in Green Bay, run for the roses in Louisville, or bank a turn at Talladega. Whichever you choose, don't forget to take a victory lap!

For any NASCAR fan who's always dreamed of driving a lap around a real racetrack, the Talladega 21000 offers the next-best thing to getting behind the wheel. Photo courtesy of Jeff Smith

Talladega 21000
Feel the need for speed

· ·

Jeff Smith

LOCATION: Talladega Superspeedway, just outside Lincoln, Alabama
DATE: September
DISTANCE: half marathon, 5K
FIELD SIZE: 1,200
WEBSITE: www.talladegahalfmarathon.com
RACE HIGHLIGHTS: run on one of NASCAR's most famous racetracks at Talladega Superspeedway; take your finisher's photo in Victory Lane

The Talladega 21000 and 5K Lap Around the Track allow NASCAR enthusiasts to race at the renowned Talladega Superspeedway in Alabama.

Attending a race at 'Dega is high on my bucket list, so running on the track gave me the perfect opportunity to pretend I was one of the 43 drivers racing around the 2.66-mile track at speeds over 200 miles per hour. (Okay, perhaps my speed was more like two miles per hour.)

Hearing the familiar NASCAR phrase, "Ladies and gentleman, start your engines," made most of the 1,200 participants laugh and certainly got me pumped for the race to begin. Both the half marathon and 5K races start near the exit of Turn 4 at the beginning of Pit Road.

Running on Pit Road made me think of all the great NASCAR races here—and also how I could run past a pit stall in the same amount of time a pit crew can change four tires and refuel a car (15 seconds).

As we exited Pit Road into Turn 1, the famous quote from the movie *Talladega Nights: The Ballad of Ricky Bobby*—"If you ain't first, you're last"—appeared on a small sign, letting me know I had to pick up the pace.

Making the turn and heading into Mile 1, I saw the impressive 33-degree banking that defines this racetrack. It's hard to imagine three cars side-by-side going around this turn safely! Luckily, we raced on the flat "apron," a 12-foot shoulder for the racetrack. The long backstretch was a nice straight shot and the perfect spot for a "caution flag," aka a hydration break.

The half-marathoners (21,000 meters is 21 kilometers, or 13.1 miles) exited the backstretch before Turn 4. They ran along the racetrack and through service roads, where thousands of RVs and automobiles will park four weeks later when NASCAR returns for its semi-annual takeover of this rural Alabama area.

The runners then go along Speedway Boulevard, the county road leading to the racetrack. Several police cars with blue lights flashing, along with orange safety cones, mark the race route for runners. The half-marathoners also got to run through grandstands and the underground tunnel that takes you from the road into the track infield. At about 12.5 miles, the half marathon route rejoins the 5K route at the beginning of Turn 4.

As we made the final turn onto the frontstretch, the next batch of *Talladega Nights* signs appeared—"I'm gonna come at you like a spider monkey!"—as added motivation, but not before I noticed the other defining characteristic of 'Dega: the start/finish line is at the end of Pit Road instead of at the beginning, the way it is at Daytona International Speedway, or in the middle, the way it is at most other oval NASCAR racetracks.

I imagined all the fantastic finishes here, like Jimmie Johnson's record-tying, 0.002-second victory over Clint Bowyer in April 2011. I secretly hoped they would switch the piped-in upbeat music to an announcer calling that race, but then I thought of Ricky Bobby: "Slingshot: Engaged!"

In the final tenth of a mile, I spotted a lady 20 years older than me about 10 yards ahead of me. I immediately started to "draft" off her—a very common technique used by NASCAR drivers at this track. As we darted toward the finish line, hundreds of supporters cheered us on. In the closing seconds, I pulled the "Shake and Bake" slingshot and passed her at the finish line amidst the waving checkered flags.

The race provides a unique experience for fans or foes of NASCAR. I loved pretending I was a driver on the track, but the non-fans enjoyed themselves as well. Talladega is known for its parties, and the post-race celebration didn't disappoint. A live band played country music as runners chowed down on delicious Southern barbeque and drank free beer. Now that's what I call racin'!

INDIANAPOLIS 500 FESTIVAL MINI MARATHON
Gentlemen (and ladies), start your engines!

The size of the Indianapolis Motor Speedway is incredible. At 253 acres, the oval could accommodate Churchill Downs, Yankee Stadium, the Rose Bowl, the Roman Colosseum, and even Vatican City.

In fact, the Speedway is the world's largest spectator sporting facility, and since 1911 it has been home each Memorial Day weekend to the Indianapolis 500.

LOCATION: Indianapolis, Indiana
DATE: first Saturday in May
DISTANCE: half marathon, 5K
FIELD SIZE: 40,000
WEBSITE: www.500festival.com
RACE HIGHLIGHTS: run a 2.5-mile lap of the Indianapolis Motor Speedway oval; enjoy entertainment from bands along the course and a huge post-race festival

You can experience the same banked curves and straightaways that the Indy cars cover during that 500-mile race, albeit at much, much slower than the 160 miles per hour those race cars travel.

In the middle of the Indianapolis 500 Festival Mini Marathon (or half marathon), the course enters the famed racetrack and treats runners to a lap around the 2.5-mile track. The track has four turns banked at 9 degrees, and the two long straightaways are $5/8$ miles each.

What has become the country's largest half marathon almost wasn't a running race at all. The idea started as a bicycle race, though it was changed to a half marathon after organizers decided it would take away from another bicycle race in Bloomington. The mini marathon started in 1977 and featured Olympic champion runners Frank Shorter and Bill Rodgers. Two years later, the race officially became a 500 Festival event.

The 500 Festival plans events such as a parade and concert throughout the month of May, leading up to the Indy 500. The mini marathon is on the first weekend of the month, a few weeks before the car race.

Today, the half marathon boasts 35,000 participants, plus another 4,000 in a companion 5K, and more than 80 bands along the course. The post-race party is in Military Park in downtown Indianapolis.

KENTUCKY DERBY FESTIVAL MARATHON
Run for the roses

Break out the mint juleps and fancy hats: it's time for the Kentucky Derby!

Celebrate the annual rite of spring and first leg of the Triple Crown of horse racing with the Kentucky Derby Festival Marathon or miniMarathon (half marathon) in mid-April, a couple weeks before the legendary horse race.

The highlight of both the marathon and half marathon is a lap through the infield of Churchill Downs, the stadium that hosts the famous horse race. Runners enter the stadium through a gate, run under the grandstands and through a tunnel into the infield, where they make one lap inside the mile-long track. (Sorry, the actual dirt track is reserved for the horses.)

LOCATION: Louisville, Kentucky
DATE: late April
DISTANCE: marathon, half marathon, marathon relay (five runners)
FIELD SIZE: 14,000
WEBSITE: www.derbyfestivalmarathon.com
RACE HIGHLIGHTS: run around the infield of Churchill Downs, home of the Kentucky Derby

Soak in the history while you're running the infield. Churchill Downs has hosted more than 125 years of horse racing. This is where War Admiral started his Triple Crown run in 1937, and where Secretariat set the track record in 1973, a record that still stands today. More history will be made here just days after your marathon, when another horse wins the roses and raises hopes of another Triple Crown winner.

The Kentucky Derby Festival that leads up to the horse race also includes Thunder over Louisville, one of the largest fireworks displays in North America, the weekend before the marathon.

The mini is by far the more popular race here, with halfers outnumbering marathoners six to one. That makes sense, because the miniMarathon was the original Derby Festival race with a history spanning more than 40 years. The marathon wasn't added until 2002.

The races start and end together in downtown Louisville, with the marathon splitting off at Mile 11.

GREEN BAY MARATHON
Make your own "Lambeau Leap"

There is nothing in the sports world quite comparable to Green Bay fans' love of the Packers. They wear foam blocks of cheese on their heads, wait decades for the chance to purchase season tickets, and suffer snowstorms and subzero temperatures while watching their beloved football team at

LOCATION: Green Bay, Wisconsin
DATE: mid-May
DISTANCE: marathon, half marathon, marathon relay (two to five runners), 5K
FIELD SIZE: 8,000
WEBSITE:
www.cellcomgreenbaymarathon.com
RACE HIGHLIGHTS: finish with a lap around Lambeau Field and a tailgate party in the parking lot

Lambeau Field.

Wouldn't it be great to experience even a fraction of that fan support while running a marathon?

The Green Bay Marathon prides itself on having some of the greatest fans and spectators to cheer runners on. Laura Broullire, who lives just outside Green Bay in De Pere, Wisconsin, said she loves seeing the fans, especially her husband and daughters, at several points along the course.

"The course is great," she said. "It's mostly residential for the first half, tree-lined streets. It's mostly flat and it's very spectator-friendly."

Plus, runners can experience a lap inside Lambeau Field, getting high-fives from spectators in the stands during their final mile.

"Coming into Lambeau is definitely a highlight," Broullire said. "It kind of gives you that final push to want to run strong to the finish. My whole family was there waiting for me."

The finish is in the parking lot and is followed by a classic tailgate-style after-party, complete with beer and brats.

Broullire, who grew up a Packers fan and had her first date with her husband at a tailgate, said she's had family members from the Duluth and Cincinnati areas come into Green Bay to run the race just for the privilege of running in Lambeau. They loved that experience and the rest of the event so much, they hope to make it an annual trip.

"The lap is definitely a highlight, but it's not the only draw," Broullire said. "It's still a very well-organized and great race."

The marathon and half marathon are capped at 8,000 runners combined, plus 250 relay teams of two to five runners each. The 5K and a kids' run do not have caps.

RUNYON 5K AT YANKEE STADIUM

"Turn left at concessions..."

Turn-by-turn directions for most races read something like this: "Left on Main Street, right on Second Avenue..."

But take a look at this course description for the Damon Runyon 5K at Yankee Stadium:

Run/walk two laps around the 100 level concourse. After second lap, near Section 126, turn left at concessions, then take ramp to sub-zero level. Run/walk through the sub-zero level. Exit the sub-zero level between the Bullpen and Monument Park, turn right onto warning track.

LOCATION: Bronx, New York
DATE: mid-August
DISTANCE: 5K
FIELD SIZE: 4,000
WEBSITE: www.runyon5k.kintera.org
RACE HIGHLIGHTS: run the concourses, stairs, and warning track at Yankee Stadium

The Runyon 5K doesn't just take participants around the parking lots or onto the playing field at Yankee Stadium. The race actually takes runners *through* the stadium—along the concourses, the Great Hall, up the stairs in the stands, and even along the outfield warning track.

There are a total of 286 stairs along the course—a little more than six stories—split into several sections. The start is on the 100 concourse level, with a finish in the Great Hall, a 31,000-square-foot special event space lined with banners of the Yankee greats.

The whole experience of touring the new stadium, which opened in 2009, is a must-do for Yankees die-hards or any baseball fan.

The event carries a fund-raising requirement for the Damon Runyon Cancer Research Foundation, which helps support scientists early in their careers and encourages new ideas in cancer research.

Runyon was a New York author who began his career as a baseball writer and whose short stories were later made into the Broadway hit *Guys and Dolls*. Runyon died of throat cancer in 1946, and the foundation that carries his name has long had ties to the New York Yankees: Joe DiMaggio was a board member in the 1950s, and Babe Ruth and Mickey Mantle were supporters as well.

FINISH AT THE 50
Feel like an NFL star as you cross the finish line

Sitting in the stands during an NFL game, who hasn't daydreamed about sprinting across the field, the fans going wild as you pass the yard lines, on your way to the winning touchdown. He's at the 30, the 40, the 50...he could go all the way!

LOCATION: various
DATE: various
DISTANCE: various
FIELD SIZE: various
WEBSITE: various
RACE HIGHLIGHTS: experience the exhilaration of finishing a race on the 50-yard line of an NFL field; at some races, get players' autographs and test your football skills

It might not be quite the same feeling as scoring a touchdown in the Super Bowl, but you can run on the field and finish your race at the 50-yard line as road racing is making its way into NFL stadiums around the country. Some stadiums have hosted runs for a decade or more, while the NFL itself started a run series in 2013 to help encourage fitness and allow fans to meet players.

Here's a sampling of races that let you finish on the field:

- **Soldier Field 10 Mile (May; Chicago, Illinois):** Chicago sports fans will love this race, where runners finish the 10-miler at the longtime home of Da Bears. (www.soldierfield10.com)

- **Finish at the 50 (July; Foxborough, Massachusetts):** A scenic 10K or 5K route around Foxborough with a dramatic finish inside the New England Patriots' stadium. (www.harvardpilgrimfinishatthe50.com)

- **Fifty-Yard Finish (June; Orchard Park, New York):** Finish this half marathon or 5K in the middle of the field at Ralph Wilson Stadium, home of the Buffalo Bills. (www.eclipsemultisport.com/fiftyyardfinish)

- **NFL Back to Football Run Series (various stadiums):** In conjunction with its Play 60 campaign encouraging kids to be active, the NFL has started a 5K run series to celebrate the return of the season each fall. Runs include fan festivals with football skill challenges and autograph opportunities. Select teams, such as the Dallas Cowboys, Denver Broncos, and Washington Redskins, participate. (www.nflrunseries.com)

018

STUDY YOUR HISTORY

How well do you remember your high school history class?

Yeah, that's what I figured.

Take a refresher course with any of these races, which take you on runs through different periods of history.

In the East and South, you can work on your Civil War history with races through battlefields, including Antietam. The West celebrates its American Indian heritage with a run at the Crazy Horse Memorial. You can even run back in time through the geologic eras and see dinosaur footprints in Utah, and the Vigilante Run in Tombstone takes you back to the days of the Wild Wild West.

The Little Grand Canyon Marathon in Utah takes runners into the canyon itself and features a post-race party at the bottom. Photo courtesy of Shirley Davis

LITTLE GRAND CANYON MARATHON
Get ready for Paleontology 101

Descending through the Little Grand Canyon in eastern Utah is like descending back through Earth's history.

The Little Grand Canyon Marathon events put on by Mammoth Marathons drop into the canyon—and give runners a geology and paleontology lesson along the way.

LOCATION: Price, Utah
DATE: early September
DISTANCE: marathon, half marathon, 10K
FIELD SIZE: 600
WEBSITE: www.mammothmarathons.org
RACE HIGHLIGHTS: descend into the Little Grand Canyon; see dinosaur footprints and a large pictograph drawn by ancient inhabitants

The marathon course begins at 5,650 feet and climbs slightly in the first four miles. Then it's mostly flat until you hit the canyon about 16 miles in. The course descends about 550 feet over the end of the marathon, a nice easy decline that shouldn't be too hard on runners' legs. The half marathon and 10K events are mostly downhill, using the latter miles of the marathon course. (Runners are bused back out of the canyon after the race and a party at the bottom.)

"It's kind of a hidden treasure," said Jared Haddock, owner of Mammoth Marathons. "It's a dirt road all the way out there and all the way back. It's a logistical nightmare to put on a marathon in, but I think the beauty of it makes it all worthwhile."

On the way down, runners pass through the different geologic eras— cretaceous, jurassic, triassic. First, the blue shale from an ancient seabed. Then sandstone and red rock characteristic of the Western desert.

Haddock said the race partners with a local museum to post signs pointing out the different layers and their origins. The runners will also pass by dinosaur footprints (some competitors even go off the course to stop and see them) and a large pictograph, known as the Buckhorn Wash Panel, drawn by a prehistoric civilization.

VIGILANTE DAYS 10K
Battle the Hill Too Tough to Climb, in the Town Too Tough to Die

LOCATION: Tombstone, Arizona
DATE: mid-August
DISTANCE: 10K
FIELD SIZE: 200
WEBSITE: www.tombstonevigilantes.com
RACE HIGHLIGHTS: challenging, hilly course that starts in downtown Tombstone; stay for Vigilante Days festival and Old West reenactments

The scene: downtown and outside Tombstone, Arizona.

The time: 6:30 AM (high noon is just too hot).

The battle: runners vs. the Hill Too Tough to Climb.

Instead of a Shootout at the OK Corral, the Tombstone Vigilante Days 10K features a showdown between about 200 brave runners and a tough race in the high country that promises to be quite the duel.

Vigilante Days celebrates Tombstone's place in Old West history with reenactments by the Vigilantes group, 1880s fashion shows, a chili cookoff, and other entertainment. The 10K gets started early on the Sunday of the festival in mid-August. The race started in the late 1980s to draw more people to the festival, director Steve Reeder said.

The 10K starts in downtown Tombstone, on Allen Street, one of the most infamous streets of the Old West, home to the OK Corral and now located inside the city's historic district. Then, just outside town, the race gets even more interesting.

There's a steep downhill from about Mile 1.3 until 2.5, when the course hits a wash and climbs back up until about Mile 3. Then there's a loop at the end before runners head back the way they came, down the first hill then back up between Miles 4 and 5. This was the first hill they had come down.

Together, this part of the course is known as the "Hill Too Tough to Climb," a play on the city's nickname of the "Town Too Tough to Kill," earned by surviving several booms and busts. Reeder described it as being like a roller coaster, and the hill seems like it keeps going up, and up, and up.

"It's the toughest 10K you'll ever run," Reeder said. "I always urge anybody to go drive that course beforehand so they know what they're in for mentally."

The tough course can be compounded by the heat for runners who take much longer than an hour to finish. Though it's usually in the 60s when the race starts, the temperature rises quickly into the 80s.

The race mercifully ends back on flat land, at Tombstone's City Park. Age group winners are given unique tombstone and noose awards, symbolic of the town's history of hangings and the Vigilante group's reenactments. (Reeder himself is an actor in the shows; he usually plays a bad guy, he said.)

Afterward, stick around for some good photo ops with race volunteers who dress up, or head to the Vigilante Festival for some Old West reenactments and entertainment.

OLD NEW CASTLE RUN
A trip back to colonial times

William Penn, founder of the British colony that became the state of Pennsylvania, is one of the great figures of American history. Penn was among the first to urge unification of the colonies of the New World, and the government he set up in Pennsylvania with the goal of harboring religious tolerance and political freedoms, is largely considered the basis for the American style of government.

So how would you like to see the spot where Penn first stepped foot in the New World?

LOCATION: New Castle, Delaware
DATE: late May
DISTANCE: 5K
FIELD SIZE: 200
WEBSITE: www.oldnewcastlerun.com
RACE HIGHLIGHTS: pass historical sites such as Delaware's first capitol and courthouse; see the spot where William Penn landed in the New World

The Old New Castle Run in Delaware is a 5K through the historic area of Old New Castle along the Delaware River. It is home to attractions such as the New Castle Court House Museum, housed in Delaware's first capitol and courthouse, and three museums of the New Castle Historical Society (the Old Library Museum, Dutch House, and Amstel House, all along the race route).

New Castle was originally settled by the Dutch West India Company in 1651, according to a history by the Greater Wilmington Convention and Visitors Bureau. The town changed names and ownerships several times, and in 1680, the area (along with a large area west of New Jersey now known as Pennsylvania) was given to Penn by King Charles II of England to settle a debt the king had with Penn's father.

In October 1682, Penn stepped off a boat and into the New World for the first time.

Historic Old New Castle encompasses 3.2 square miles and is home to nearly 5,000 people. It is second only to Williamsburg in the number and authenticity of historic structures, according to the visitors bureau.

Hatfield & McCoy Reunion Marathon and Half

Help settle the infamous feud once and for all!

Denise Malan

The first rule of the Hatfield & McCoy Reunion Marathon: if someone hands you a mason jar full of "water," don't drink it!

LOCATION: Goody, Kentucky, to Williamson, West Virginia
DATE: early June
DISTANCE: marathon, half marathon, 5K
FIELD SIZE: 900
WEBSITE: www.hatfieldmccoymarathon.com
RACE HIGHLIGHTS: historic markers such as the Pawpaw Tree Incident, in which three McCoy men were killed; meet descendants of the Hatfield and McCoy families and compete with them in the marathon or half

I didn't actually come across any moonshine in this scenic Appalachian race, but the history and the camaraderie were incredible.

The reunion marathon and accompanying festival are the remnants of the most famous feud in American history, between the Hatfields of West Virginia and McCoys across the Tug Fork in Kentucky. Today, the families still compete, only now it's with softball games, tug-of-war competitions, and, luckily for us, a marathon.

The race director, David Hatfield, is a direct descendant of the Hatfields, and many family members compete in the race. Even runners who aren't members of the families get placed on a team, and the family with the lowest time wins bragging rights for that year.

When I got my bib the morning of the race, I immediately turned it over to find out which family I would represent. As it turned out, I was a Hatfield, the family led by Devil Anse Hatfield during the decades of the feud in the late 1800s. I definitely didn't want to let down any family with the Devil in it.

The race started with shotgun blasts from a bearded Hatfield and a McCoy in the parking lot of a grocery store in Goody, Kentucky, just south of Williamson, West Virginia, where the race ends. The June morning was cool, in the 60s, and foggy, perfect for racing.

I admit I had to brush up on my Hatfield-McCoy history before the race.

Many believe the feud between the formerly friendly families started when McCoy family patriarch Randall accused Devil Anse's cousin of stealing McCoy's pig in 1878. A trial with a jury made up of six Hatfields and six McCoys acquitted the Hatfield (one of the McCoys voted with the Hatfields), and the fight was on. (The feud also could be traced further back to when the Hatfields were suspected of killing Randall's brother as he recovered from a wound suffered in the Civil War.) Estimates are that up to 150 family members and their allies were killed during the worst decades of the feud.

After the first few miles, the marathon course travels through the heart of "Feud Country." We passed the home of Randall McCoy and the graveyard where five of his children killed in the fighting are buried. Later, we also passed the site and historic marker showing where three of his sons—Tolber, Bud, and Pharmer—were tied to pawpaw trees and shot by the Hatfields in retaliation for killing Devil Anse's brother Ellison during an Election Day celebration.

Miles 6 and 7 are uphill, first gradually and then steeper, leading up Blackberry Mountain, the worst hill along the course. After reaching the top, I felt like I was practically flying down the other side. After we made it through that, the rest of the course is mostly rolling hills, though some were rather steep.

At the foot of Blackberry Mountain we passed the site of the infamous Hog Trial, which also is near where the Election Day stabbing took place. We turned and followed a creek that led us over the Tug Fork and into Matewan, West Virginia, the site of more Hatfield-McCoy lore and a separate historic event. A gunfight between miners and coal company agents trying to prevent union organization killed seven of the agents and three townspeople, including the town's mayor, in 1920.

Matewan also marks the halfway point of the marathon. There was a finish line for people running the first half of the race, and a starting line for those who chose to run the second half instead, a new option the race offered in 2013.

After Matewan, we crossed back into Kentucky and turned onto River Road, which started as a narrow paved road and devolved into a muddy, gravelly trail. Though there were fewer spectators out here, this part of the course was very scenic and one of my favorite sections.

Somewhere in Mile 18, we emerged into the Tug Valley Country Club golf course, which straddles the two states, and crossed the river into West Virginia again on a wooden plank bridge. A volunteer stationed at the entrance to the bridge advised us to walk because of the bounce.

By the time we reached the golf course, the sun had burned off the fog and clouds, and the temperature was rising fast. The aid stations stocked with ice water each mile were a welcome sight.

The race ends in Williamson, West Virginia, with the Hatfield and McCoy who started the race with their shotguns posted at the finish line, ready to high-five all the runners as they crossed.

After I got my medal and cooled down a bit, I was sure to get my other finisher's trinket, one of the most unique I've seen: a mason jar emblazoned with the Hatfield & McCoy Reunion Marathon logo.

There was a finish line festival well stocked with fruit and Powerade for the runners, along with vendors selling Hatfield-McCoy collectibles and T-shirts. The families have succeeded in turning their bloody feud into a positive economic force for the area.

After the race, you can stick around to hear actors perform monologues from historical figures such as the Hatfield and McCoy patriarchs, and Johnse Hatfield and Roseanna McCoy, who fell in love despite their families' bad blood. Back in Matewan, another part of the reunion festival includes a tug-of-war between the families. I got there just in time to see the McCoys lose and begin a chant of "Hatfields suck! Hatfields suck!" from across the river.

The next day, when I checked the race results online, I felt like I had let the family down. The McCoys had prevailed in the marathon and both halves. I might have to return to this race to seek my revenge—and enjoy this one-of-a-kind event all over again.

FREEDOM'S RUN
"An event for health and heritage"

With four national parks and three Civil War towns on the course, there's so much history packed into the Freedom's Run Marathon that it's hard to know where to start.

LOCATION: Harpers Ferry to Shepherdstown, West Virginia (with most of the race in Maryland)
DATE: mid-October
DISTANCE: marathon, half marathon, 10K, 5K
FIELD SIZE: 3,000
WEBSITE: www.freedomsrun.org
RACE HIGHLIGHTS: tour four national parks; run through the solemn Antietam National Battlefield

So let's just take it from the beginning.

The marathon starts in the Harpers Ferry National Historical Park, where the Potomac and Shenandoah rivers meet. It's also the site of several historic events, including John Brown's famous raid and the largest surrender of Federal troops during the Civil War. The first loop is around Murphy Farm, where John Brown's fort was moved and preserved before being moved back to its original location.

From there, the course crosses the Potomac on a footbridge and turns north along the Chesapeake and Ohio Canal, another national park better known as the C&O Canal, that remains as a testament to early transportation, engineering, and westward expansion.

After about 10 miles on the canal towpath, the course jogs inland to the solemn Antietam National Battlefield, site of the bloodiest one-day battle in American history, where 23,000 soldiers were killed, wounded, or went missing after 12 hours of combat. The battle ended the Confederate Army of Northern Virginia's first push into the North.

From the battlefield and nearby Sharpsburg, the course passes back across the Potomac to Shepherdstown, West Virginia, where the steamboat was built and tested, and a finish in the football stadium of Shepherd University.

The half marathon starts in Shepherdstown and runs down the canal before joining the marathon course into Antietam. The 10K and 5K are run mostly along the canal.

Besides the marathon and related races in October, Freedom's Run offers several other races through historic sites in the area. Check out the Harpers Ferry Half Marathon, Run through History, or American Odyssey Relay (see the "Get Some Friends Together" chapter).

RUN CRAZY HORSE
Honor the Native American spirit

The Crazy Horse Memorial is a work in progress—and has been since 1948.

That's when sculptor Korczak Ziolkowski and Lakota Chief Henry Standing Bear officially started the world's largest mountain carving in the South Dakota Black Hills.

The sculpture is a monument to the Native American people; Crazy Horse was chosen as a

LOCATION: Hill City, South Dakota
DATE: early October
DISTANCE: marathon, marathon relay (five runners), half marathon, 5K
FIELD SIZE: 1,000
WEBSITE: www.runcrazyhorse.com
RACE HIGHLIGHTS: start at unfinished Crazy Horse Memorial

subject because of his courage, humility, and tragic death, according to the memorial foundation. In the planned sculpture, the great leader is riding a horse, his hand pointing straight ahead.

Ziolkowski died in 1982, 16 years before the completion of Crazy Horse's massive, 87-foot-high head. Work continues today on the 22-story horse's head. When completed the full carving will be 641 feet long and 563 feet high, though there's no estimated completion date.

You can honor the spirit of Crazy Horse and check out the unfinished carving with the Run Crazy Horse marathon and half marathon, which start at the memorial and descend into downtown Hill City. The race, which also offers the Fast 5K the day before, started in 2010.

Take in even more history the day before the race: the event partners with nearby Mt. Rushmore to offer a tour of that famous monument on the Saturday before Run Crazy Horse. You can also take a trip on the 1880 Train through the scenic Black Hills.

BATTLE FOR CHATTANOOGA
A historic competition among runners

The fall of 1863 saw some of the fiercest fighting of the Civil War near the Tennessee-Georgia border. Union and Confederate armies were fighting for control of Chattanooga, a key rail center and what many saw as the gateway to the Confederacy and the Deep South.

LOCATION: Chattanooga, Tennessee, and Fort Oglethorpe, Georgia
DATE: April, August, November
DISTANCE: marathon, half marathon/15K, 5K/4.7 miles
FIELD SIZE: various
WEBSITE:
www.battlefieldmarathon.com/battle.html
RACE HIGHLIGHTS: tour major battle sites key to the outcome of the Civil War

Collectively known as the Battles for Chattanooga, months of fighting near Chattanooga and along Chickamauga Creek ended in November, with the Union Army controlling Chattanooga and most of Tennessee. The city was used as a supply base the next spring when Maj. Gen. William T. Sherman made his famous March to the Sea, carving a path of destruction through Georgia.

With the Union victory and the ensuing marches through the South, the Battles for Chattanooga became known as the "death knell of the Confederacy."

The battlefields were preserved as the Chickamauga & Chattanooga National Military Park, the first designated U.S. national military park, established in 1890.

Now, runners can compete in a modern day "Battle for Chattanooga," a series of three races at the park and a nearby battle scene. Overall prizes are awarded to the runners with the lowest combined times in all three

Running in the Chickamauga Battlefield Marathon also serves as a tour of a Civil War battle site. Photo courtesy of Charlene Simmons

races, and everyone who completes all three receives a special Battle for Chattanooga medal.

- **Chickamauga Chase 15k & 5k (April):** Chattanooga's oldest continuously run road race, the Chickamauga Chase started in 1968 and passes many of the historical markers and monuments in the military park. Only the 15K counts for the race series, but there also is a competitive 5K and trail run, a scenic walk, and a kids run.

- **Missionary Ridge Road Race (August):** This 4.7-mile out-and-back course runs atop Missionary Ridge, the scene of a battle in which Union soldiers charged the Confederate rifle pits at the base of the ridge. Missionary Ridge is about three miles east of downtown Chattanooga, rising about 500 feet above the valley.

- **Chickamauga Battlefield Marathon & Half Marathon (November):** The marathon is two loops around the park, while the half marathon is one. (Only the marathon counts toward the race series.) The course is mostly paved, scenic, and challenging, but not too tough.

019

STAY UP LATE

Calling all night owls: this chapter is for you.

There's something special about being up and running while everyone else is asleep. There's less traffic, and no sun glaring in your eyes or beating down on your skin. Everything is more still, more quiet, especially if you're out on a trail.

These races take advantage of the novelty of running in the dark. Some were founded out of necessity, to find respite from the summer heat. Some were made to show off the glittery city lights. Some require headlamps to run out in the wilderness.

In any case, these events can be a challenge for runners who are used to getting up and running early in the morning, like many of us do.

Reset your body clock, at least for one night, and take on a night owl race.

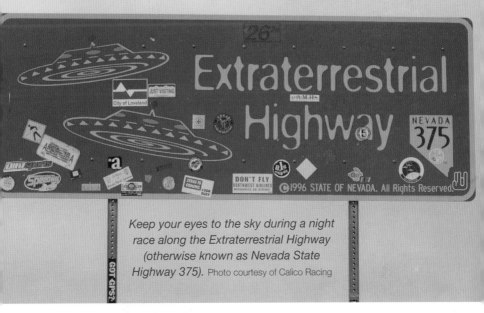

Keep your eyes to the sky during a night race along the Extraterrestrial Highway (otherwise known as Nevada State Highway 375). Photo courtesy of Calico Racing

E.T. FULL MOON MIDNIGHT MARATHON
Run the dark fringes of Area 51

Is that a UFO? A plane from nearby Nellis Air Force Range? Or are the runners just hallucinating because of the midnight start time?

It could be any of the above at the E.T. Full Moon Midnight Marathon.

LOCATION: Rachel, Nevada
DATE: mid-August
DISTANCE: 51K, marathon, half marathon, 10K
FIELD SIZE: 800
WEBSITE: www.calicoracing.com
RACE HIGHLIGHTS: run along the "Extraterrestrial Highway" near Area 51 in Nevada; finish at the Little Al'E'Inn, a kitschy hangout for alien fanatics

Although Joyce Forier's company, Calico Racing, hosts several running events throughout the year near Las Vegas, she knows if something weird is going to happen, it happens at the E.T.

"It challenges runners in a lot of different ways," Forier said. "I think most runners are morning people. Most people don't have the luxury of changing their training schedule, so they go out of their minds."

Runners can minimize their sleep deprivation–induced craziness by napping before the race on buses chartered from Las Vegas for the event and by staying hydrated and watching what they eat for dinner. But there's always going to be an element of the weird at the E.T. Midnight Marathon.

The E.T. is the perfect race for UFO and sci-fi enthusiasts. Many runners show up in costumes honoring *Star Trek* and even *The Jetsons*, Forier said.

The starting line (for all races but the 10K) is at the famous "Black Mailbox," which is now painted white, a popular gathering spot for UFO chasers. Runners take off at midnight, enjoying cool desert temperatures during the night, even in August.

The route follows remote State Highway 375, which the state tourism commission renamed the "Extraterrestrial Highway," on the fringes of Area 51, a federal military base where conspiracy theorists believe the government stored and studied crashed alien spacecraft. The course is open range, making it more likely the runners will see cattle than aliens.

After climbing to Coyote Summit (elevation 5,591 feet) the racers descend into Rachel, a small town that caters to UFO tourists. After the finish, runners are treated to breakfast at the Little Al'E'Inn—and a spectacular sunrise—before heading back to Las Vegas to live among the Earthlings.

MAKE IT BY MIDNIGHT MARATHON
Don't turn into a pumpkin!

LOCATION: Macon, Georgia
DATE: mid-July
DISTANCE: marathon, half marathon
FIELD SIZE: 175
WEBSITE:
makeitbymidnight.homestead.com
RACE HIGHLIGHTS: start any time you want to finish by midnight; receive a tiara if you make it, a pumpkin if you don't

The Make it by Midnight Marathon is a backward race.

Instead of starting together, the goal is for everyone to finish around the same time—specifically, as close to midnight as possible.

Racers must predict their own time in the half or full marathon, and then back up their start times from midnight. Someone who wants to run the marathon in four hours, for example, would start at 8:00 PM. A two-hour half-marathoner would start at 10:00 PM.

There is some room for error, of course; the finish line closes at 1:00 AM. You'll also want to allot some extra time for the hilly course and the oppressive heat and humidity of the Georgia summer. Some runners start as early as 3:00 PM, when temperatures are in the 100s, and temps usually only fall to the high 90s after the sun sets.

The idea, like many other good ones, started as a joke. Running buddies Deborah Botkin and Andrew Strickland were on a marathon kick, running one or two a month, and they couldn't find one nearby in July. They did some research and found out they only needed five official starters (three of whom finish) and a website to announce the race and publish results—and presto, it's an official marathon.

So they decided to get a few friends together and run loops around Strickland's gated community. A night race would provide relief from the sun, at least, if not from the stifling humidity.

The genius of the Make it by Midnight—the differing start times—was Botkin's idea. "It was totally selfish," she said. "I am a slow runner. When I'm done, there are no people; there's no food. I thought, *Wouldn't it be nice to finish with a bunch of people?*"

Naturally, a Cinderella theme emerged for the race, with those who make it by midnight being awarded tiaras and those who don't receiving pumpkins for their efforts.

Though that first race had only a few participants, word spread and by the sixth annual running in 2013, the 175-runner cap was reached less than a month after registration opened. The residential community has gotten behind the race, with homes competing for a $50 prize for best runner support. Some have impromptu water, beer, or even ice cream stops.

The 6.6-mile loops around the subdivision (four for the marathon, two for the half) provide another unique aspect of the race. Because everyone starts at different times, when a runner passes you it's impossible to know if they are just starting or making a kick toward the finish. Everyone really must run his or her own race.

Botkin and Strickland still run their race every year, starting a little earlier so they can be at the finish line when runners are coming in. They've been surprised to see runners from as far away as South Korea, Panama, and Germany compete in a small race in the middle of Georgia.

"It really captures people's imagination," Strickland said.

RACE REPORT

Charley Melvin Mad Bomber Run for Your Life
A dynamite race

Denise Malan

Many know of Carrie Nation, the crazed prohibitionist who attacked bars around Kansas smashing liquor bottles with a hatchet during the early 20th century.

LOCATION: Iola, Kansas
DATE: mid-July
DISTANCE: 5K
FIELD SIZE: 300
WEBSITE: www.madbomberrun.com
RACE HIGHLIGHTS: an entertaining street festival leading up to the 5K start at precisely 12:26 AM; a "drag race" sprint relay for men dressed as women (or women dressed as men)

Lesser known, but just as crazy, is the story of Charley Melvin, a fellow Kansan who, like Carrie, had developed an extreme dislike of alcohol.

Now Melvin is getting his due as the small southeast Kansas town of Iola, where Melvin dynamited three saloons one night in 1905, has started a street festival and 5K to turn the destruction into something constructive for their city.

As a native Kansan myself, I couldn't resist signing up for the Charley Melvin Mad Bomber Run for Your Life. It would be my first night run, and I was intrigued by the history of the small town near where I grew up.

(One note about the race's name: I ran the Mad Bomber in 2013, several months after the Boston Marathon bombing. The race organizers, sensitive in the wake of the bombing, put a note at the top of the race website explaining that Melvin's actions targeted buildings and alcohol, not people. A portion of the Mad Bomber's registrations was donated to the fund for Boston victims.)

As the Charley Melvin story goes, in early 1905, he was having trouble sleeping. His co-workers at a concrete plant recommended whiskey and beer, which Melvin, a strict prohibitionist, was desperate enough to try. Instead of quieting his nerves, the alcohol only served to make Melvin feel even worse. He felt so bad, in fact, that he vowed to take down Iola's illegal saloons. (Kansas was a dry state decades before national Prohibition.)

After his first plan to shoot several local barkeepers was foiled, Melvin was placed in an insane asylum. He was released several months later, and at 12:26 AM the morning of July 10, 1905, the first of two great explosions rocked the Iola square. The second followed about a minute later. Three of the boomtown's bars had been destroyed by 400 sticks of dynamite. Miraculously, no one was killed. Melvin was caught a month later and pleaded insanity, though he was found guilty and sentenced to prison for his crimes.

More than a century later, the town of Iola (population 5,700) gathers on the weekend closest to the anniversary and commemorates the bombing with the 5K Run for Your Life and a pre-race street festival unlike any other I've seen.

I was a bit worried how I would stay awake until the race kicked off just after midnight, well past my regular bedtime. But the festivities around Iola's town square did not disappoint and were enough to keep me wide awake (with the aid of some caffeine, of course).

Before the race, we stopped at a gazebo on the square and listened to a man reading the Melvin story, with backup from an old-fashioned barbershop quartet singing key lines. Then came "killer karaoke," in which the singers were subjected to pies in the face, sticking their hands in boxes of mystery animals, and other distractions. The singing was terrible, but the show was hilarious!

One of the other main attractions is a "drag race," where a surprisingly high number of the town's boys and men put on wigs, makeup, and dresses, and sprint in a short relay race where they have to pass a garter on to the next runner. I'm not sure the drag race has anything to do with Melvin or the history of the town, but it was truly funny to watch.

A country band then entertained the crowd until it was time to line up for the race. About 1,000 people registered for the 5K run and 3K walk, an impressive number given the size of Iola (though only about 300 residents were in the run). The starting line was on West Street, where the saloons were hit with Melvin's dynamite. The last 20 seconds until the race were counted down with a tick-tock, tick-tock, and the starting gun was a blast through the loudspeakers.

We took off through the streets of Iola, which were dark and peaceful except for the occasional dog barking or resident sitting outside to cheer on the runners. I didn't bring a headlamp, though at times I wish I had one. The air was relatively cool for July and there was a nice, light breeze. I felt right at home running in the dark and any fatigue had left me in the pre-race countdown.

The quick and flat course finished back at the square, where a well-lit finish line and a line of volunteers ringing cowbells greeted all the finishers. It was a rousing finish that kept me awake on the drive home in the wee hours of the morning.

PIGEON FORGE MIDNIGHT 8K
A road running classic

The Pigeon Forge Midnight 8K actually started as neither a midnight race nor an 8K.

David Morris, who had moved to Tennessee from Florida, started a running club in Sevier County in 1981. He brought the idea of a night race with him from Florida, and in 1991, the group started the five-mile Pigeon Forge Twilight Road Race.

"We had it at 9:00 PM, and we were overwhelmed," Morris said. "We had a lot more runners than we expected. Traffic was an issue because it was summertime."

LOCATION: Pigeon Forge, Tennessee
DATE: first Saturday in August
DISTANCE: 8K
FIELD SIZE: 700 to 800
WEBSITE: www.ktc.org
RACE HIGHLIGHTS: unique distance and flat, fast course that practically guarantee an 8K PR

So the club pushed it back from July to the first Saturday in August, after the rush of tourism season in the mountain resort town. The race was changed to an 8K some years later to qualify as an 8K championship race.

Morris and another runner co-directed the race for about 15 years, and it became a road racing classic during running's heyday in the 1990s. Known as a fast, flat course—especially for eastern Tennessee—the race is a loop along the Parkway, the main drag in town.

Morris handed over the reins to the local police department and high school, which weren't able to keep up with demand. The race went dormant for a few years, until the Knoxville Track Club, about 30 miles away, asked Morris to revive it in 2009.

The first year back, the race attracted about 400 runners, and now it's leveling off at about 700 to 800 runners.

"Moving it to midnight actually helped with the traffic, and people actually seemed to like the fact that you can start at 11:59 and finish the next day," Morris said.

The unique distance and prize purse also attract some elite runners from around the Southeast, Morris said. Since its reboot, the Pigeon Forge Midnight 8K has served as the Tennessee State 8K Championship and the Road Runners Club of America Southern Region 8K Championship.

"You see a lot of 5Ks and 10Ks," Morris said. "[The 8K is] nice for people who are wanting to move up but not ready for the 10K yet. A lot of people make a weekend outing of it."

Las Vegas Rock 'n' Roll Marathon
See the Strip at night

Amber Tafoya

The Rock 'n' Roll Las Vegas Marathon and Half Marathon tests runners way beyond the course itself.

LOCATION: Las Vegas, Nevada
DATE: mid-November
DISTANCE: marathon, half marathon, quarter marathon
FIELD SIZE: 25,000
WEBSITE:
  runrocknroll.competitor.com/las-vegas
RACE HIGHLIGHTS: avoid temptation of Sin City long enough to complete an evening run on the Strip and through old Vegas

Constant temptations, from the poker table to decadent food, tried to lure participants away from their goals and deep into Sin City. The marathon and half marathon started at night, which helped set the tone. This race was about the party, not just the run. Throw in some Elvis impersonators and a few thousand runners congregating on the Las Vegas Strip, and this was one of the most energetic races I've ever participated in.

With thousands of participants, this was easily the largest-attended event I've run. And like any event with large crowds, there are some positives and negatives.

I wanted to make this my first half marathon because the course is, for the most part, flat. But the race had some unexpected challenges— most outside of the course and in Sin City itself.

When arriving in Las Vegas the first thing some may want to do is grab a cocktail and a chair at the nearest poker table. You just have to know your limits. I turned my head away at most of these vices but did splurge on a rich pasta meal and a couple glasses of wine the night before the race.

On race day, my friends and I grabbed breakfast and took the rest of the day to prep for the race. Ignore that blackjack table! We knew that there would be shuttle buses ready to take us to the starting line, and we headed out about an hour before start time. This was definitely not enough time. The line for the shuttles stretched several blocks long, and the waiting runners grew anxious. This was not the best way to kick off a race.

We finally got on a bus and the driver reassured us he would get us there, somehow, as he navigated heavy traffic. And while the runners were laughing and having fun, many were still annoyed that we would be getting at the starting line late.

We jumped off the bus and made it in time to start with one of the later waves. After a mile or so we were closer to one of the highlights of the race—running down the colorful Las Vegas Strip. We also ran by one of many stages featuring a band playing pop and rock music. Thousands of people lined the streets to cheer the runners on, and their cheers, mixed in with the bright lights and music, created a wonderful energy. The runners themselves also made the event interesting. I saw a few Elvises running, and one man, who was dressed as a young Elvis, dropped to his knee and proposed to his girlfriend (she wore a sparkly white cape and a black wig styled like an old Elvis).

After running through the Strip the course took us through old Vegas, where the atmosphere was calmer. Many stopped to take photos by iconic signs and landmarks, while the more serious racers pushed on. A few miles later we hit the Strip again and pushed through our last leg. By then, I was exhausted but the huge crowd motivated me to finish. I crossed over with relief—that I completed my first half and finally allow myself to have a little fun.

This was one of the most chaotic, fun, and energetic races I've ever participated in. And isn't that what Vegas is all about?

INSOMNIAC NIGHT SERIES
These races will keep you awake

You know you're in for some fun when the race day forecast includes moonrise and moonset.

LOCATION: Arizona
DATE: May–September (one per month)
DISTANCE: 7K to 100K
FIELD SIZE: 200 to 400
WEBSITE: www.aravaiparunning.com
RACE HIGHLIGHTS: nighttime trail runs with varying distances from beginner to ultra runner; camping available in most of the parks

Aravaipa Running in Arizona offers the Insomniac Night Series of five nighttime trail races around the Phoenix area, each race with its own forecast according to the moon. For example, the moon during one of the runs in August will be in waxing crescent phase, offering only 15 percent illumination, so the race is scheduled for 9:20 PM. You'll definitely want to carry a flashlight for that one!

Jamil Coury, who founded Aravaipa Running, said the company took over a popular Javelina 100 ultra marathon trail race several years ago and started a training run at night, to dodge the blazing desert sun. At first, the event was informal, but as word spread, Aravaipa turned it into an official event, complete with registration, T-shirts, and awards.

"All of a sudden, once we started doing that, it got really popular," Coury said. "We had a lot of people who said it was their first time ever running at night or at night on a trail. We thought it was really cool, so we wanted to create more opportunities for people."

So in 2013, Aravaipa started the Insomniac Night Series that run throughout state and regional parks near Phoenix. The races are all set up in loops so runners can choose distances from about six miles to about 40 miles. The longer distances start earlier, around sundown, to give runners plenty of time to finish before sunrise.

Runners should carry a flashlight or headlamp, though on nights with full moons, extra light probably isn't necessary. The courses are well marked with reflective markers and lights.

"I think it's just kind of a magical experience, something that you don't get running in the day," Coury said.

Here's a look at each of the five races (and the swag you can collect for running all five):

- **Sinister Night Runs (May):** One, three, or six loops of a 9K trail in San Tan Mountain Regional Park. Technical shirt for all participants.

- **Adrenaline Night Runs (June):** One, two, or five loops of a 13.3K trail in McDowell Mountain Regional Park. Campsites and tent rentals available, plus a singlet for all participants.

- **Vertigo Night Runs (July):** One, three, or six loops of the 10.4K Sonoran Competitive track in White Tank Mountain Regional Park. Campsites and tent rentals available, plus a sport bag to all participants.

- **Hypnosis Night Runs (August):** One, two, or four loops of the 15.5K loop in Estrella Mountain Regional Park. Campsites and tent rentals available, plus trucker hats to all participants.

- **Javelina Jangover Night Runs (September):** One, two, three, or four 25K loops on the Pemberton Trail Loop in McDowell Mountain Regional Park. A shorter 7K option is available on the Scenic Trail. Camping available, plus technical shirts for all participants.

The Javelina Night Run started several years ago as an informal night training run in Arizona and has grown into a full-fledged race. Photo courtesy of Aravaipa Running

LIGHTED NIGHT RUNS
You'll rave about these runs

LOCATION: various
DATE: various
DISTANCE: usually a 5K
FIELD SIZE: various
WEBSITE: various
RACE HIGHLIGHTS: light up the night with neon lights and glow in the dark costumes; dance the night away to electronic music

Just like the adventure obstacle course race, the lighted night race has become ubiquitous around the country. Several companies now offer races where runners dress with glow sticks, neon paint, and crazy costumes and party into the night with music and laser shows.

Runners can get extremely creative with their costumes for these races. Try wearing a black sweatsuit with only a glowing stick figure painted on it. Or fashion some unique accessories (glasses, headbands, or even wigs) out of glow-in-the-dark necklaces.

Here are a few ideas to find an illuminated night race near you:

- **Firefly Run:** With locations across the country, the Firefly Run hosts a costume contest and post-race laser light show and concert. (www.fireflyrun.com)

- **The Rave Run:** The Rave Run's lighting effects are designed by rave artists and industry experts, leading to a fun electronic dance and running event. This race does have one major difference, though, from an actual rave: a strict no-drug policy. (www.theraverun.com)

- **The Glo Run:** This race series brings its "sensory overload" mostly to Midwestern cities. All runners receive a glow-in-the-dark T-shirt, and on-course DJs provide entertainment during the race. (www.theglorun.com)

- **Electric Run:** Runners travel through different "lands" along the course, each with their own flavor and mood, with lighting features synchronized to music. You could experience fountains of lights, illuminated trees, and glowing arches. (www.electricrun.com)

MIDNIGHT SUN RUN

Talk about throwing off your body clock!

The Midnight Sun Run in Fairbanks, Alaska, is unique to the northernmost state. In Fairbanks, which is about 200 miles south of the Arctic Circle, the sun shines well past midnight on the summer solstice toward the end of June. (Inside the Arctic Circle, the sun shines for 24 hours on the solstice.)

LOCATION: Fairbanks, Alaska
DATE: late June
DISTANCE: 10K
FIELD SIZE: 3,500
WEBSITE: www.midnightsunrun.us
RACE HIGHLIGHTS: run in daylight in the middle of the night

So though this 10K starts at 10:00 PM, you won't need a flashlight or headlamp like you would at most other races in this chapter. And it's not like you would find it easy to sleep while the sun is out, so you might as well go for a run!

The Midnight Sun Run has been held annually since 1983. It's an interesting tidbit that the first race was held at 9:00 AM, and therefore didn't showcase the actual midnight sun, according to a race history on the website. By the second year, though, the event was moved to the bright nighttime to fully celebrate the midnight sun.

That year, the race director also introduced a costumed division in hopes of making the Midnight Sun Run into Fairbanks' own version of Bay to Breakers, known as one of the most eccentric races in the country (see the "Party Hardy" chapter for more on Bay to Breakers).

The race winds through many different Fairbanks neighborhoods, and the course often is lined with spectators who cheer on the racers and even spray them with hoses if the weather is too hot (yes, temperatures can reach into the 70s in Alaska).

After the sun sets near 1:00 AM, you should be able to get plenty of rest and be ready for the next day's Midnight Sun Festival, when the town of Fairbanks basks in the long-lasting sun and celebrates the end of a long, cold winter.

020

IS A BRIDGE TOO FAR?

Reaching the top of a steep bridge is one of the best feelings a runner can experience.

You just conquered a tough hill, but you also get to enjoy a view that thousands of people zoom by each day with barely a notice.

While many races include bridges in their course designs, these events were chosen for the bucket list because each one made a bridge (or in the case of Chattanooga, seven bridges) the centerpiece of the race.

From covered bridges in New England to the Florida Keys' miles-long causeway to the Golden Gate in San Francisco, these bridge races are the best the country has to offer.

Pacer Ryan Shrum comes down the Walnut Street Bridge during the Seven Bridges Marathon in Chattanooga, Tennessee, with Lookout Mountain directly behind him.
Photo courtesy of Whitney Allison

SEVEN BRIDGES MARATHON
Finish on top of the world

Chattanooga shows off its best assets with the Seven Bridges Marathon. There's the art district, Tennessee Aquarium, the River Walk, and, of course, all those bridges.

The full marathon course crosses seven bridges in total. Six of those cross the Tennessee River, plus a bonus bridge crossing a smaller creek. The marathon's sister races are aptly named by the number of bridges included: the Four Bridges Half Marathon and Two Bridges 5K.

"The course goes through all the best parts of Chattanooga," said Benj Lance, a runner from nearby Dellrose, Tennessee. "And as you're running you can look around and see all the mountains."

LOCATION: Chattanooga, Tennessee
DATE: late October
DISTANCE: marathon, half marathon, 5K
FIELD SIZE: almost 2,000
WEBSITE: www.sevenbridgesmarathon.com
RACE HIGHLIGHTS: crisscross the Tennessee River several times; the approach to the finish line is a wooden, pedestrian-only bridge filled with cheering spectators

The course has some hills but is pretty tame for a Tennessee race, Lance said. Even with seven bridges, the total course ascent is less than 400 feet. The toughest part is the Chickamauga Dam Bridge, which, unfortunately, comes in the later miles of the marathon. But after that, the final 10K through the River Walk is a breeze. The last bridge is a pedestrian-only wooden bridge filled with spectators cheering runners on.

The grand finale is a finish in Coolidge Park, where runners cross an inlaid-brick globe, finishing "on top of the world."

"This is a race I think I'll probably do every year," Lance said. "There's something special to me about Chattanooga. It's just such a beautiful city."

RACE REPORT

Harbor Half Marathon
A strong start and finish

· ·

Denise Malan

The Harbor Bridge is a towering mass of steel and concrete.

As I stand below it, watching the sun rise over Corpus Christi Bay, I am more than a little intimidated that I'm about to run across it. Twice.

LOCATION: Corpus Christi, Texas
DATE: late October
DISTANCE: half marathon, two-person relay, 10K
FIELD SIZE: 800
WEBSITE: www.harborhalf.com
RACE HIGHLIGHTS: view from the Harbor Bridge about 140 feet above the water

The bridge opened in 1959 and spans more than a mile over the Corpus Christi Ship Channel. Oil tankers and other ships must pass under it to reach the city's refineries and chemical plants. Color-changing lights along its steel trusses have made it a tourist destination in its own right in this popular vacation city.

The Harbor Half starts in the shadow of the bridge, outside Whataburger Field, home of the Corpus Christi Hooks minor league baseball team and named for the hometown favorite burger chain. The stadium is locally famous for another reason, too. Justin Timberlake, who portrayed a fictional Hooks player in *The Open Road*, filmed the movie's opening scenes here during an actual game in 2008.

After the runners take off, we have less than a mile to warm up before hitting the bridge. The early course winds through the city's entertainment district, passing the American Bank Center arena and Heritage Park, where the city moved 12 Victorian homes and restored them.

After a couple more turns, we hit the on-ramp to the Harbor Bridge.

The bridge has three lanes of traffic in each direction. For the race, one lane is closed to traffic, but cars and 18-wheelers whiz by on the left, often honking at the runners. On the right is a low concrete barrier and a narrow walkway, which few pedestrians ever brave. The walkway is bounded only by a couple steel rails.

Beyond those rails, if you're brave enough to look down, are some of Corpus Christi's most popular tourist attractions. The unique, pointy-roof architecture of the Art Museum of South Texas, was the first to catch my eye—and take my mind off the burning in my legs. Beyond that, just on the other side of the ship channel is the Texas State Aquarium, which has dolphin shows, a stingray touch tank, and a splash park.

Hulking in the water is the Lexington Museum on the Bay, a World War II era aircraft carrier turned museum. The flight deck, where scenes were filmed for the 2001 movie *Pearl Harbor*, is filled with aircraft.

With all the scenery, the first ascent of the bridge, about a half mile, actually goes by faster than I expected. When I feel the hill crest then start to slope downward under my feet, I pump my arms in the air to celebrate. The worst part—of the first half, at least—is over.

On the way down, I take care not to let my legs go too fast, reminding myself that there's still plenty of race left.

After the bridge, we take an off-ramp to an access road, where those running the 10K turn around, only to face the bridge again. The rest of us follow the access road for about a mile before entering the Nueces Bay Causeway.

This middle part of the run is peaceful. Endangered brown pelicans float on the bay waters surrounding the causeway, and laughing gulls soar overhead. The air is starting to feel steamy from the Gulf Coast sun and humidity.

After another couple of miles, we enter Indian Point Park and run along its paved trail through coastal wetlands. This out-and-back along the trail is the final stretch of the first half, and faster runners who have already made the turn stream past me.

Finally I reach the halfway point, where the two-person relay hands off and the rest of us turn around. The course winds back exactly the way we came, with the Harbor Bridge looming in the distance. The dread of running back up the bridge nearly overshadows the rest of my run.

When I hit the bridge my sole focus is on not stopping. The second ascent is much steeper than the first...or maybe my legs are just tired. Either way, it's definitely tougher. I am bolstered, though, each time I pass someone who has had to walk or stop to catch their breath. Just don't stop.

I am so proud of myself when I reach the top without walking, but I don't have as much energy to celebrate as I did during the first ascent. I just want to make it to the finish line.

Soon after I start descending, I pass the 12-mile marker and feel home free. This is the reward for the climb.

I wind my way back through the entertainment district and the finish line at Whataburger Field. Waiting for me is the perfect memento—a finisher's medal with a silhouette of the Harbor Bridge.

WOODROW WILSON BRIDGE HALF MARATHON
Bridge along the Beltway

. . . .

The bascule bridge memorializing Woodrow Wilson spans the Potomac River, carrying Interstate 95/495 (the Capital Beltway) traffic into Washington, D.C.

A half marathon crossing the bridge started in 2010 and within four years was named one of the top 27 half marathons in the country by *Runner's World* magazine readers—no small feat for such a young race. Runners raved about the course and scenery.

LOCATION: Alexandria, Virginia, to Maryland
DATE: early October
DISTANCE: half marathon
FIELD SIZE: 5,000
WEBSITE: www.wilsonbridgehalf.com
RACE HIGHLIGHTS: start at historic home of George Washington; run the Woodrow Wilson Bridge, a drawbridge with views of Washington, D.C.

The destination half marathon begins at the historic Mount Vernon home of George Washington in Alexandria, Virginia, crosses the Woodrow Wilson Bridge, and ends at the National Harbor in Maryland, just south of Washington, D.C.

There is a bit of a buildup to the bridge; the first eight miles are on the George Washington Memorial Parkway that runs along the Potomac. Then the bridge span is about a mile and a half, and the final couple of miles run around National Harbor, a resort, shopping, and entertainment area in Prince George's County, Maryland.

US HALF MARATHON
A must-see bridge hosts a must-run race

When it comes to bridges, there are few more iconic than the Golden Gate Bridge in San Francisco.

Marking the span where San Francisco Bay meets the Pacific Ocean, the Golden Gate Bridge was the longest suspension bridge in the world when it opened in 1937, and it remained so for about three decades. Its copper-colored towers are an unmistakable symbol of the Bay Area.

LOCATION: San Francisco, California
DATE: early November
DISTANCE: half marathon
FIELD SIZE: 5,000
WEBSITE: www.ushalf.com
RACE HIGHLIGHTS: cross the Golden Gate Bridge twice; enjoy views of Alcatraz, the city skyline, and parks

This must-see civil engineering "Wonder of the Modern World" should be a must-run on your list. And you can actually run across it not once but twice during the US Half Marathon in San Francisco.

The early November race starts on the waterfront in Aquatic Park and winds through the Marina and the Presidio (a national park and former military base for three countries) to the Golden Gate. Runners cross the bridge twice, out and back along pedestrian walkways on each side of the span. The course then returns to Aquatic Park along the Golden Gate Promenade.

The park is a destination to be enjoyed in its own right, with great views of the bridge, the infamous Alcatraz island prison, and the city skyline. After the race, enjoy music, food, and massages at the finish line festival.

COVERED BRIDGES HALF MARATHON
Experience the romance and history of
New England's covered bridges
· ·

The covered bridges of New England are a popular tourist attraction. Vermont, with 106 covered bridges and even a covered bridge museum, is a prime destination to tour the historic structures.

So it's no surprise, then, that the Covered Bridges Half Marathon in Vermont is one of the most popular races in the region—the 2013 event sold out in a mere 14 minutes (with a cap of 2,300 entrants).

The race, founded in 1992, starts in the Suicide Six ski area in South Pomfret, travels through Woodstock, and finishes in the village of Quechee. Along the way, runners will pass two covered bridges and run through two more.

The first bridge runners encounter is the Meadow Covered Bridge before running through the Middle Covered Bridge. The course then follows the Ottauquechee River to the Taftsville Covered Bridge and past the Quechee Covered Bridge. The finish line—and the beer tent—is in the Quechee Polo Field.

LOCATION: near Woodstock, Vermont
DATE: early June
DISTANCE: half marathon
FIELD SIZE: 2,300
WEBSITE: www.cbhm.com
RACE HIGHLIGHTS: course runs through two covered bridges and past two more

7 Mile Bridge Run

Join a lucky group of runners for a one-of-a-kind view

· ·

Beth Moyes

Every year, thousands of people awake one February morning before the sun comes up and park themselves in front of their computers, poised to register for a highly competitive, extremely beautiful seven-mile run across a bridge in the Florida Keys. All are willing to face the elements along a historic, exposed concrete bridge—which is usually solely for automobiles— in blistering heat and pouring rain.

> **LOCATION:** Seven Mile Bridge near Marathon, Florida
> **DATE:** early April
> **DISTANCE:** 6.8 miles
> **FIELD SIZE:** 1,500
> **WEBSITE:** www.7mbrun.com
> **RACE HIGHLIGHTS:** entire race completely surrounded by water

The 7 Mile Bridge Run has been an annual tradition since 1982, when the new bridge opened. The bridge traverses the span between the city/island of Marathon and the next island, Ohio Key (about 118 miles from Miami and 47 miles from Key West). The bridge is lovingly called the "Eighth Wonder of the World," and it really is a wonderful sight to see. To see it outside the confines of a car is a unique experience, so it's understandable that this is one of the most famous bridges to run in the world. Just to be one of the lucky 1,500 entrants is a feat to be celebrated.

I am a runner and the owner of a racing business, Theme Runs, as well as a longtime resident of the Florida Keys. I was lucky enough to experience the 7 Mile Bridge Run firsthand in April 2013. I was one of the lucky 1,500 because my close friend had donated money that year to The 7 Mile Bridge Foundation in support of the local high school sports teams. As a thank-you for the donation, he was guaranteed one entry to the race, and it was generously given to me.

My two running partners were not as lucky. To secure their enrollment, they each woke up at 5:45 AM on February 7 to attempt to register for the race. There were two dates for registering—local county residents were allowed to register on February 7 before registration was opened to the public on February 12. The process is similar to buying concert tickets for a coveted event. People visit the website online before tickets are even open for sale and then hit "refresh" until tickets are available to purchase. Sometimes, despite these efforts, the event can sell out before you even have a chance to purchase. Both friends tried pressing the refresh button until their fingers ached, but neither one got in. I was very disappointed for them and for me, as I wanted their support and drive to push me to perform on the big day of the race. Thankfully, there was another chance to get in. Both friends would have to try to register on the open registration day, along with thousands of people from around the world who also want to face the challenge of the race. As it turned out, only one of my running partners got in.

On the morning of the race both of us got up at 5:00 AM, which we figured was plenty of time to get to the race, drive to the start, and wait to get our number bibs. We wore matching homemade sweatbands with our team name on it for solidarity. Team *Beat the Bus* was ready to race. I ate my usual breakfast: oat bran with cocoa powder, and an apple. I stuffed Gatorade chews in my sports bra for energy during the race. Yes, they get a little salty as I run, but it's worth it for the boost. Plus, I don't like to weigh myself down with a runners fanny pack. We arrived at the parking lot at the base of the bridge but the car in front of us snagged the last spot in the lot. Now we had to find a place to park, run to the bridge to get our numbers, and hope to beat the starting gun! We made it with about a minute to spare.

When the gun went off, it seemed strangely far away, and those of us toward the back of the crowd had a slow beginning, crossing the start line roughly 60 to 90 seconds later. I couldn't resist taking pictures with my phone as we were running because seeing 1,500 people on this two-lane bridge I'd driven over hundreds of times was such an impressive sight.

For the first mile I kept pace with my friends, but then some fell behind, some shot ahead, and I was left to enjoy the sights and people-watching while chugging along with my one running partner and friend. I was impressed to see a firefighter running the race in full gear and holding a flag to commemorate 9/11. The sight gave me goose bumps—which is not easy to do when it's 80 degrees and the humidity is over 80 percent—and I snapped a quick pic while trying to keep pace.

I passed the first couple miles with ease before the bridge began to ascend. It's a tough incline but we all leaned into it. The view from the top, which is a little short of the halfway point of the bridge, was the most exciting: runners as far as you could see in either direction. To keep us cool, there were buckets of water with sponges and a fire truck that had its hoses hanging above us like shower heads.

The race was almost over but I didn't want it to end. Though it was a tough journey, it was also beautiful. I felt strong and connected to this community of runners. Just when I thought it couldn't get any better, I passed the Mile 6 marker and had my first runners high. Even though I run all the time, I had never felt anything like it; my vision seemed to tunnel, I felt elated, and my breathing was totally relaxed. This race experience was even better than I could have imagined. It was like a tropical vacation, right in my backyard.

COOPER RIVER BRIDGE RUN
Now on its third bridge

The Cooper River Bridge Run, one of the largest 10Ks in the country, has outlasted two bridges over the Cooper River in Charleston, South Carolina.

The run faced an uphill battle from the beginning. A local group wanted to start the race to promote health and fitness, and thought a new bridge over the Cooper River would be a big draw.

But it almost didn't happen. That first year, in 1978, the Cooper River Bridge Run required the intervention of a state senator to close the Silas Pearman Bridge to traffic for the race, according to a detailed history of the race written by Cedric Jaggers, a running journal editor.

By the third year, the race had to switch to the older Grace Memorial

LOCATION: Charleston, South Carolina
DATE: early April
DISTANCE: 10K
FIELD SIZE: 35,000
WEBSITE: www.bridgerun.com
RACE HIGHLIGHTS: run across the 2.5-mile-long Ravenel Bridge with 575-foot-tall towers; a flat, fast course that attracts world elites as well as casual runners and walkers

Bridge, before switching back to Pearman in 1995, according to Jaggers' history. Both of those bridges were demolished after the opening in 2006 of the stunning Arthur Ravenel Jr. Bridge, where the race is run today.

The Ravenel Bridge is a 2.5-mile-long structure with an incline from 1.8 percent to 5.6 percent (though most of the distance is a manageable 4 percent). The first year for the race on the Ravenel Bridge also saw its peak participation, with nearly 46,000 runners and walkers.

The bridge provides great views of Charleston and is a marvel in itself. Two diamond-shaped towers reach heights of 575 feet, with 128 cables supporting the main span.

LOUISIANA BRIDGE RUN SERIES
One river, three unique races

LOCATION: New Orleans, Louisiana
DATE: April, early June, and mid-June
DISTANCE: 5K/10K, 4 miles, 5K
FIELD SIZE: various
WEBSITE: various
RACE HIGHLIGHTS: cross the Mississippi River on three unique bridges; earn finisher's items for each race, plus a unique series medal for finishing all three

Ah, the Mississippi River. The Mighty Mississippi. The Big Muddy. Old Man River.

Whatever you want to call it, the Mississippi River and its many bridges are just waiting to be conquered.

The Louisiana Bridge Run Series represents the joint venture of three races over the Mississippi in the springtime in and around New Orleans. Complete all three to earn a special finisher's medal, plus receive all the individual race swag (like a trucker hat for the Huey P. Long run). If you're a strong runner, you can compete for the title of King or Queen of the Mississippi River by earning the lowest combined time.

Here are the details on the three unique races:

- **United Way of St. Charles Bridge Run (April):** This 5K/10K crosses the Mississippi River on the Interstate 310 bridge, just west of New Orleans, from Destrehan to Luling. As a fund-raiser for the United Way, this race has become ever more popular, with nearly 2,000 runners and walkers in 2013. (www.uwaysc.org/bridge-run)

- **Crescent Connection Bridge Run (early June):** This evening race starts in New Orleans' West Bank and crosses the Crescent City Connection Bridge, at a height of 300 feet above the river and with great views of the city at sunset. The four-mile race ends in the trendy Warehouse District. (www.ccc10k.com)

- **The Great Huey P. Long Bridge Run (mid-June):** Start in Bridge City and cross the river into Jefferson on the Huey P. Long Bridge, which opened in 1935 and was named for the popular governor who was assassinated that year. The bridge still carries rail and road traffic and was widened in 2013. (www.hueyprun.com)

021

FINISH AN INTERNATIONAL DESTINATION RACE

For many runners, an overseas destination race is near the top of their bucket lists. Not only do these races offer unique histories, scenery, and international fields, but they also provide a great excuse to take an extended vacation and explore an entirely new country.

When choosing an international destination race, you might want to start with deciding which country you'd like to visit, then find some potential races there.

From the thousands of available races around the globe, a few stand out, be it for their location, history, course length, or popularity.

A truly international field takes part in the Marathon de Paris, which begins beneath the Arc de Triomphe. Photo courtesy of Kyle Taylor/kyletaylor.com

MARATHON DE PARIS
Ah, Paris in the springtime…

You definitely won't feel out of place as a tourist at the Paris Marathon. About two of every five runners are from one of 100 countries other than France.

LOCATION: Paris, France
DATE: second weekend in April
DISTANCE: marathon
FIELD SIZE: 40,000
WEBSITE: www.parismarathon.com
RACE HIGHLIGHTS: one of the world's five largest marathons; take in views of the iconic Arc de Triomphe, Place de la Bastille, Notre-Dame Cathedral, and the Eiffel Tower

With more than 40,000 entrants, the Paris Marathon is typically one of the five largest in the world (along with New York, London, Berlin, and Chicago).

The Marathon de Paris actually predates the marathon sport as we know it today. It was first run in 1896 at a distance of 40K, the actual distance of

Pheidippides' original run from Marathon to Athens. The official marathon race distance of just more than 42K was set 12 years later in the 1908 Olympics.

The race starts at the foot of the Arc de Triomphe, the iconic 162-foot-tall arch built in the early 1800s in honor of those who fought for France in the Napoleonic Wars.

After that kind of start, you can't help but triumph over the rest of the course, which heads down the famous Champs-Elysees and down the Rue de Rivoli, past the Palace de la Bastille and the Notre-Dame Cathedral before passing the base of one of the most recognizable landmarks in the world, the Eiffel Tower, in the 19th mile.

The race finishes back near the Arc de Triomphe, a fitting place to celebrate your personal victory.

RACE REPORT

Great Wall Marathon
5,164 steps into history

Robert Muilenberg

When my sister Lynette and I flew into Beijing, the race organizers with Adventure Marathon tours and several other participants were there to meet us. Early on, I had a feeling that we were at sort of a sleepaway camp for runners. There was a very camp-like feel, with the group riding in buses and eating in large dining halls. There were participants from all over the world, and most everyone seemed to

LOCATION: Huangyaguan, China
DATE: May
DISTANCE: marathon, half marathon, 8.5K
FIELD SIZE: 2,500
WEBSITE: www.great-wall-marathon.com
RACE HIGHLIGHTS: steps, steps, and more steps (5,164 of them); planned race package from Adventure Marathon with accommodations in Beijing

enjoy the international spirit of it. We were shuttled to the hotel in Beijing, a trip during which we got our first taste of the famous traffic.

On our second day, we were taken to the race site at Huangyaguan, Tianjin Province, where we were able to inspect the portion of the Great Wall we were going to run. I was pretty winded and intimidated by just walking the wall, so I was a bit apprehensive about running. When I saw the uneven stairs and the steep climbs and descents, I had a feeling I would not be running my best time.

The start of the race left from the Yin and Yang Square. Runners departed in waves. The run started with a three-and-a-half-mile climb up some pretty steep and winding roads. The pack of runners started to separate with the hard early climb, which helped as we started to climb onto the wall. There were many bottlenecks at the points where runners were getting on and exiting the wall. Often you would find yourself waiting for slower runners. Luckily, most runners were very patient. The biggest problem running on the wall was that no two stairs were the same size — they ranged from a slight rise to an arduous stretch.

The first part of the run took us about nine kilometers up and over the wall. Marathoners ran this section twice, while those running only the half ran the wall section once. There were also many bottlenecks at the guard towers where only one person at a time could go through. Again, patience seemed to be the order of the day.

I took some time to take in the sights and appreciate my location on the inspection day, so I spent my time on the wall during the run trying to stay upright and not completely exhaust myself before hitting the remaining two-thirds of the race. At most times while I was on the wall, the idea of running seemed a bit far-fetched to me. At other times, it seemed downright dangerous. There were areas where there were breaks for drainage. They were not big, but if a runner were not paying attention, he could trip. There were also areas with no railings and a pretty steep descent.

Needless to say, it was a huge relief to get off the wall and run on a flatter surface. My legs were aching a bit from all the climbing, but I was able to hit a comfortable stride. It was really nice to be greeted and cheered by the people in the village, mostly children. I could have spent my entire run giving kids high-fives. They seemed to get a charge out of it. Most of the people in the village took little notice of the people running through their streets. The traffic was controlled but there was some dodging of carts and running alongside cars and trucks.

As I wound through the village we got back to the uneven running I had grown so fond of on the wall. The route went from paved to gravel roads to dirt trails, which made me wish I had trail running shoes (it was my fault I didn't, because there was plenty of warning about the running surfaces in the runner information packet).

I struggled much for the last few kilometers, even slowing to a brisk walk at times, which I had not resorted to in quite some time. I was not used to the elevation and the hills, so those took their toll on me by the end of the run. I finished the half marathon about 30 minutes slower than my usual half marathon time. According to the race literature and the officials at the run, that is the normal adjustment. There is much more walking and even some waiting that aren't a part of other races. Nonetheless, I finished much sooner than my sister Lynette, so I had a lot of time to inspect the fare. The post-race food left a lot to be desired, and the swag was a bit limited at this race. After I finished my sandwich, I took a very cold shower in the living quarters at the site and got a massage from some hardworking locals under the race tents.

The medal was ornate with an etching of the Great Wall, but not as big as I was hoping. Still, it is great to have a medal from this particular run. The only thing that differentiated the medals is the small distance pin ranging from the fun run to the full marathon that decorated the ribbon. The finisher shirt was a standard white that I still wear proudly when working out today.

With most races I run, there is a relief and warm feeling of accomplishment when it ends. However, when Lynette and I finished the Great Wall race, we were both exhausted and a bit sad. Finishing a race is an accomplishment; participating in this race seemed much bigger. The overwhelming feeling of being at a site with such rich culture and history, combined with the encounters with the wonderful people we had the opportunity to meet, made it more meaningful than any race I had previously run. Just as it was tough to leave camp when we were kids, it was sad to leave China.

ATHENS CLASSIC MARATHON
In the footsteps of Pheidippides

This is it, the place where the legend of the marathon began.

In 490 B.C., the messenger Pheidippides was dispatched from the plains of Marathon into Athens, about 25 miles away, to spread news of the Athenian victory in a battle with their Persian invaders. He arrived in Athens, delivered the message—either by saying "Rejoice! We conquer!" or the Greek word for victory, "Niki," depending on which version of the legend you believe—and then collapsed and died.

Although it is hard to say how much truth there is to the legend, the story nonetheless inspired the entire sport of marathoning.

When Greece hosted the first modern Olympic Games in 1896, the country honored Pheidippides with a footrace from Marathon to the Olympic Stadium in downtown Athens. (That first race was about 25 miles, just like Pheidippides' run. The current distance of 26.2 miles wasn't set until the 1908 Olympics in London.)

LOCATION: Marathon to Athens, Greece
DATE: mid-October
DISTANCE: marathon, 10K, 5K
FIELD SIZE: 18,000
WEBSITE: www.athensclassicmarathon.gr
RACE HIGHLIGHTS: run the route of the legendary Pheidippides, who inspired the sport of marathoning; finish in the 1896 Olympic Stadium in Athens

The Athens Classic Marathon started in 1983 to honor the legend and the history of the marathon (featuring the modern-day distance of 26.2 miles, of course). And now all runners have the chance to experience the emotional, yet very challenging, original marathon.

The route starts in Marathon and circles the burial mound and memorial for Athenian soldiers who died in that battle 2,500 years ago, before heading down Marathonos Avenue. There are some hills between 10K and 17K, but the real challenge of the race is right in the middle, with the steady climb between the 20th and 31st kilometers.

The finish is perhaps the most inspirational part of the Classic. After all those hills, runners descend into Athens and sweep in for the final 170 yards inside the Panathinaiko Stadium, the horseshoe-shaped, white-marble stadium that hosted the original 1896 Olympics.

THE BIG FIVE MARATHON
The ultimate safari run

No fence, no moat or river, no invisible electric field.

There is nothing separating you from the African savannah wildlife—rhinos, elephants, buffalo, lions, and leopards—you will see on this safari marathon through the Entabeni Safari Conservancy, a private game reserve.

The Big Five Marathon, which gets its name from the Big Five game preserves in Africa, is one of the four annual events produced by Adventure Marathons/Albatros Travel (the Great Wall Marathon is another).

LOCATION: Entabeni Safari Conservancy, Limpopo Province, South Africa
DATE: mid-June
DISTANCE: marathon, half marathon, 10K
FIELD SIZE: 200
WEBSITE: www.big-five-marathon.com
RACE HIGHLIGHTS: see wildlife in the wild; vacation and marathon travel package

It's hard to say which is more intimidating: the wildlife or the race elevation chart. The Big Five Marathon, which offers a companion half marathon and 10K, is also one of the tougher marathons you'll come across. Before the halfway mark, it dips into a valley and along a lower plain, known as "lion land," before heading back up to the upper plateau.

As with all Adventure Marathon races, the marathon comes with a complete travel package. Runners can choose from five- or seven-day itineraries that also include game drives, a pre-race drive along the route, and a marathon after-party on the African plain.

COMRADES MARATHON
The "Ultimate Human Race"

The Comrades Marathon bills itself as the "Ultimate Human Race," and with good reason; only 54 percent of those who set out to race the grueling South Africa course finished in June 2013.

Though it is called a marathon, Comrades is actually usually around 54 to 56 miles, more than twice the length of a true marathon. The sun and hills are relentless, but the aid stations are well stocked with fluids, fruit, and carbohydrates, plus sunscreen and Vaseline.

Overcoming the challenges and finishing the Comrades is one of the truly great achievements in running.

Vic Clapham, a South African World War I veteran, envisioned the race as a tribute to soldiers in the Great War. Running about 90 kilometers through the sweltering South African heat would be a fitting physical challenge to help memorialize the hardships these soldiers endured.

LOCATION: Pietermaritzburg to Durban (or vice versa), South Africa
DATE: late May or early June
DISTANCE: about 87K
FIELD SIZE: 20,000
WEBSITE: www.comrades.com
RACE HIGHLIGHTS: one of the most grueling ultra marathons on the planet; course alternates between "up" and "down" years

It took some convincing, but Clapham eventually got the League of Comrades of the Great War, a group of former soldiers, to agree to the race. The first Comrades Marathon in 1921 had 34 entries. It has been run every year since, except several years during World War II.

Today, tens of thousands attempt the Comrades each year. Finishers are given medals according to the times they cross the line. The top 10 men and women receive gold medals; all the rest earn different-colored medals or those honoring Comrades historical figures. Anyone finishing out of the gold but under six hours earns a Wally Hayward medal in honor of the famous South African marathoner who won the Comrades five times. Medals continue on down the line until the Vic Clapham medal for finishers from 11 to 12 hours, the official race cutoff time.

The course alternates running from Pietermaritzburg to Durban or vice versa. From Durban to Pietermaritzburg is known as the "up" course, because of the relentless uphill for the first third of the course. Alternating years are known as "down" years, when the course runs from Pietermaritzburg to Durban. As the course varies year to year, the distance can vary slightly as well.

MARATHON DU MÉDOC
A 26.2-mile party

Leave it to the French to come up with a race this indulgent yet charming.

The Médoc wine growing region of France is host each fall to the Marathon du Médoc, a 26.2-mile party with wine at each aid stop—more than 20 in all—and even food stations with oysters, ham, and sorbet.

You can see why the Médoc is also known as "le marathon le plus long du monde," or "the longest marathon in the world."

The race was created in 1984 by a group of marathon fans, and it has become quite popular both inside and outside France—more than 20 percent of racers are foreigners. The founders have kept four principles—health, sport, conviviality, and fun—at the forefront of the Médoc.

Health and sport are pretty obvious at a marathon (though the Médoc does

LOCATION: Médoc region, France
DATE: September
DISTANCE: marathon
FIELD SIZE: 8,500
WEBSITE: www.marathondumedoc.com
RACE HIGHLIGHTS: wine and gourmet food stops; great finisher's gifts; recovery walk the next morning

take that one step further by requiring medical certificates for all its runners), so let's talk about the conviviality and fun. The field is limited to 8,500 runners each year so that organizers can keep it intimate. Each runner who crosses the finish line gets a bottle of Médoc wine, an art print, sports bag, medal, T-shirt, and other gifts. The night after the race, everyone is invited to a ball featuring fireworks and entertainment, and the next day is Médoc's famous recovery walk and a mountain bike ride through the Moulis wine region.

None of that compares to the fun had during the race, though. More than 90 percent of runners dress in costumes with a different theme each year. But the 22 refreshment stands (including wine), 21 food stands, and special gourmet stands (oysters, ham, steak, cheese, and ice cream) are the main draw to the Médoc.

The wine can really take the edge off running a marathon, and some runners even imbibe on their training runs so they can be prepared for the Médoc. Just remember, there's also *water* at those stops, so be sure to stay hydrated!

SPARKASSE 3-COUNTRY MARATHON
Three foreign countries in one scenic race

What's cooler than a marathon in a foreign country? How about a marathon through *three* foreign countries?

The Sparkasse 3-Country Marathon ("3-Länder Marathon" in German) takes advantage of the proximity of the borders of three countries—Germany, Austria, and Switzerland—around Lake Constance in Central Europe.

The race starts on an island in Germany and runs along Lake Constance, soon leaving Deutchland for Austria. Runners continue counterclockwise along the tip of the lake (in fact, about 60 percent of the course is on Lake Constance) through Lochau and Bregenz.

The course leaves the lake at Hard, Austria, and bends down toward Switzerland, where runners only spend a couple kilometers, but still enough to count it as a third country. Then the marathon loops back toward a finish at a stadium in Bregenz. (It should be noted that courses for the companion half marathon and quarter marathon run through only two countries, Germany and Austria.)

LOCATION: Lindau, Germany, to Bregenz, Austria
DATE: mid-June
DISTANCE: marathon, half marathon, quarter marathon, marathon relay (four runners)
FIELD SIZE: 5,000
WEBSITE: www.sparkasse-marathon.at
RACE HIGHLIGHTS: hit three countries (Germany, Austria, and Switzerland) in one marathon; flat and scenic course mostly along the shores of Lake Constance

ANTARCTICA MARATHONS
Chills and thrills way down under

The temperature is regularly below zero, with blowing winds. There's nothing but ice for miles and miles and miles. You literally are near the end of the Earth.

Wait a minute…why is Antarctica such an appealing destination for races again?

Apparently the challenge of overcoming the freezing cold and isolation are just the thrill some runners are looking for. Plus, a race on Antarctica can be the crowning achievement for those runners who want to join the Seven Continent Club.

Two companies offer popular race destination packages to Antarctic marathons:

LOCATION: Antarctica
DATE: March and November
DISTANCE: 100K, marathon, half marathon, 1 mile
FIELD SIZE: 100
WEBSITE: www.marathontours.com, www.icemarathon.com
RACE HIGHLIGHTS: finish a marathon on the seventh continent; experience views few people ever get to see

- **Antarctica Marathon and Half Marathon (March):** Marathon Tours & Travel organizes this event and is the exclusive tour company. The course is on King George Island, off the tip of the Antarctic

Peninsula, on marked gravel roads that connect several scientific research bases. Runners embark on a boat from South America to reach the peninsula. Antarctic weather on the island in March is a balmy 15 to 20 degrees with light snow flurries. With the gravel roads, you won't need any special shoes. This race is limited to only 100 and can sell out a couple years in advance. (www.marathontours.com)

- **Antarctic Ice Marathon (November):** This race goes even farther south, just a few hundred miles from the Antarctic Circle near the Ellsworth Mountains. It's also the colder of the two events, with temperatures dipping below zero. The race recommends three layers of clothing—a base layer, a thermal layer, and a wind layer—plus goggles, gloves, two pairs of socks, and trail shoes.

The Ice Marathon, offered by Polar Running Adventures, includes several distances for thrill-seekers of all running abilities, from the Antarctic Mile, perfect for friends and family of marathon runners, to the Frozen Continent Half Marathon, Ice Marathon, and 100K Ultra Race. (www.icemarathon.com)

PALIO DEL DRAPPO VERDE
The world's oldest footrace

This race has quite a lot of history to live up to.

The Palio del Drappo Verde (or "Race of the Green Cloth") 10K in Verona, Italy, is the world's oldest foot race, dating all the way back to 1208, according to the Association of Road Racing Statisticians, the authority on road racing data around the world.

LOCATION: Verona, Italy
DATE: March
DISTANCE: 10K
FIELD SIZE: 500
WEBSITE: http://xoomer.virgilio.it/stscevar
RACE HIGHLIGHTS: experience living history in the world's oldest foot race; the course crisscrosses the heart of Verona

Though the Drappo Verde was interrupted for a couple hundred years, it was brought back in 2008. As of 2013, the ARRS counted 596 official runnings of the Drappo Verde.

The race was modeled after a popular Verona horse race and used the same course, according to ARRS. The Drappo Verde apparently was started to celebrate the city of Verona's victory over feudal counts to become its own self-governing city; its name refers to the green cloth awarded to the winner. The Drappo Verde apparently was so popular it was mentioned in Dante's *Divine Comedy*.

Though the course distance likely varied throughout the years, the latest incarnation of the Drappo Verde is a 10K that tours the heart of Verona. The ARRS advocated for its revival, and an amatuer sports club worked with the city to bring it back.

Italy is a long way to travel for a 10K, but it might just be worth it to experience this slice of running history.

ZEVENHEUVELENLOOP 15K
Run with the world's elite through the Dutch hills

"Zevenheuvelenloop" is quite a mouthful, so let's just call this race by its English name: the Seven Hills Run.

The event is aptly named for the seven hills spread over the 15K course. The race started in 1984 and has grown to international prominence, with 15K world records set here for both men and women. Running superstar Haile Gebrselassie has run this race, as have Paul Tergat and Lornah Kiplagat.

With a large field approaching 30,000 runners, the Seven Hills Run is open to all runners from around the Netherlands and other countries, allowing recreational runners to join the elite for a run in the hills.

LOCATION: Nijmegen, Netherlands
DATE: November
DISTANCE: 15K
FIELD SIZE: 30,000
WEBSITE: www.zevenheuvelenloop.nl
RACE HIGHLIGHTS: course featuring seven hills; run with elites in this race in which the men's and women's 15K world records have been set

The course leads the runners from Nijmegen to Groesbeek and back to Nijmegen via the village of Berg en Dal.

022

SEEK ADVENTURE

At some point, the same old road races can become dull and monotonous. It's easy to get bored hitting the pavement mile after mile.

Enter the adventure and obstacle course races that have been soaring in popularity the last several years. Running USA reported in 2012 that participation in such races grew from just a blip on the radar to more than 1 million in only 10 years. And there's no end in sight.

Race series such as Warrior Dash, Tough Mudder, and Spartan Race are dominating the market with events across the United States (and some other countries), but there are also smaller, one-of-a-kind races that take advantage of local terrain or urban environments to give runners an extra challenge.

So get going—boredom is no longer an excuse!

JAMES RIVER SCRAMBLE
Urban landscape turned obstacle course

If it weren't for the skyline of downtown Richmond, Virginia, in the background, you might forget you're in the city during this unique 10K.

The James River Scramble starts on the roads but quickly turns down some stairs onto a canal walk, a floodwall, bridges, a trail, more stairs, and even boulders that you must hop to get to an island.

"It's one of my favorite races I've ever done," said Drew Sullivan of Richmond. "I'm definitely more into the trail and adventure-type races that aren't just monotonous road racing."

Highlights of the event include the Buttermilk Trail mountain biking trail, a series of steep steps known locally as the "Mayan Ruins," and views of downtown Richmond from the floodwall. You'll also have to jump boulders to get across the riverbed to Belle Isle, an island turned city park in the middle of James River.

"You've got to take your time," Sullivan said of the boulder hopping. "Nobody's sprinting. They're all laughing."

The James River Scramble ends on Brown's Island, an artificial island formed when a canal was built along the river. The race is limited to 1,500 participants to limit damage to the James River Park System.

The race is on the Saturday evening of the Dominion Riverrock Festival, a weekend-long adventure sports competition and concert festival. So you can stick around after the race to watch freestyle bikes, stand-up paddleboarding, or even dog jumping contests.

There's also a mud run 5K on Friday night that would make a perfect warm-up for the James River Scramble.

LOCATION: Richmond, Virginia
DATE: mid-May
DISTANCE: 10K
FIELD SIZE: 1,500
WEBSITE: www.dominionriverrock.com
RACE HIGHLIGHTS: jump rocks to get across the riverbed; stay and watch the Dominion Riverrock Festival

The James River Scramble in Richmond, Virginia, gives runners an obstacle course feel with an urban backdrop. Photo courtesy of Jesse Peters/Sports Backers

LIVING HISTORY FARMS RACE
One of the first adventure races

The FAQ section of the Living History Farms Race website is refreshingly short:

- Will it be cold? Probably!
- Will I get wet? Probably!
- Will I get dirty? Probably!
- Do I need gloves? Yes!
- Exactly how far is it? 7 miles

LOCATION: Urbandale, Iowa
DATE: Saturday before Thanksgiving
DISTANCE: 7 miles
FIELD SIZE: 7,500
WEBSITE: www.fitnesssports.com
RACE HIGHLIGHTS: nine water crossings, steep gullies, and farm animals

That's about all you need to know about the Living History Farms Race, which bills itself as the country's largest cross-country race. Living History Farms in Urbandale, Iowa, outside Des Moines, is an outdoor, nonprofit museum that educates people on rural Midwestern life.

And with its creeks, gullies, fences, and farm animals, it is the perfect setting for the race that has been giving runners a thrill since 1979, long before the surge in popularity of traveling obstacle course races.

The Living History Farms Race typically sells out its 7,500-runner cap in less than two days. Runners love to dress up in costumes that are guaranteed to end up muddy and wet after the nine water crossings along the course.

Keep in mind that the race is in November, so it's bound to be cold, too. Runners warm up with a hot meal afterward including beef stew, biscuits, cider, and coffee. It makes for a satisfying way to end an adventurous day on the farm.

Berserkr Games
Non-stop adrenaline rush

Alissa Mejia

When a race director contacted me about a new event called the Berserkr Games in a small town near Kingsville, Texas, he described mud, water, sand, shooting, and jumping from helicopters into a pond.

LOCATION: Ricardo, Texas
DATE: two to three per year, various dates
DISTANCE: about 5K to 20K
FIELD SIZE: 400 to 500
WEBSITE: www.berserkrgames.com
RACE HIGHLIGHTS: 44 obstacles (per loop), muddy and sandy terrain, and a helicopter-drop start

The event was going to be huge. Oh, and it was happening in two weeks. I decided he had to be either pranking me or crazy.

It turned out that I was right on one of those counts.

The host organization, Rifles Only, is devoted to outdoor adventure. Its 488-acre ranch provides tactical training for elite long-range military, government, and civilian shooters. Although newcomers to the obstacle race business, the Rifles Only crew knows how to plan a top-notch event. They also know how to host a party. The Berserkr course delivers every bit of the promised adventure, plus a dose of Texas-style hospitality.

The first thing to know about Berserkr Games is to never expect the same course twice. Organizers are always looking for ways to expand and improve the obstacles. However, participants can expect a few common threads. The 20-foot-tall "giant stairs" are a staple of Berserkr courses. Each race features at least one rifle shooting challenge. (If you have not shot before, don't fear—trained staff members assist, and competitors advance through this challenge whether they hit or miss their targets.) And, of course, there is the signature event: the helicopter drop into a pond. It does feel disconcerting to step onto the runner of a hovering helicopter, but turquoise well water, only about six feet below, beckons refreshingly in the Texas heat. After a "3, 2, 1, drop" signal from the co-pilot, competitors let go in pairs and the race is off with a splash.

Other obstacles have included a vertical climbing "mouse trap," full-body hurdles, giant ladders, tire jungles, logs, ladders, nets, balance beams over water, a 25-meter pond, ammunition boxes, and, of course, mud. The longest mud obstacles can reach 400 meters. In fact, the Berserkr Games stands out from other obstacle races for its sheer number of challenges. In a recent running they managed to cram 44 obstacles into a single lap, so those completing the entire four-lap course faced 176 obstacles.

Each lap is approximately five kilometers long. However, even seasoned 5K or 10K runners should not be fooled by the lap distances. Throw in 40-plus obstacles, plus terrain of either slippery mud or soft sandy loam throughout, and your typical road race times can more than double. Plan on at least three to five solid hours of strenuous full-body activity to complete the four loops.

Only a multi-pronged training approach of both distance running and strength training can prepare you for this full-body endurance effort. Because many of the challenges—the full-body hurdles, the mud pits, and the giant stairs—require pulling one's body weight over the obstacles, some of the most effective training would be to practice climbing or to get in and out of a pool without using the ladder. Strong calf muscles are a must. The ideal clothing and shoes will stay on snugly while wet or dry.

Since the Berserkr Games is a team event, it also helps to pick teammates with similar levels of stamina to your own. Teams can consist of two or more members. Organizers wait to start each team's clock until all members have completed the helicopter drop.

Volunteers keep the course stocked with water bottles, and all competitors are greeted at the finish with drinks, music, and Texas barbecue. Kids under 10 can get muddy in a special 600-yard miniature Berserkr course.

RIVER VALLEY RUN
One of the top-ranked trail races in the country

Organizers of the River Valley Run caution that theirs is no leisurely trail run. Facing features like "Rocky Ridge trail scramble" and "Dead Man's Hill," you'll be glad you were warned.

The race is held in the River Valley Ranch, a Christian summer camp in Carroll County, Maryland, with the Gunpowder Falls River flowing through it.

LOCATION: Manchester, Maryland
DATE: mid-August
DISTANCE: 10K, 5K
FIELD SIZE: 1,100
WEBSITE: www.rivervalleyranch.com
RACE HIGHLIGHTS: challenging course with options for crossing rock outcroppings and a river; receives rave reviews and accolades from running websites

The 10K starts on paved roads and groomed trails but quickly takes off onto a hill overlooking the camp's Western Town. Runners then hit wooded trails, with moderate to steep hills, then the Rocky Ridge scramble, an outcropping of rocks where you choose your own path.

After a bit of a break through Cigar Tree Field, you'll face the short but very steep Dead Man's Hill before descending to the Gunpowder Falls River, where you make another choice between two adventurous options: charge straight through the river or stay dry by crossing a single-lane tree bridge.

The worst (or best, depending on your point of view) of the race over, the rest of the trails follow the river and Grave Run Road before going through Western Town and across a covered bridge to the finish.

The course is scenic and challenging enough to have earned the River Valley Run several accolades from racing websites and a spot in the 2013 *Trail Runner* magazine Trophy Series. There's also a 5K option on roads in the campgrounds for those wary of the trails. Both runs raise money for camp scholarships and related programs.

TOUGH MOUNTAIN CHALLENGE
A combination of natural and manmade obstacles

The Sunday River Resort in Maine is outfitted with 1,900 snowguns and 72 miles of pipe for creating the perfect snowpack for skiers.

But one Saturday in late July, the snowmaking equipment becomes part of the obstacle course 5K known as the Tough Mountain Challenge.

LOCATION: Sunday River Resort, Maine
DATE: late July
DISTANCE: 5K
FIELD SIZE: 3,000
WEBSITE: www.toughmountain.com
RACE HIGHLIGHTS: face the ski resort's snowmaking equipment turned obstacles; less crowded course than many similar events

The race is short but packed with back-to-back obstacles, both natural and manmade, that will make you glad it's over in 3.1 miles. The course is a little different each year, but the 2012 course had obstacles like "Hurricane Alley," a sprint up South Ridge while facing the snowmaking guns; and "Snow and Steady," where the pipes are transformed into balance beams over muddy, cloudy water.

And that's just the first two challenges—of 16!

The natural obstacles include the "Trench of Terror" ravine and the affectionately named "WTF," a slope so steep organizers hang ropes just in case they're needed.

The race is limited to 3,000 entrants, who run in heats to ensure the course doesn't become too crowded.

After you finish—an obstacle in itself, splashing down a twin slip-n-slide, with your friends and family watching below—stick around the Sunday River Resort for a full day of entertainment. The resort provides outdoor music, barbecues, beer garden, ziplines, geocaching, and chairlift rides—if you're not too worn out from the race.

TOUGH MUDDER

"The toughest event on the planet"

The Tough Mudder pledge reads as follows:

- I understand that Tough Mudder is not a race but a challenge.
- I put teamwork and camaraderie before my course time.
- I do not whine—kids whine.
- I help my fellow mudders complete the course.
- I overcome all fears.

LOCATION: various
DATE: various
DISTANCE: 10 to 12 miles
FIELD SIZE: various
WEBSITE: www.toughmudder.com
RACE HIGHLIGHTS: obstacles that test your physical and mental grit; focus on teamwork and camaraderie rather than finishing time

It's clear this race is more about teamwork and finishing together than about coming in first.

The Tough Mudder events aren't for the faint of heart: 10- to 12-mile obstacle courses designed by British Special Forces. (The race was created by Will Dean, a former British counterterrorism agent who was tired of boring road races.) You can sign up by yourself or as a team, but either way you'll need your fellow Mudders to make it through many of the obstacles.

Some of the obstacles you'll encounter include "Arctic Enema," which necessitates completely submerging yourself in an ice bath; "Electroshock Therapy," running through live wires carrying as much as 10,000 volts of electricity; and "Twinkle Toes," balancing on narrow wooden planks over a freezing pond.

George Doup of Dauphin Island, Alabama, completed a Tough Mudder with his family in South Carolina.

"I'm retired military, and my sister is active reserve in the Navy," Doup said. "She was trying to get the rest of my family to be more physically active."

Doup's two nephews ran ahead while he and his three siblings worked their way through the obstacles. The toughest, Doup said, was the ice bath.

"We're all kind of lean, so we didn't have much fat to keep us warm," Doup said.

The best part, though, was bonding with his family.

"I've done those things all my life, so it wasn't unique to me," the retired Navy corpsman said. "But it was cool to share it with someone who hadn't."

You can find a Tough Mudder in more than 30 U.S. locations, plus Australia, Canada, and some European countries. More than 1 million people have run a Tough Mudder so far, raising more than $5 million for the Wounded Warrior Project.

Though the obstacles are tough, Mudders don't take themselves or the race too seriously. Finishers are greeted with a beer and party at the finish line, and in some locations you can even get tattooed for an extra 70 bucks.

"Have fun; that's the most important part," Doup said. "Everyone on the course supports the team aspect of it, so if you need some help, they will be there."

RACE REPORT

Warrior Dash
Be a warrior for a day

Denise Malan

LOCATION: various
DATE: various
DISTANCE: 5K (Warrior Dash), 15 miles or more (Iron Warrior Dash)
FIELD SIZE: thousands
WEBSITE: www.warriordash.com
RACE HIGHLIGHTS: obstacles including cargo climbs, hay bales, and old gutted cars; test your skills against thousands of other warriors

My Warrior Dash started with a quest for adventure and ended with a tetanus shot.

Like many runners, I was tired of the same old 5Ks. I wanted to try something that would challenge my all-around fitness, including upper body strength. So I signed up for the Warrior Dash obstacle race nearest my hometown. (There were 39 locations in North America in 2013 alone, so there's bound to be one close to you.)

I was excited just to be racing in a rancher's field and to get off the roads for a little while. And I couldn't wait to wear the warrior helmet, a furry hat with horns given to each runner.

The Warrior Dash takes off in waves to prevent crowding on the obstacles, though it's impossible to alleviate that entirely. I took off in a 10:30 AM wave with a friend but soon lost him and didn't see him again until the end.

We encountered the first obstacle—a smattering of gutted, rusty cars— right off the bat. It would have been easy to simply run around the cars, and many people were.

But I was here to be a warrior. I was going to tackle and conquer every obstacle head on.

I jumped into one of the car's empty engine compartments, feeling like a badass already. But I was quickly brought back to reality as I felt the car frame scratch my knee as I leapt back out.

Leave it to me to injure myself on the first obstacle.

I looked down. Although the cut burned, it didn't seem too deep; I was barely bleeding. I had to warrior on.

The other obstacles weren't as hard as I'd imagined. We scaled small walls, climbed a slippery slope, scrambled over piled hay, and high-stepped through old tires.

Probably the most physically demanding for me was running through a muddy creek. My feet seemed to stick in the creek bed with every step, and I was gasping for breath by the time I made it out.

The final two obstacles were perhaps the ones that made me feel most like a warrior—leaping over a bed of fiery coals, and crawling under wires through a manmade mud pit. If you're not dirty by then, the final mud pit will make sure you're covered.

By the end, I was caked in mud but also pretty satisfied with the effort I'd put into the obstacle course. I found my friend and we washed off via the provided firehoses, a cold but welcome shower. We threw our ruined shoes into a donation pile and changed our clothes before getting in the car.

It was then that I started to worry about the gash on my knee. It's a common misconception that tetanus is caused by rust; it's actually caused by a bacteria found in dirt that gets into deep cuts. I had just cut myself and run through a pretty dirty course. And I couldn't remember the last time I had a tetanus shot.

I went to my doctor the next day and felt pretty cool explaining why I was there. After all, even warriors need tetanus shots.

HASH HOUSE HARRIERS
Find adventure in nearly any city

Technically, the Hash House Harriers are not competitive and do not run races, but you'll be hard-pressed to find a more adventurous or accessible run around the globe.

Hashers have chapters in most cities in the United States and many around the world. In fact, the idea of "hashing" started in Malaysia among a group of British officers and expats before World War II, according to hasher history websites. Participation diminished during the war, but hashing later saw a revival during recovery from the war and spread through Europe and eventually most other countries since the 1970s.

LOCATION: Most mid-sized to large cities
DATE: usually weekly
DISTANCE: various
FIELD SIZE: various
WEBSITE: www.half-mind.com (U.S. directory) or www.gthhh.com (world homepage)
RACE HIGHLIGHTS: race-like feel but unorganized event; run through parts of your city you otherwise might never see

So what exactly is hashing?

The sport likely evolved from a combination of running groups and a child's game called Paper Chase, or Hare and Hounds.

Today, Hash House Harriers, who like to call themselves drinkers with a running problem, form clubs called "kennels." They give themselves nicknames (often R rated) and meet for weekly or monthly runs with a "hare" leading the way. The hare takes off usually 10 to 15 minutes before the other runners and marks his or her trail with chalk, flour, paper, or by some other method. The other runners follow, sometimes singing songs from the Hash Hymnal (also often R rated).

Ideally the hare leads its kennel through rugged, cross-country terrain, though many times clubs must run in urban environments. And, of course, the runs usually end in drinking, revelry, and socializing for the adventurous hashers.

HALFWIT HALF MARATHON
Compete for a horse's ass award

LOCATION: Reading, Pennsylvania
DATE: mid-August
DISTANCE: half marathon
FIELD SIZE: 300
WEBSITE: www.pretzelcitysports.com
RACE HIGHLIGHTS: tough, technical routes that include steps and running through the woods without a trail

Making the Halfwit Half fun is just a way of coping with how hard it is.

"You almost have to be a halfwit to run this race," said race director Ron Horn of Pretzel City Sports. "It's difficult."

In fact, this Pennsylvania trail race is so tough, the organizers make it a habit to insult the runners, saying only people with "limited gray matter and low SAT scores" do it every year. The insults don't stop; even the trophies are "horse's ass" awards.

The trail race has numerous rocky sections, a long set of "stairs to hell" on a 45 percent incline, and even a section that has no trail, just running through the woods. Though these aren't obstacles per se, the race is hard-core enough that it qualifies as an adventurous run.

The Halfwit is a half marathon, but it is probably equivalent in effort to an 18- to 20-mile road run, Horn said.

To help runners deal, the race instituted some unique and fun provisions. There is a beer stop runners pass going each way. No one has to drink, but there is a special award for the person who drinks the most and still comes in under three hours. The record is an unbelievable 28 eight-ounce beers, Horn said.

The age group awards are "horse's asses," and runners are subjected to the lighthearted ribbing deserving of anyone who is halfwit enough to run this half.

RUN FOR YOUR LIVES
Would you survive the zombie apocalypse?

The zombie infestation has started! Are you fast and clever enough to survive?

Find out by entering the Run for Your Lives 5K, a series of races across the United States. If the regular 5K obstacle run doesn't thrill you anymore, this one with zombies nipping at your tail should do the trick.

LOCATION: various
DATE: various
DISTANCE: 5K
FIELD SIZE: various
WEBSITE: www.runforyourlives.com
RACE HIGHLIGHTS: choose to be a zombie or regular runner; see if you are ready to survive a zombie apocalypse

Thousands of runners race through obstacles such as a blood pit and a maze while trying to outrun the zombie horde. Runners wear flags they must protect from the zombies scattered throughout the course. Lose your two health flags to a zombie and you're deemed "infected," though you're not automatically transformed into a zombie and you can't chase the other runners.

At the finish line, runners will receive medals designating them as a "survivor" or "infected."

You can also join the ranks of the undead before the race. Sign up for Run for Your Lives as a zombie and you'll be transformed by professional makeup artists into a horrifying zombie. It's up to you whether you're a "chaser"—a fast zombie who can sprint after runners—or a "stumbler."

5K THE HARD WAY

Navigate some of Nebraska's toughest terrain

The signature obstacle of this locally owned mud run is a 100-foot waterslide straight into a mud pit.

Before you get there, though, you'll have to scale an old school bus; plunge into a creek and climb out up a ladder wall; venture into "Goodyear Canyon" loaded with tire obstacles and a cargo climb; weave through a vineyard; and navigate Nebraska's version of a jungle.

LOCATION: Fremont, Nebraska
DATE: several in the summer
DISTANCE: 5K
FIELD SIZE: 1,200 (in small waves of 100 to 150)
WEBSITE: www.5kthehardway.com
RACE HIGHLIGHTS: 100-foot waterslide into a mud pit; natural obstacles such as a creek and gorges

And that's just the first half.

This is how you do a 5K the Hard Way.

The 5K the Hard Way race in Fremont, Nebraska, just northwest of Omaha, prides itself on being a locally owned and operated obstacle course run. Kevin Simonson's brother and sister-in-law were avid marathoners and mud runners and traveled to other races around the country before the family realized they could use their land for something even better.

"There wasn't really a local version of this type of run," Simonson said. "We just had the perfect property for this. It's like running through the jungle."

The land includes a ravine, vineyard, orchard, creek, and plenty of wildlife, including turkeys, beavers, and even bald eagles. Runners cross a balance beam over a giant beaver dam, zigzag through a vineyard and an orchard, and have to cross the creek several times in several different ways.

"Because of our rugged terrain, we tried to create obstacles that would complement what we already have," Simonson said.

If you do get tired in the middle of the race, take a break at the Lucky Bucket Lounge, where you can grab a shot of Gatorade, water, or even the alcoholic Jungle Juice (a secret recipe, Simonson says) to help you get started again.

The 5K the Hard Way has another advantage over other traveling obstacle course races, Simonson said.

"These are permanent obstacles, so we can keep building on them," he said. "We try to change up the course every run. We do get a lot of repeat runners."

The race is held several times throughout the warm months, so check the race website for details. Though there are 1,200 or so signed up for each date, runners are separated into small heats of 100 to 150 to keep them moving smoothly through the course.

023

GET SOME FRIENDS TOGETHER

Covering 200 miles or more with a team of your best running buddies, spending a weekend living off Pop-Tarts in a stinky van, and missing two days' worth of sleep.

What's not to love about a relay race?

Relays are becoming increasingly popular, especially with the Ragnar series that hosts events from coast to coast. Runners love being part of a team and building a sense of camaraderie, even if that means smelling way more of your friends' sweaty funk than you ever wanted to.

Though many relays cover a couple hundred miles and keep runners going well through the night, you can get a taste of a relay in some shorter races where your team only has to cover a marathon distance or a little more.

So get some of your craziest friends together, think up a clever team name, and pick your favorite relay race.

The Green Mountain Relay travels smaller, scenic roads from Jeffersonville to Bennington, Vermont. Photo courtesy of Road Less Traveled Relays

ROAD LESS TRAVELED RELAYS
(Or the road less run)

LOCATION: Iowa, Vermont, Colorado, Oregon, and California
DATE: various
DISTANCE: various
FIELD SIZE: 50 to 150 teams
WEBSITE: www.rltrelays.com
RACE HIGHLIGHTS: small races with intimate feel and rural scenery

Paul Vanderheiden admits to being a bit of an elitist when it comes to his races.

He once drove the roads around Austin, Texas, looking for a suitable course for one of his Road Less Traveled Relays. And though it was an admittedly beautiful part of the country, Vanderheiden didn't find a single possible route. It seemed like every road he drove led to a four-lane highway, a definite no-no on his courses.

"Anybody can design a course if you're running along roads or sidewalks or bike paths," Vanderheiden said. "You just pick two points and have people run between those two points, and you don't care what's in between. I really care about what's in between."

The first relay Vanderheiden ran was the Colorado Relay, before it was bought by Ragnar and the course was changed. He said he liked parts of the former course, the more scenic legs, but would ditch running on the bike paths along Interstate 70.

So he decided to start his own relay in Colorado.

Vanderheiden started with the Wild West Relay, a 36-leg, 200-mile race from Fort Collins to Steamboat Springs. He loved the scenic, rural route, and that became a theme for other races as his company, Timberline Events, began to expand. After visiting a friend in Vermont, he decided that state was the perfect setting for a second overnight relay. The Green Mountain Relay is a 200-miler covering farmland, small villages, and seven covered bridges.

"I struggled for years to find other routes that matched the scenic routes and values that those two routes have," Vanderheiden said. "I went to Texas, Pennsylvania, New Mexico. It wasn't until I got to Iowa that I found another route that kind of met my standards." That route became the Heartland Relay, the company's longest race at 205 miles, which had its first running in 2013.

Road Less Traveled also has some shorter relays, including two 160-mile races in California and Colorado, and two sprint "civil war" relays (about 55 miles) between rival college towns in Oregon and Colorado. The races are smaller than many relays, with fewer than 150 teams for long races and 50 teams for the sprints.

But Vanderheiden wouldn't have it any other way. It's a lot easier to manage 150 teams than the 1,000 that can be found in larger races. "I want to co-exist with all the communities we're going through," he said. "I'm not trying to overwhelm them."

RAGNAR RELAY SERIES
"A slumber party without sleep, pillows, or deodorant"

More than a dozen Ragnar Relay Series races have sprung up around the country, helping popularize the overnight, long-distance relay race.

Named after a legendary ninth-century Norse king and adventurer, the Ragnar phenomenon started in 2004 with the Wasatch Back Relay from Logan to Park City, Utah. Today, tens of thousands of runners participate in Ragnar events in Las Vegas, Napa Valley, Massachusetts, Tennessee, Florida, and elsewhere.

A Ragnar team is made up of six to 12 runners, each completing three legs to cover a distance of about 200 miles during the course of two days and one night.

The Ragnar website calls its races "a slumber party without sleep, pillows, or deodorant," which is almost exactly how the members of Team 2 Days and Confused described their experiences. The runners can tell stories all day about portable toilets; cranky, sleep-deprived women; and living off Diet Pepsi and Hot Tamales.

LOCATION: various
DATE: various
DISTANCE: various
FIELD SIZE: various
WEBSITE: www.ragnarrelay.com
RACE HIGHLIGHTS: more than a dozen to choose from across the country; variety of leg lengths and difficulty levels makes races accessible to beginners and challenging for experienced runners

"There's something from every race that you take with you," said Krissie Summerhays, who started the team along with her husband, Mike. "I have just an overwhelming sense of laughter and bonding with my friends."

The team, based in Utah near the headquarters for Ragnar, has done the Wasatch Back for several years and also branches out to other destination races, such as Northwest Passage and Vegas. The team has the same eight to 10 core runners but usually needs a couple different runners for each race. They divide runners into girls' and boys' vans.

"Most of us have run at least one marathon," team member Tori Bergstrom said. "There are several of us who have run 10-plus marathons. We have one team member who has been an ultra runner. We have some who have never even run a competitive 10K."

For teammate Tim Lawlor, the running is the easiest part.

"It's probably deprivation of sleep," he said of the largest challenge presented by the Ragnars. "Driving at 3:00 in the morning after doing an eight-mile run? The actual running is not the hardest part. It's actually the most relaxing part."

They have so much fun in the vans, though, that they have trouble thinking of "clean" stories to tell.

"The best memories are just the things that happen in the van," Lawlor said, "and the laughs that you get."

RACE REPORT

Beach to Bay Relay Marathon
The granddaddy of all relays

Denise Malan

The country's largest relay-only marathon comes with six legs, 15,000 runners, and a whole lot of chaos.

LOCATION: Corpus Christi, Texas
DATE: Armed Forces Day (third Saturday in May)
DISTANCE: marathon relay (six runners)
FIELD SIZE: 15,000 (2,500 teams of six)
WEBSITE: www.beachtobayrelay.com
RACE HIGHLIGHTS: America's largest relay-only marathon; controlled chaos at handoff points and creative ways to find your team members

Beach to Bay, run each year on Armed Forces Day in May, is a mostly local and Texas-wide race, but it also attracts relay teams from around the country. The point-to-point race starts on North Padre Island and ends with pizza and beer in downtown Corpus Christi.

The race is less about running and more about having fun and trying to outsmart the logistical nightmare that comes with so many people running a relay. I've run Beach to Bay several times, and every year my team gets a little better at that part.

Each leg is about 4.4 miles, though they vary from 3.4 to 4.9. If you're worried about the South Texas heat and humidity—which you should be—pick one of the first two legs. Leg 1 also happens to be on the beach and is the shortest section. It's not unusual in the later stages for temperatures to reach the high 80s with a heat index near 100. (Cruelly, the last leg is also the longest and the hottest.)

Besides the heat, the main challenge of Beach to Bay is getting to your leg's handoff on time. My teammates and I always estimate our times before the race and determine when each team member should be at each handoff, then plan to get there a little earlier in case we're ahead of our expected paces.

But that's the easy part. The race provides bus transportation to most handoffs (except the last one, which is easily accessible by car), so catching a bus on time is crucial. The provided buses also don't prevent a sizeable number of runners from trying to drive to each handoff, creating the worst traffic jams this beach town sees all year. So traffic chaos is the variable that can keep even the most prepared runners from arriving on time.

The second-hardest aspect of the race is finding your teammate when you arrive at the baton handoff. A volunteer with a microphone yells out team numbers as runners arrive, but with 2,500 runners at each exchange, that is of limited use. I've been on teams that lost as much as 10 minutes at a single exchange.

My advice is for each teammate to carry a cell phone and text the next runner shortly before they arrive. It helps to pick a specific meeting location at each exchange. I've seen teams wearing crazy wigs and bright neon shirts or carrying giant foam noodles for batons so their runners can see them.

Hey, whatever works to get you to the after-party fastest!

GRAND TETON RELAY
A full day of gorgeous views

Potential wildlife sightings along the 180-mile Grand Teton Relay include skunks, bears—and Bigfoot.

Of course, while there have been reported Bigfoot sightings in this area of Idaho, no one knows for sure if he exists. He is still listed as a potential

LOCATION: Ashton, Idaho, to Jackson Hole, Wyoming
DATE: mid-August
DISTANCE: 180 miles (six or 12 runners)
FIELD SIZE: 100 teams
WEBSITE: www.grandtetonrelay.com
RACE HIGHLIGHTS: gorgeous views of the Teton Mountains; overnight sections on Rails to Trails

"course gem" of the Grand Teton Relay, and race organizers say there could be some fun extra prizes in it for you if you are crazy enough to run the relay in a full Sasquatch costume.

The Teton Range is a portion of the Rocky Mountains just south of Yellowstone National Park. Its highest peak is Grand Teton, at almost 14,000 feet. But don't worry—you won't have to run over it. You will just be treated to spectacular views of the peak and the entire range.

Starting in Ashton, Idaho, and snaking along the Idaho-Wyoming border, this 12-person relay also features a view of the Sleeping Indian natural monument and a stop at the Grand Targhee resort. Three of the overnight legs are on a section of Rails to Trails (a former railroad transformed into a running trail) where the terrain was smoothed and flattened. The highlight of this portion is the Conant Bridge, a former railroad bridge that towers hundreds of feet over a creek.

The 36 legs are nicknamed according to their terrains, many with clues to their difficulty ("Best Kept Secret" and "Paradise City" are easy, while "Teton Pass Upper" and "Down Teton Pass" are listed as very hard).

You might have to fight your teammates for the "Conant Bridge" leg, or draw straws to decide who has to run the stretch named "Sasquatch."

AMERICAN ODYSSEY RELAY
A relay through our country's history

The American Odyssey Relay is a must-run for Civil War history buffs.

The relay starts in the battlefields at Gettysburg, site of the Civil War's bloodiest battle and a Union victory that marked a turning point in the war. It then passes through Fairfield before crossing the Mason-Dixon Line, the demarcation line between the North and the South during the war.

Runners will pass through the Antietam Battlefield during the wee hours of the morning and past Harpers Ferry, another famous battlefield and now a national park. The final legs run along the Potomac River, and the last runner finishes in the Southwest Waterfront area of Washington, D.C.

LOCATION: Gettysburg, Pennsylvania, to Washington, D.C.
DATE: last weekend in April
DISTANCE: 198 miles (12 runners)
FIELD SIZE: 150 teams
WEBSITE: www.americanodysseyrelay.com
RACE HIGHLIGHTS: run through sites steeped in early American history; an "oasis" break for Van 1 runners

In the middle of the race is another of its unique features, known as the "Odyssey Oasis." Leg 16 ends at Boonsboro High School in Maryland; Legs 17 and 18 are run like cloverleafs from the school, so all the team members in the first vans can hang out on campus and take advantage of the food, showers, and massages offered at the oasis.

The race has 36 legs and is best suited for teams of 12, but organizers will allow teams with fewer people.

BREW TO BREW
How fast can you run for the beer?

Sure, any race can have an after-party. But how many races also have a pre-party?

The Brew to Brew relay starts with a couple of beers for each runner at local favorite Boulevard Brewing Co. in Kansas City, and the party continues across the state line, all the way to a meal and more beer at Free State Brewing Co. in Lawrence, Kansas—44.4 miles away.

LOCATION: Kansas City, Missouri, to Lawrence, Kansas
DATE: early April
DISTANCE: 44.4 miles (two-to-10-runner relay or solo), 27.4 miles
FIELD SIZE: 3,200
WEBSITE: www.brewtobrew.com
RACE HIGHLIGHTS: beer, beer, and more beer; relaxed rules allowing solo runners or teams of two to 10 runners

And we're not talking about your everyday light beers that you find at most races. Both companies make brews for any taste, from regional favorite

This crew won the spirit award at Brew to Brew in Kansas City for their clever—and accurate— Boulevard Brewery beer costumes. Photo courtesy of SeeKCrun

2012 Brew to Brew

unfiltered wheat to pale ales and oatmeal stouts.

In fact, race founder and experienced marathoner Lou Joline likes to talk about the beer just as much—if not more than—he likes to talk about the running. And he speaks very highly of both Boulevard and Free State beer.

Perhaps that's why the Brew to Brew ended up with its route.

In 1994, lamenting a lack of ultra marathon races in the Kansas City area, Joline put on a 24-hour race.

"It was a success," he said, "except 24-hour runs appeal to a very narrow segment of the population. If you have 25 people, you have a crowd."

So the next year, Joline decided to broaden the appeal of his race by copying a relay that was having success on the other side of Missouri: the River to River Relay that starts at the Mississippi River outside St. Louis.

In Kansas City, there had already been a couple fun runs to Lawrence, giving Joline the idea for ending his relay there. And bookending the race with the breweries in each town was a major bonus.

The Brew to Brew started in 1995 with 250 runners and now has been capped at 3,200 runners to keep traffic under control. Its course runs along the north side of the Kansas River and has changed only slightly through the years. Some exchange points are even on family farms.

One of the best aspects of the Brew to Brew, besides the beer? You can actually earn handicap minutes and decrease your team's time by fund-raising. Any team that raises at least $200 for the Cystic Fibrosis Foundation gets one minute taken off its time for every $10 donated.

And how far you actually have to run to make it to the beer is up to you. There is a solo race the day before the relay for anyone who wants to tackle all 44.4 miles on their own.

For everyone else, all teams have to cover 10 legs of about four miles each, though teams can have anywhere from two to 10 runners. There's also a shorter "Six Leg Special" option for teams of two to six runners to run only six legs (27.4 miles), drive the rest, and make it to the beer faster.

RELAY IOWA
Set your own legs

There is a single goal of Relay Iowa: make it across the state.

There are no pre-determined legs, no set team size, and no awards for the winners.

Just make it all 336 miles, any way you can.

LOCATION: Sioux City to Dubuque, Iowa
DATE: early June
DISTANCE: 336 miles
FIELD SIZE: 25 teams
WEBSITE: www.relayia.org
RACE HIGHLIGHTS: no set leg distances; two and a half days of running

"Unlike other relays where you have to stay in a certain order and you have to run a certain amount, this is so long, people get blisters, there are problems and concerns that come up," founder Bill Raine said. "It's more, 'Let's make it across Iowa together as a unit,' as opposed to, 'Let's race this other team.'"

There are a few rules, of course. The team can't have more than 12 people, you'll have to check in at certain points, and your team needs to keep up at least a 10:30-minute-mile pace to make it under the 60-hour time limit.

Yes, that's two and a half days straight.

Because this relay is so much longer and less structured than the average race, the first thing you'll need is a good plan so each person on your team has an idea of how much he or she will be running. And then you'll need the flexibility to adapt when your plan goes straight out the window after a couple hundred miles.

Plus, you'll need plenty of food. The relay will provide runners three meals, and residents of the small towns on the route also like to feed the participants. But bring along plenty of food and water to keep your team fueled on the road.

Much of the route covers smaller farm roads, some of them gravel. Unfortunately for runners, Iowa's roads aren't as flat as in neighboring Midwestern states. The teams have to deal with about 120 miles of hills over the entire course. Raine likes to say the relay is so long, it will be both the flattest and the hilliest relay you've ever run.

"It's as mentally challenging as it is physically challenging," Raine said. "Sleep deprivation is the biggest part of it. Most people get about six hours of sleep over the course of a Friday through Sunday."

With such a long distance, it's no surprise the race is small, with about 25 teams competing.

"Many runners have said they've learned why they enjoy running again doing this relay," Raine said. "We've heard from so many teams and so many runners about the appreciation they have for their fellow runners."

HOOD TO COAST
The most famous of all relays

LOCATION: Mount Hood to Seaside, Oregon
DATE: late August
DISTANCE: 199 miles
FIELD SIZE: 1,050 teams (12 runners each)
WEBSITE: www.hoodtocoast.com
RACE HIGHLIGHTS: the country's "Mother of All Relays"; start at Mount Hood and run to the beach in Seaside

A race has to be pretty legendary to warrant an entire full-length documentary.

That must put Hood to Coast among the most famous of all races in the country, never mind among relays. A 2011 movie followed four Hood to Coast teams, their training, and their preparations on a quest to finish the 199-mile relay from Mount Hood to the Oregon coast.

So if you're looking for the biggest, baddest, "Mother of All Relays," this is it.

Oregon has long been known for its running community. Relay founder Bob Foote had already run 35 marathons and 13 ultras when he decided he needed a new challenge. He got some friends together for an adventurous point-to-point relay, and eight teams ran that first Hood to Coast in 1982, with the course judiciously measured in five-mile segments.

The Hood to Coast relay in Oregon is one of the largest and most famous relays in the country. Photo courtesy of Eddie Higgins

That was long before the relay craze had started across the country, so word spread fast of Foote's new race. The next year saw 64 teams, then 150 the third year. By 1998, registration was filling up on the very first day it opened, and it has done so ever since.

The race today is capped at 1,050 teams of 12 runners for the 36-leg journey. Most legs are from four to six miles, but there are a couple seven-milers sprinkled in. The total mileage for each runner ranges from 13.6 to 19.7 miles, and the race website provides handy rankings for each runner based on total distance and difficulty.

So find 11 friends, sign up early for the race, and watch the Hood to Coast movie for inspiration.

GOLDEN GATE RELAY
"California's longest party"

. . . .

If you want to win the Golden Gate Relay, you have to be organized.

The Google1 team, made up of workers from the famous technology company who all happen to be former collegiate runners, won the race four consecutive times, from 2007 to 2010. Besides their obvious running chops, they had another advantage: their technical expertise.

LOCATION: Calistoga to Santa Cruz, California
DATE: first weekend in May
DISTANCE: varies from 190 to 200 miles (36 legs of 3 to 8 miles each)
FIELD SIZE: 200 teams (12 runners)
WEBSITE: www.therelay.com
RACE HIGHLIGHTS: run the Golden Gate Bridge in the middle of the night; start in wine country and end in gorgeous Santa Cruz

"We've run simulations before," team member Eddie Higgins said. "We feed everything into the computer and ask it to formulate every possible runner and leg and see the best possible outcome."

Most teams won't be that advanced, but everyone needs to at least know their expected finish times. Those must be turned in before the race so the start can be staggered to facilitate the race's most unique feature: all teams pass over the Golden Gate Bridge around midnight, at about the halfway point of the race.

Known as "California's longest party," the Relay covers about 200 miles from Calistoga to Santa Cruz, though it has varied from 193 miles to 200 miles depending on small course changes through the years. Its 36 legs vary in difficulty and in distance, from three to eight miles each.

Higgins advises that teams put their best runners on Legs 10 and 11, and then fill in other runners from there. Because each team needs two vans

to carry six runners each, the most dependable runners need to be Nos. 1 and 7 (so they can be at the exchanges at the right times), and you'll also need at least two trusty drivers.

The Google1 team is a four-time winner of the Golden Gate Relay, a 200-mile race from Calistoga to Santa Cruz in California. Photo courtesy of Eddie Higgins

"A big part of the logistics is just recruiting people," Higgins said. "You need yourself and 11 other people who are crazy enough to do this."

And be sure to bring plenty of sugary food for the team members to nosh on while they're riding in the vans.

"You will eat some pretty disgusting stuff over this race," Higgins said. "You will look back and think, 'Oh my gosh, I didn't think six bananas and some Pop-Tarts and some PowerBars would get me through 24 hours.' Whatever your body is asking for, it's best to just give it to it."

Even with the staggered start that helps everyone finish the first half around the same time, the teams usually get pretty spread out in the second half, with the winners typically coming in between 20 and 21 hours, and the last finishers taking 36 hours or more. So it helps that the relay has a 10-hour after-party with plenty of wine, beer, food, and desserts.

ZILKER RELAYS
Don't worry about logistics for this relay

Zilker Metropolitan Park in Austin, Texas, is a much-beloved oasis in the hipster town, with a spring-fed natural pool, botanical gardens, and access to Lady Bird Lake. Just across the lake from downtown, Zilker Park is the site of many concerts and events, including the Zilker Relays each Labor Day weekend.

LOCATION: Austin, Chicago, Milwaukee, and Minneapolis
DATE: Friday before Labor Day
DISTANCE: about 10 miles (four legs of 2.48 miles each)
FIELD SIZE: 200 teams (four runners each)
WEBSITE: www.zilkerrelays.com
RACE HIGHLIGHTS: known as Austin's best post-race party; easy logistics because every leg starts and ends at the same place

Race founder Paul Perrone, of The Genesis Agency, was out for a run one day in the park when the idea of the relays came to him. He styled his after the Beach to Bay Relay Marathon, which he'd run many times in nearby Corpus Christi, but trimmed it down to about 10 miles instead of a full marathon, and limited each team to four runners instead of six.

Though the Zilker Relays are a favorite among experienced runners, the race also is perfect for beginners wanting to try a relay. Each runner only has to complete one leg of 2.48 miles, and the logistics are simple: every leg starts and ends at the same start/finish line.

That means there's only 2.5 miles between you and what is known as Austin's best post-race party. Because the race is on a Friday evening, you'll get more than the typical bananas and Gatorade found at the finish line of many morning races.

"It's just one leg," Perrone said. "Then you're cheering your teammates on from the beer garden and listening to the band in the background, eating some Taco Deli."

The relays also are family-friendly, with a 4x600-meter relay for kids, who then can tie-dye their own race T-shirts afterward.

"There are a lot of races that get voted 'best race in Austin' because they have 10,000 people or whatever," Perrone said. "But I consistently get told this is the best race in Austin, I think because it's less about the winning and more about the camaraderie and the teamwork and having fun."

The Zilker Relays are so popular, Perrone decided to expand the brand, with new events in 2014 in Chicago, Milwaukee, and Minneapolis. Watch for this relay series to continue to grow.

GREAT LAKES RELAY
Get a little bit of rest

. . . .

LOCATION: Michigan's Lower Peninsula
DATE: late July
DISTANCE: varies (around 270 to 300 miles)
FIELD SIZE: about 80 teams (up to 10 runners each)
WEBSITE: www.greatlakesrelay.com
RACE HIGHLIGHTS: handicapped times determine the winners; each leg has surprises and unique terrain

A sampling of leg names in a recent version of Michigan's Great Lakes Relay: "Let me be brave in the attempt," "Puff on Huff," "The Bam-Bam Run," and "If You're a Pansy This One's for You."

That last one describes one of the race's shortest legs, a 2.5-mile run on the Shore to Shore Trail. Most of the other legs are from three to six miles long and many feature varying degrees of hills, narrow trails, and even sand and swamps.

Some of the terrain is so remote it's accessible only to the runners, so the teams' support vehicles have to take detours. The race organizers detail each leg—both for runners and for vehicles—with maps, turn-by-turn directions, and ratings for difficulty and scenery.

Here's the catch: the legs and the entire route can vary year to year. Some will be the same, some different, and some recycled from a few years before. That means much of the terrain won't be familiar to the runners, leading to some potential navigation issues—and part of the fun of the Great Lakes Relay. Teams can lose a lot of time if they veer off course and add too much unnecessary mileage.

Every year, it seems like someone gets lost, said Joel Dalton, who has run the race with the long-standing team Nasty Boys Glee Club.

"It's not always well marked, and sometimes it's not marked at all," Dalton said of the race course. "Sometimes you're out there running by yourself for a long time, and you see people running the other direction."

In the Great Lakes Relay, teams of up to 10 people run 270 miles over three days. Each team member would run at least 24 miles during the entire course; teams with fewer than 10 people would have higher mileage per runner.

Unlike other relays where teams run nonstop throughout the night, the Great Lakes Relay leaves time for runners to sleep. How much sleep you get is up to you, though: each of the three days starts at 6:00 AM, and teams finish anywhere from 4:00 PM to midnight. Another nice feature of the GLR: runners on the same team can run concurrent legs if they see they're not going to finish in time. Two (or more) of the runners take off on different legs and just add their times up later.

One of the race's coolest features is the handicap. You don't actually have to be the fastest team to win; each team's three-day total time is recorded, then calculated according to a formula that handicaps for age and sex.

The final "leg" no doubt will be your favorite. The after-party is given the moniker of "Food Leg" and includes awards, food, and music. All runners receive a T-shirt and a handmade ceramic mug as souvenirs.

024

RUN WILD

Man's best friend is a great running companion. But have you tried running with your donkey on a leash? How about trading off with a friend between running and riding a horse?

If you like your animals in a cage instead of on a leash, you could take a run through a zoo or animal theme park. Or if you don't like to get too close at all, you can run a race that benefits animal conservation groups.

Either way, the races in this chapter are guaranteed to be a hit with animal lovers.

Runners and their furry companions gather before the start of the New Lease on Life run, a fund-raiser for the Zumbro Valley Mental Health Center and Paws and Claws Humane Society in Rochester, Minnesota. Photo courtesy of Pam Eggler

BRING YOUR DOG ALONG
Ruff running

Maybe it's time Fido gets in shape.

LOCATION: various
DATE: various
DISTANCE: 1.5 miles to 15K
FIELD SIZE: various
WEBSITE: various
RACE HIGHLIGHTS: pet-friendly atmosphere and perks such as pet health information booths and dog treats

A host of races across the country now pride themselves on being pet-friendly and invite runners to bring their dogs for some tail-wagging fun. If your dog has been training with you for some time and already is in good shape, you can even find 15K trail runs to challenge both of you.

Here's a selection of some of the best and most unique dog-centered races out there:

- **UC Davis Dog 'n' Jog (March; Davis, California):** Run a 1.5-mile, 5K, or 10K race through the University of California–Davis campus with the goal of raising awareness of pest-borne diseases that can affect both dogs and humans. Afterward, visit the veterinary health fair to learn how to keep your pooch healthy. The race is sponsored by the UC Davis School of Veterinary Medicine and the Students for One Health Organization. (www.vetmed.ucdavis.edu)

- **Dirty Dog 15K Trail Run (May; Charleston, West Virginia):** The longer distance, combined with the single-track, mountainous trail, means this race is definitely for the more in-shape dogs (and people!). You can take your dog off the leash after the first mile, and there is a special prize for the Top Dog. (www.wvmtr.org)

- **Hair of the Dog 5K (May; Robbinsville, New Jersey):** Earn some treats for your dog and a wine tasting for yourself at this 5K, hosted by Silver Decoy Winery. Proceeds benefit local pet rescues, so dogs are welcome and encouraged to run with their owners. (www.hairofthedog5k.com)

- **Hair of the Dog 5K (January; Bethany Beach, Delaware):** This race shares a name with the previous race but it is a much different event. A New Year's Day celebration, this Hair of the Dog also features a fun party and an Eskimo Plunge after the race. And award winners are honored with stuffed dog "trophies." There also is a 10K, though dogs are allowed only in the 5K. (www.seashorestriders.com)

TRIPLE CROWN OF BURRO RACING
Just a runner and his ass

There's nothing quite like the bond between a runner and his burro.

Take it from Curtis Imrie.

"I was lucky enough to understand right away that it was about the animal, not me," Imrie says.

Those are sage words of advice from one of the most seasoned pack burro racers and a three-time world champion.

What's that? Yes, there is indeed a World Championship of Pack Burro Racing. More than that—there's an entire Triple Crown of the sport that is native and unique to Colorado. And there's even a Western Pack Burro Ass-ociation (their spelling, not mine) to promote the sport and its five annual races.

Pack burro racing, as you've probably guessed by now, involves a person running and leading a burro, or donkey, by a rope (or is it burro leading a runner?). The donkey must be carrying a load of 33 pounds (for donkeys of a certain height), harkening back to the sport's beginnings in 19th century mining country.

LOCATION: Fairplay, Buena Vista, Leadville, Georgetown, and Idaho Springs, Colorado
DATE: May through September
DISTANCE: 4 to 29 miles
FIELD SIZE: usually a few dozen
WEBSITE: www.packburroracing.com
RACE HIGHLIGHTS: push, pull, or carry your burro—but never ride him; experience a sport unique to Colorado

The legend, according to the Ass-ociation, is that two miners found gold in the same location and raced back to town, vying to be the first to stake the claim. They couldn't ride their burros because of the load, leading to the No. 1 rule of pack burro racing: no riding the animal. (A secondary legend holds that a couple drunken miners invented pack burro racing as an easier way to make money than actual mining.)

Today, pack burro racing has been named a summer heritage sport in Colorado, with a season that runs from May to September and includes five races that are part of festivals celebrating each town's history. The Triple Crown races are in Fairplay, Leadville, and Buena Vista, and the other two are in Georgetown and Idaho Springs. They range from four to six miles in Idaho Springs, a great race for first-timers, to the 29-mile World Championship race through rough, mountainous terrain in Fairplay.

There are a few rules for pack burro racing. First, the animal must be a donkey, or burro, not a mule or a horse. The animal's load must include a pick, shovel, and gold pan, and it must be led by a rope.

Most importantly, no riding is permitted. You can push, cajole, and bribe your burro to run, but you can never hop on his back or use any kind of electric prodding device.

As a seasoned pack burro racer, Imrie rounds up wild burros from the Colorado back country and trains them. He also breeds and sells them.

"They're great pack burro racing animals because they're tough," Imrie said. "If you can just come to terms with the wildness in them. They taught me a lot about being free and the joy of movement."

It can be tricky dealing with a 1,200-pound animal known more for its stubbornness than its athleticism—especially in the beginning of races when the pack mentality can take over. But the burros also can be the force that keeps runners going in the tough terrain, through creeks and over obstacles.

"When something goes wrong, it's usually my problem, not theirs," Imrie said. "They pull me on the uphills and break me on the downhills. I've just never had anything but fun, even though it's very hard grinding out that many miles."

Beginners to the sport can rent burros to take on one of the races, but the experience is not likely to match the one you'd have with an animal you've raised, trained, and come to love and trust.

"To me, it's pretty clear you have to put in some time," Imrie said. "People forget it's a team sport, and your partner has veto power."

TOUR THE ZOO
Run through a concrete jungle

LOCATION: various
DATE: various
DISTANCE: 5K, 10K
FIELD SIZE: various
WEBSITE: various
RACE HIGHLIGHTS: tour scenic zoos, including some behind-the-scenes areas; support animal care, conservation, and research efforts

Many large city zoos host fun runs to help draw new visitors for their parks and to raise money for their foundations. The benefit for runners: a refreshingly fun course that is much more scenic than your average 5K. Plus, entry to the park, usually before other visitors, and a race that would be easy to convince the kids to run!

Here are just a few of the runs in some of the country's top-notch zoos; chances are there is a race at a zoo near you.

- **Zoo Run Run (January; Nashville, Tennessee):** The Zoo Run Run 5K and walk at the Nashville Zoo takes runners on a looping course through the park, passing animals from the giraffes and elephants to the tigers and kangaroos. A portion of the course is off road, though most of it is on public pathways. Runners also are served dinner when they finish the afternoon race. (www.nashvillezoo.org)

- **Run for the Wild (April; Bronx, New York):** This 5K family fun run raises money for the Wildlife Conservation Society and gives runners a tour of one of the best zoos in the world. Participants are asked to raise money to help save elephants and other wildlife. This zoo run is extremely popular: it draws more than 5,000 runners! (wcsrunforthewild.org)

- **Zoo Run Relay (September; San Antonio, Texas):** Each person on a four-runner team completes two miles in the Zoo Run Relay. That means each runner takes a loop through the zoo and through San Antonio's Brackenridge Park. (www.sazoo-aq.org)

- **Run for the Zoo (June; Chicago, Illinois):** The Lincoln Park Zoo hosts this 5K/10K that also takes runners through some residential streets and along lakeshore paths. There's even a Safari Stampede mini obstacle course for the kids. (www.lpzoo.org)

- **Safari Park Half Marathon (May; San Diego, California):** This point-to-point half marathon takes runners through vineyards, horse farms, golf courses, and through behind-the-scenes areas of the San Diego Zoo's Safari Park. The race supports rhino care at the park and conservation in the wild. (www.safariparkhalf.com)

RIDE AND TIE
35 miles, two runners, and a horse

How do you train a horse to run a marathon?

Pretty much the same way you'd train a human.

"I'm training an Arab horse now," said Ben Volk of the Ride and Tie Association. "I ride him three times a week. I try to get in one hill run, one speed workout, and one distance run, up to 20 or 22 miles."

But *why* would you want to train a horse to run a marathon?

The answer to that one is Ride and Tie, an endurance race that involves one horse and two people who take turns riding the horse and running. The typical Ride and Tie is 10 to 20 miles, though they range from four to 50, with a few even at 80 or 100 miles. The annual world championship is a middle distance of 35.

LOCATION: various (mostly in California but also in the Midwest and Southeast)
DATE: various
DISTANCE: varies from 4 to 100 miles
FIELD SIZE: usually 10 to 50 teams
WEBSITE: www.rideandtie.org
RACE HIGHLIGHTS: conquer a course working with both man and beast

Ride and tie goes like this: the three-member team takes off, with one person running and the other riding ahead on the horse. After a mile or so (the distance is up to the team), the rider jumps off and ties up the horse, then takes off running. Eventually the first runner makes it to the horse, hops on, and starts riding. The second rider will pass the runner, go up the trail a bit, tie up the horse, and so on and so on.

"It seems like about the time you're getting tired, there's your horse waiting for you and ready to run," Volk said. "The horses get into it, too. They'll see you coming down the trail and whinny. They catch on pretty quick."

The sport of ride and tie has its roots in necessity. When people traveled by horse, they sometimes only had one animal and two people who needed to get somewhere. Ride and tie founder Bud Johns writes in his book *What Is This Madness?* that he even found a reference to the method in 18th century England.

Johns wrote that he came up with the idea for the new sport in 1960 when he was a newspaper reporter researching the history of Pine Valley, California, where he worked. He found an old article recalling a rustling incident in which all of a ranch's horses were stolen, except one. The owner and his son rode the horse ride-and-tie style all the way to San Diego, covering 40 miles a day.

Johns held onto the idea until a decade later, when he was the public relations director at Levi Strauss & Co. The company, still small at the time, was looking to sponsor a sporting event and Johns saw his chance. The first Levi's Ride and Tie Race was June 5, 1971, north of San Francisco in the

Ride and Tie events, held around the country, pair two runners with one horse for a truly unique racing experience. Photo courtesy of Thom Vollenweider

Mayacamas mountain range, Johns writes in the book.

Levi's sponsored the races for about 20 years, Volk said. The Ride and Tie Association formed in 1988 to set rules, organize the annual world championship race, and promote the sport. Today, the association has about 550 members. Sanctioned races are still mostly in California, though they have spread to Oregon, Washington, and to a lesser extent, the Midwest, Texas, and Southeast.

Races make sure the horses' health is of the highest importance. The animals are checked by veterinarians before the race and during at least two vet stops on the endurance courses.

"The runners we don't care about; we figure they should know when to stop," Volk said. "But the horses we are pretty careful about."

Runners who don't own horses but want to try their hand at the adventurous sport can try to find partners through the Ride and Tie Association website.

"I can always seem to find runners who are willing to try it," Volk said. "It's a challenge to find horses."

RACE REPORT

SeaWorld Run for the Fund
Penguins, seals, and a python...Oh my!

Jacqueline Trenz

LOCATION: San Antonio (similar runs at SeaWorld in San Diego and Orlando)
DATE: early October
DISTANCE: 10K, 5K
FIELD SIZE: various
WEBSITE: www.seaworldparks.com
RACE HIGHLIGHTS: run past sea lions, dolphins, wild birds, and reptiles; park admission for the day included for all registered runners

Do you love animals and wildlife? How about visiting amusement parks? Anyone want to sign up for a 5K, a 10K, or a brisk family fun walk?

I had the privilege of being part of the inaugural SeaWorld

10K Run for the Fund in 2010 (I also participated in 2011 and 2012) and would recommend this event to anyone—not only for the exercise benefit but also for the great amenities included and the events' contribution to the SeaWorld & Busch Gardens Wildlife Conservation Fund.

October is perfect for a competitive 10K, a wake-up 5K effort, or a lively walk for a boisterous family. The entry fee includes the run, free parking (if you arrive before 8:00 AM), and access to SeaWorld park for the remainder of the day. Early access to the parking lot makes for close proximity to the park entrance. The run begins before the park opens, so event participation puts you first in line for the rides when the park does opens. Same day re-entry into the park is allowed if you get your hand stamped before exiting.

Don't leave to go home and shower after the race, though. You're going to get very wet later anyway in the Shamu Theatre at the special Shamu performance you'll be treated to!

The race begins near the front of the park, just outside the park entry gates. Approximately the first 1.5 miles of the run is alongside the parking area, out and back, and then around to the far east side of the parking lot. About the time when my heart rate started to go up from effort, I had my first animal encounter. What a great distraction! I knew I was going to like this race a lot.

Throughout the course, I made mental notes of the animals I saw, so that I would be sure to visit their area when the race was done. I felt like a kid as the race weaved and zigzagged around the park, westward, and back out to the parking lot toward SeaWorld Drive. Then it's back into the park, more animal encounters, more winding curves, under roller coaster rails and then onward to the finish line in front of Shamu Theatre. Along the route is an intersection point where people running the 10K and 5K meet, and I caught sight and waved hello to a 5K running buddy I had traveled with.

Just after the run, a snack-style breakfast awaited. It was refreshing and delightful, with chilled honey crisp apples and homemade sugar cookies set up in theatre prop wooden boats, as well as bottled water and juices in iced-down containers, all in self-serve fashion. Massages were also available, and a few vendors provided token giveaways.

Animal encounters remained set up during the after-party. A variety of animal trainers were present to answer general questions and explain how contributions for the SeaWorld Conservation Fund are used for each unique animal.

Many of the up-close animal encounters allowed a distinctive opportunity to view animals out of their habitat as the trainers talked about everyday ways to protect wildlife. A portion of the race entry fee supports the conservation fund, whose programs include awareness campaigns to educate and encourage human behaviors and decisions that positively affect wildlife, and to insure funding and resources for animals in crisis situations.

Some animal encounters along the 5K and 10K routes include penguins, seals, walrus, a parrot, a sloth, monkeys, and a yellow python (who, by the way, is very handsome, soft to the touch, and very scary...yikes!). In some instances, actual handling the animals was allowed.

Awards ceremonies were held in the Shamu Theatre just prior to the special Shamu performance.

All in all, one entry fee provided a full day of enjoyment. The weather was pleasant enough to enjoy time in the park afterward, including shows and catching some thrills on the Great White roller coaster (and 360-degree flips), the Steel Eel roller coaster (vertical drop of 15 stories), and Rio Loco circular water raft.

The race ensures a safe place to run, terrific animal interactions, and an opportunity to run for a good cause.

RUN FOR THE WHALES
Beautiful run for a good cause

In some cases, animal lovers can't necessarily run with the animals they care about, but they can run *for* the animals.

The Run for the Whales in Hawaii is a perfect example. The race is part of an annual Maui Whale Festival that celebrates the return of the great mammals to the area each spring. It also is one of Maui's largest road races. Best of all—it's in Maui!

The half marathon, 10K, and 5K courses travel along the scenic Makena and Wailea coast, with ocean views along the way. There also is a 2K run for kids.

LOCATION: Maui, Hawaii
DATE: early February
DISTANCE: half marathon, 10K, 5K
FIELD SIZE: 600
WEBSITE: www.mauiwhalefestival.org
RACE HIGHLIGHTS: raise money for the Pacific Whale Foundation; overall and age group winners receive whale watching tickets

Overall winners and age group winners in each race will win a lei, medal, and whale watching tickets from the foundation.

The race directly benefits education programs provided to children by the Pacific Whale Foundation.

Since 1980, the Pacific Whale Foundation has provided whale watches, tidepool explorations, and science lab programs in its Discovery Center to thousands of schoolchildren each year, plus training for teachers to help them incorporate environmental and marine science education into their classrooms.

025

HAVE A LAUGH

Don't take yourself so seriously!

Runners tend to get so caught up in time goals, training regiments, and racking up the miles that we can forget to stop and smell the roses. Or, you know, explore the world's largest corn maze.

Give yourself permission to run like a kid again. Leave your watch at home, take along a running buddy, and laugh your way through these lighthearted events.

They will remind you why you started running in the first place.

Humorous signs posted along the course of the Laugh and a Half Marathon in Nebraska keep runners motivated—and laughing! Photo courtesy of Laugh and a Half Marathon

LAUGH AND A HALF MARATHON
Heeeere's a great half marathon!

Did you hear the one about the race between the lettuce and the tomato? The lettuce was a "head" and the tomato was trying to "ketchup."

What do you get when you run in front of a car? Tired!

What do you get when you run behind a car? Exhausted!

LOCATION: Norfolk, Nebraska
DATE: mid-June
DISTANCE: half marathon, half marathon relay (four runners), 10K, 5K
FIELD SIZE: 600
WEBSITE: www.laughandahalfmarathon.com
RACE HIGHLIGHTS: jokes along the course and a feel-good atmosphere; see the Great American Comedy Festival while you're in town

Ha! Don't you just love cheesy running jokes?

These are just a few of the zippy one-liners you'll find posted along the course of the Laugh and a Half Marathon in Norfolk, Nebraska.

This feel-good race in Johnny Carson's hometown is a

great reminder that running is meant to be fun.

The Laugh and a Half Marathon actually is on the weekend of the Great American Comedy Festival, an annual event that attracts talented comedians to Norfolk. (In 2013, the headliner was Drew Carey.)

The race started in 2010 when local radio station 94 Rock Radio, Faith Regional Health Services, and the Norfolk Convention and Visitors Bureau came together to put on a half marathon.

"Runners can come into town, kick their feet up, and enjoy some laughs before or after their races," said Jodi Richey, with Faith Regional Health Services, which remains a major sponsor of the event. "And with all that Johnny Carson has done for Norfolk, including sponsoring our theater at the Norfolk Senior High, his donation to the Faith Regional Carson Cancer Center, and his overall support of Norfolk, we wanted to give back to him, as well."

Along the course, there are strategically placed jokes; bands; performances from cheerleaders and young gymnasts; and volunteers handing out Laffy Taffy and jelly beans. Spectators also get in on the act by holding fun signs and wearing costumes to help entertain the runners.

"The course atmosphere first and foremost is to find creative ways to help entertain and motivate runners along the course," Richey said.

After all, you know how the saying goes: "Laughter is the best medicine."

WORLD'S LARGEST CORN MAZE RUN
Get lost in this "corny" 5K

The race gurus at All Community Events in the Chicago area were looking for a new idea, something no one else had thought of.

"We thought that there would be nothing more crazy than running through a corn maze," said Peter Starykowicz, the maze race director with All Community Events. "So we got in touch with the World's Largest Corn Maze. We figured if it's the largest in the world, then we can probably fit a 5K in the middle of it."

The World's Largest Corn Maze is an attraction at Richardson Adventure Farm in Spring Grove, Illinois, about 60 miles northwest of Chicago. (The farm also has a zip line, giant slides, and wagon rides if you're looking for even more adventure.)

LOCATION: Spring Grove, Illinois
DATE: late October
DISTANCE: 5K
FIELD SIZE: 1,000
WEBSITE: www.allcommunityevents.com
RACE HIGHLIGHTS: 250 turns within the world's largest corn maze; different maze and different course every year

The race cordons off the maze to make only one path, roughly a 5K with about 250 turns, so racers don't have to worry about getting lost. There are at least 1,000 participants who take off in three-second intervals according to their projected finish times so the maze doesn't get too congested.

Each year, Richardson Farms changes the maze, so the 5K course becomes different as well.

"You have to have people who are very good at reading maps," Starykowicz said. "It takes up a lot of hours to set up a course like that. It usually takes an entire night of people setting up the course."

The race attracts all kinds of runners, including those just looking to have fun and even some faster runners looking for a challenge.

"The fun people see it as a really fun themed event, and the really fast people see it as a crazy trail run," Starykowicz said. "It kind of attracts different people in different ways."

MARTIAN INVASION OF RACES
A playful contest between Earthlings and our Martian neighbors

The Martians are coming! The Martians are coming!

There's nothing to fear, though. Apparently, all they want from Earth is a little friendly running competition.

The Martian Invasion of Races has a clever hook to elevate this Dearborn, Michigan, event to must-run status.

LOCATION: Dearborn, Michigan
DATE: mid-April
DISTANCE: marathon, half marathon, 10K, 5K
FIELD SIZE: 8,000 (including 2,000 in the kids' marathon)
WEBSITE: www.martianmarathon.com
RACE HIGHLIGHTS: walker-friendly and emphasis on fun; playful Martian theme complete with hundreds of giant aliens lining the course, costumes, and alien medals

The race website includes an illustrated, if somewhat convoluted, explanation of why Earthlings should race the Martians. In a nutshell, Mars is Earth's closest planetary neighbor, plodding along in its orbit just outside the Earth's. Because the Earth is on the inside lane, it catches up to and passes Mars every two years.

So there you have it—a race between the planets.

"A cheesy theme for a race makes it more fun, it smoothes the serious edge off, and allows the mid- and back-of-the-pack runners to shine," race creator Randy Step explained. "No matter what your pace, you can dress up and get more attention than the winner. The Flying Pig was taken, so we chose Martians!"

Runners love to dress up for the Martian Invasion, with *Star Trek* and *Star Wars* outfits being particularly popular. Plus, the course is decorated in giant aliens, the finisher's medals are green alien heads, and the emphasis of the entire race is on having fun.

"Hundreds of six-foot inflatable aliens in green, purple, and blue can seriously change the look of this planet!" Step said. "They are great course marshals that never leave their posts. They do a good job holding directional arrows, mile markers, and signs for the bathrooms."

HAIRY GORILLA HALF MARATHON AND SQUIRRELLY SIX-MILER
"When running and insanity mix…"

Expect lots of Halloween hijinks along this trail race.

The costumes are just the beginning of the insanity at the Hairy Gorilla Half Marathon and its companion race, the Squirrelly Six-Miler, which are run in late October in a state park about 15 miles southwest of Albany, New York.

First of all, the course is not easy. It's a quite technical trail race that will add considerable time to your road race half marathon time.

LOCATION: John Boyd Thacher State Park, Voorheesville, New York
DATE: late October
DISTANCE: half marathon, 6 miles
FIELD SIZE: 600
WEBSITE: www.hairygorillahalf.com
RACE HIGHLIGHTS: banana-carrying and gorilla impersonation contests; stuffed gorilla finisher's "medals"

As the race organizers, the Albany Running Exchange, put it: "The course is a roller coaster ride with mud, muck, roots, steep drops, big puddles—and the occasional grave that may have your name on it."

That would be the Halloween hijinks part.

The course runs through numerous "graveyards" with customized headstones, some bearing the names of lucky—or are they unlucky?—pre-registered runners. Also watch out for potential zombies, costumed volunteers, and other general insanity along the course.

Then there's the gorilla theme, with a prize going to the best gorilla impersonation at the finish line (not necessarily for the best gorilla costume) and another special award to the person who can find and carry the most bananas along the course to the finish, without the aid of any bag, rope, or other device. (A man in 2006 won this competition with an incredible 56 bananas!) There's also gorilla finisher's "medals"—small, stuffed gorillas on a string—for all finishers.

HERSHEY HALF MARATHON
Don't miss the chocolate stop!

This is your chance to tour the "Sweetest Place on Earth," on foot.

The Hershey Half Marathon starts and ends at Hersheypark Stadium. The route includes a section of Hersheypark, Chocolate Avenue—with its famous Hershey Kiss street lights—Milton S. Hershey's home, and the Milton Hershey School.

LOCATION: Hershey, Pennsylvania
DATE: mid-October
DISTANCE: half marathon, half marathon relay (two runners)
FIELD SIZE: 4,000
WEBSITE: www.hersheyhalfmarathon.com
RACE HIGHLIGHTS: a mouth-watering chocolate stop along the course; run along world famous Chocolate Avenue

But of course, the highlight has to be the chocolate stop near the end of the race!

Hershey's is the purveyor of countless chocolate candies, from the classic and simple candy bar to the Kiss candy to its popular chocolate syrup. The company was founded in 1903 by Milton S. Hershey in the middle of a Pennsylvania farm field. The resort town built up around it, with Hershey's Chocolate World, featuring a candy factory tour ride; a Reese's factory that makes Peanut Butter Cups and Kit Kat bars; and Hersheypark amusement park with rides, shops, shows, and restaurants.

All racers also receive two tickets to Hersheypark in the Dark, the amusement park's evening hours in the fall.

RACE REPORT

Color Me Rad
Color me entertained

· ·

Denise Malan

LOCATION: various
DATE: various
DISTANCE: 5K
FIELD SIZE: usually thousands
WEBSITE: www.colormerad.com or www.thecolorrun.com
RACE HIGHLIGHTS: wear a white outfit to get pummeled with brightly colored powder

I am pretty sure I'd never made so many preparations for a 5K before I tried the Color Me Rad.

White T-shirt (that I'm willing to throw away afterward)? Check. Temporary "RAD" tattoo in a visible location on my body? Phone and keys in a protective baggie? Towel for my car seat? Check, check, check.

Running takes a back seat to the colorful festivities at Color Me Rad events, held throughout the country. Photo courtesy of Whitney Olson

I also took the neon sunglasses provided in the race packet but left my watch, my good shoes, and anything else I cared about at home. I was about to get colored.

The Color Me Rad and the similar Color Run are two series of untimed, unstructured, and completely not-about-the-running races. Many of these runs take place in stadium parking lots or other wide-open and easy-to-clean spaces. But they are not supposed to be about great views.

These races are about letting loose and just enjoying the moment. And they are attracting thousands of runners at events across the country and spawning a flood of other races involving colored powder or spray, UV lights, and other gimmicks. (Color Storm, Run or Dye, Color Mania—there are so many it's hard to keep track.)

But I didn't care if this was a gimmick or not. The Color Me Rad is fun, and it encourages plenty of people who have never done a 5K to try one for the first time—definitely a good thing. Plus, I had always wanted to be part of the Holi festival, an Indian tradition in which celebrants pummel each other with brightly colored corn starch to celebrate the triumph of good over bad. This was as close as I was going to get!

At the race, volunteers at color stations along the course shower runners with fine colored powder—corn starch tinted with food coloring—that sticks to your hair, skin, and clothes.

Running with my friend Jacque, I was covered in orange, followed by yellow, pink, and green. Each time, we'd slow or even walk through the color station and twirl, throw our hands up, and goad the volunteers to throw more color on us.

My eyes were protected by the swag sunglasses, but I definitely inhaled and swallowed some of the powder. It wasn't as bad as I'd expected, just a very fine dust, though it did get a little gritty on my teeth.

Part of the course was out-and-back, and I'd never seen runners having such a good time. Everyone was high-fiving, yelling, and singing. Because neither of us was worried about time, Jacque and I even turned around in the middle and went through the pink station at the end of the loop again.

The final color station right before the finish line was purple, and it was chaotic. Toward the end of the event, the powder had piled on the ground like snow, and runners were dropping to the ground to roll in it or flap their arms and legs and make color angels. Anything to color every inch of their bodies.

Jacque and I watched the fun for a while and even ran through the purple a few more times ourselves. I think we "finished" the race three times.

The finish line chute was a color party in itself. Every runner can grab one baggie of powder before finishing, then pop it at the after-party (you also can buy more baggies when you register). If you're still starving for color, the volunteers spray more into the crowd.

For all the fun we had getting colored, by the time I made it home I was back to reality. I threw away my outfit and hopped in the shower to exfoliate. The color came off more easily than I expected. It took a few more days for the tattoo to come off, but my friends and I were still talking about the Color Me Rad months later.

SEVEN CAMPUS SCRAMBLER
A mouth-watering obstacle course

This race sounds so delicious, it's hard to resist!

The Seven Campus Scrambler is part of Biscuitville Bowl, a weeklong celebration of the seven colleges and universities and the entrepreneurial community of Greensboro, North Carolina. The event's title sponsor is local company Biscuitville, which explains how the 5K obstacle course got such a tasty twist.

LOCATION: Greensboro, North Carolina
DATE: April
DISTANCE: 5K
FIELD SIZE: 500
WEBSITE: www.biscuitvillebowl.com
RACE HIGHLIGHTS: get down and dirty in obstacles of sweet tea, grits, buttermilk, jelly, and flour

The week and the 5K started as competitions among students from the seven campuses (Bennett College,

Elon University School of Law, Greensboro College, Guilford College, Guilford Technical Community College, North Carolina A&T State University, and University of North Carolina at Greensboro). But there is also an open division for non-students in the Seven Campus Scrambler.

The race can be completed either solo or by teams of four, with each person completing a .7-mile loop and one obstacle.

Let's get to the delicious details. Here's a rundown of the four obstacles (plus a bonus), as described by the race:

- Sweet Tea Tumble: Scale a 12-foot ramp with a lemon in your mouth, then tumble down the other side into a pool of sweet tea.

- Grit-Iron: High-knee it through eight sets of tires filled with Southern-style quicksand, also known as grits.

- Buttermilk Slip 'n' Slide: Take a running leap into a 27-foot-long river of buttermilk.

- Jelly Belly: The stickiest of the obstacles, this requires an Army crawl on your elbows through a 20-foot-long pit of strawberry jelly.

- Flour Shower: Get dusted in flour as you sprint through the finish.

RACE REPORT

Hot Chocolate 5K/15K
"America's Sweetest Race"

. . . .

Amber Tafoya

The promise of a big, warm cup of hot chocolate is a surprisingly powerful motivator.

Especially on a cold, clear race day in Seattle.

Thousands of runners lined up at the starting line of the Hot Chocolate 5K/15K race a few blocks away from the Space Needle at 7:00 AM in March 2013. The race is part of a series that takes place throughout the colder months in cities across the United States including Dallas, Chicago, and Philadelphia. Weather can be unpredictable this time of year, and I was happy to see that we would get a rain-free race. But this also meant that the morning would be cold.

Runners had the option to run a 5K or 15K. I opted for the 5K, thinking I would use this race to work on my speed. The course was a perfect combination of flat terrain and an occasional hill to keep things interesting.

Plus, you get a lot of view for your buck. The race turned out to be a quick tour of many iconic Seattle destinations including a sculpture park, coffee shops, and Pike Place Market. Racers started in the popular Queen Anne neighborhood and ended closer to the Space Needle at Seattle Center. The day was clear and I had a great view of the gray-blue water of the Puget Sound, the

LOCATION: various
DATE: colder months
DISTANCE: 15K, 5K
FIELD SIZE: thousands
WEBSITE: www.hotchocolate15k.com
RACE HIGHLIGHTS: chocolate treats at the end, including hot chocolate and chocolate fondue

snow capped Olympic Mountains, and even Mount Rainier as I hit the downtown area and made my way to Pike Place Market. At the market, I hit the turnaround point and the first challenging hill. Luckily, the race attracted a positive and colorful crowd. Racers cheered each other on as they made their way back up the hill. Some runners dressed in tutus and other fun costumes—I even saw an Elvis somewhere in the crowd.

Because of the early start, we ran in weather colder than desirable. I definitely needed my gloves and hat for this one. The good thing is this race goes by fast. I hardly needed my music because of the sights of the beautiful city, and fellow runners were enough motivation to get me through.

That and the hot chocolate.

After pushing up one last hill I caught sight of the Space Needle again and ran past it to the finish line. Once my body stopped moving I immediately became cold and stood in line for my treat. There was a bit of a wait and the process was a little unorganized, but I finally claimed my prize, which was bigger than expected. A variety of snacks—including bananas, pretzels, and chocolate fondue for dipping—were served in little compartments alongside the mug of Ghirardelli Hot Chocolate. The only disappointment was the mug itself. While I could have brought it home as a keepsake, I opted to recycle it. The mug was made of thin plastic and looked like it would not make it through a few washes. Racers also received a hoodie with their packet featuring the race's logo, which was a welcome change from the usual technical shirt.

I met up with my friends at the after-party area and we ducked into an indoor public space at Seattle Center to get out of the cold. A bit warmer, we happily munched on our snacks. Finally—chocolate!

The chocolate was delicious and the accomplishment of finishing a 5K in record time left me satisfied.

ACKNOWLEDGMENTS

I'm eternally grateful to my sister, Jennifer, who, as the first person I told about this idea, didn't laugh at me. To Jen Deselms, for always telling me what I need to hear, and to Elvia Aguilar, for being my biggest cheerleader. To all my friends (Allison, Beth, Beth, Bryan, Emily, Jeff, Jeff, Katie, and Michael) and family, for at least pretending to be interested in my endless racing stories. To all the contributors, both old and new friends, who added their voices to these pages. To Don Gulbrandsen, Adam Motin, and all the folks at Triumph Books for seeing the possibilities with this book. And, of course, to Mike Davis, for putting up with all the nights I spent with my computer or traveling to races, and for baring all for the cause.

INDEX